Web Site
WIZARDRY

Web Site
WIZARDRY

Marianne Krcma

CORIOLIS GROUP BOOKS

PUBLISHER	KEITH WEISKAMP
PROJECT EDITOR	DENISE CONSTANTINE
COVER DESIGN	ANTHONY STOCK
INTERIOR DESIGN	MICHELLE STROUP
EDITOR	KATHY DERMER
PRODUCTION	PROIMAGE
PROOFREADER	STEPHANIE HOON
INDEXER	KIRSTEN DEWEY

The Coriolis Group
7339 E. Acoma Drive, Suite 7
Scottsdale, AZ 85260
Phone: (602) 483-0192
Fax: (602) 483-0193
Web address: www.coriolis.com

ISBN 1-883577-87-X : $34.99

Printed in the United States of America

10 9 8 7 6 5 4 3 2 1

acknowledgments

In writing this book, I depended on input from the Web wizards who are daily defining cyberspace. The following people were especially generous with their time and knowledge, and patient with my questions:

Bonnie Carasso of Carasso Design (http://www.carasso.com/)

Mark L. Donnelly at M-Squared Productions (http://www.m-squared.com)

Mary Jo Fahey at http://www.echonyc.com/~art/webdesign/webdesign.html

Dave Friedel of the The Coriolis Group (http://www.coriolis.com/)

Charles Goodin at http://www.tanega.com/java/java.html

Eric Harshbarger, Mark Holt, and Mark Sacoolas of Sun Microsystems' New Media Marketing Lab (http://www.xm.com/cafe/)

Michael Herrick of Matterform Media (htttp://www.matterform.com/)

Gil Kasparek of Up All Night Productions ((http://www.alnight.com/)

Leonid Katainik of ParaGraph (http://www.paragraph.com/)

Arnold Kling of ASK Real Estate Information Services (http://www.homefair.com/homefair/)

Kevin Krejci of Pop Rockets (http://www.poprockets.com/)

Graham Leggett of VWV Interactive (http://vwv.is.co.za/)

John Luoma and David Yunk of Frontier Technologies (http://www.frontiertech.com/)

Joe Maissel of Soundwire (http://www.soundwire.com/)

Scott Milener of Bulletproof.com (http://www.bulletproof.com/)

Bill Murphy of the Webology Group (http://www.webology.com/)

Steve Rimmer of Alchemy Mindworks (http://www.north.net/alchemy/alchemy.html)

Larry Rosenthal of Cube Productions (http://www.cube3.com/)

Morgen Sagen at http://www.morgen.com/main.shtml

John L. Scott of Alt.coffee (http://www.altdotcoffee.com/)

Michael Sullivan of Haywood & Sullivan (http://www.hsdesign.com/)

Moshe-Dovid Teitelbaum at http://www.wam.umd.edu/~moshman/

David Yang of QuantumWave Interactive (http://www.magic.ca/~qwi/)

Thanks, also, to my family, my friends, and the staff at the The Coriolis Group for all their help—and for listening sympathetically when I whined about how this book had completely taken over my life.

CONTENTS

CHAPTER 3   A FEW WORDS

ABOUT WORDS   77

CHAPTER 4   TABLES   103

CHAPTER 5   IMAGE MAPS: YOU CAN GET THERE FROM HERE   149

CHAPTER 6   CUSTOM FRAMING   175

CHAPTER 7   A FORM FOR EVERY FUNCTION   205

CHAPTER 8   THE SOUND OF MUSIC...OR VOICES...OR BARKING   253

chapter 9   electrifying shockwave   281

chapter 10   java: hot, fresh, and strong   303

chapter 11   vrml puts places in cyberspace   349

Introduction

What This Book Is

If you've been surfing the Web for a while, maybe even experimented with publishing a basic Web page or two, and are interested in learning the skills that really make a Web site stand out, this book is for you. If you've ever been blown away by a site and wondered, "How'd they do that?", this book is *definitely* for you. I've gone to the source, sat at the virtual feet of the Web wizards—the Michaelangelos and Edisons of the Net world—and returned with the knowledge you need to help make your Web site great.

This book is a collection of tips, techniques, shortcuts, secrets, and a few horror stories gleaned from those Web wizards and supplemented by my own experience. A basic knowledge of and access to the Web (preferably through Netscape Navigator on a Windows-based PC) and some basic software are all you need to take advantage of this information. Everything else is provided in these pages and the included CD-ROM.

What This Book is Not

If you are looking for a basic book on the Web, one that shows you things like how to understand a URL, how to "surf," and how to send email over the Net, put this book back on the shelf. It's not for you—yet. There are lots of other great books out there that teach basic Web concepts, including the *Explorer* series from the Coriolis Group. Get one of those and enjoy.

If you're wondering what the heck a "URL" is and, for some reason, you've already *bought* this book, don't panic. (And don't return it; I need the money!) Instead, just set it aside temporarily and spend some time experimenting with the Web, checking things out, finding some great Web sites, and maybe some that you don't like very much, and trying your hand at some basic HTML. Then, when you're bursting with eagerness to put up a really "kewl" Web site of your own, take this book back out and prepare to produce some powerful pages.

This book deals primarily, although far from exclusively, with HTML, the "language" of the Web. You won't find the absolute basics of HTML here, though. First of all, it's very simple to learn the basics on your own (really!), especially with the HTML editors and add-ons available today. There are even programs and Web sites that will generate a basic Web page for you, such as the Web Wizard shareware program that you can download from http://www.halcyon.com/ and the Create a Home Page site that you can find at http://theinter-net/www/future21/create1.html. With these tools, you just answer a few questions, and they take care of the tedious things like constructing basic links and indicating headings.

This leads to the second reason why this book doesn't spend time on the absolute basics of Web-site building: I wanted to concentrate on the "wow" stuff because it's more fun for me to research and write, and presumably more fun for you to read and experiment with. My goal is to give you the tips and techniques that will really impress your spouse, friends, and boss.

What's on the CD-ROM

The CD-ROM is divided into four main directories: Samples, Libraries, Tools, and Acrobat. The Samples directory contains subdirectories for each chapter. Within each subdirectory are all the files needed to follow the examples in that chapter—all the HTML files, graphics, sounds, CGI scripts, Java classes, etc. This is done so that you can open a particular Web page locally from the CD-ROM (using File|Open File in Browser from Netscape, for example) and have it look pretty much like it does in the book.

The Libraries directory contains these subdirectories:

@ Graphics

@ Sounds

@ CGIs

@ Shockwave

@ Java

@ VRML

Some of the files in these directories are repeats of the ones in the Samples directories, gathered here by category for your convenience. Others are from examples that didn't make it into the book, but which you might find useful. Still others are particularly cool examples of particular Web elements that were either donated to me by the creator especially for this book or were acquired from the public domain.

To the best of my knowledge, you can freely use everything in the Libraries directories **on your Web pages only**, *except* those in a Shockwave directory. Also, you cannot disassemble Java, Director, Shockwave, or VRML files that contain images or sound that I didn't create. (To see which ones these are, refer to the particular chapters; anything that I didn't create is credited to the author.) In other words, these Java, Director, Shockwave, and VRML files need to stay whole and intact. You can't, for example, pull a particular graphic from one of the Pop Rocket games to reuse because it is copyrighted by its creator. You **do not** have the right to sell anything in the Libraries directories unless the creators specifically say you can (and none of them do, as far as I know).

The Tools directory contains the shareware and freeware programs and utilities that help you perform the Web wizardry you'll learn in this book. Here are just a few of the programs included in the Tools directories:

- The GIF Construction Set, for making animated GIFs
- GoldWave, a sound editor
- The HTML Color Reference
- Kenn Nesbitt's WebEdit, an HTML editor
- Mailto Formatter
- MapThis
- Paintshop Pro, an all-purpose paint program
- Programmer's File Editor
- WinZip
- CuteFTP

For information on installation, usage, copyright, and registration, see the individual programs. Also, if you like the shareware programs, please register them according to their authors' instructions.

Most of the files on the CD-ROM should be usable on any Windows-based PC with the appropriate hardware. (For example, to play the audio files, you'll need a sound card and speakers.) In fact, many of the files in the Samples and Libraries directories should be usable on a Mac, too, if it's equipped to handle files in PC formats. The Acrobat directory contains an annotated gallery of cool Web pages. Since black-and-white book pages don't do justice to them, they're presented as a .PDF file. The Tools directory contains the reader program you need to view them.

"How do you know this stuff?"

In the computer classes that I teach, people often ask, "How did you find out about all this stuff?" or similarly, "How do you remember all this stuff?" The answer is simply that it's in my interest to know and remember computer "stuff." In other words, I get paid for doing that, just like other people get paid for managing finances, administering to the sick, or operating heavy machinery. The need to pay my bills provides a powerful incentive to continually expand my knowledge base, and therefore my client base. So, I'm constantly combing through technical books and journals, taking classes, talking to computer professionals, and trying out new computer programs and procedures.

Computers—and specifically the Internet—might not be your livelihood, though. Maybe you're in marketing and want to explore the use of the Web as a marketing vehicle. Maybe you're a college student with some free time, free access

Have you surfed The Spot? Millions of Web users have.

to the Web, and the desire to express your views on the state of the world to the world. Maybe you're an artist seeking a new artistic medium. Maybe you *are* a computer professional who is suddenly confronted with the need to be up-to-speed on all the latest Web wizardry, by a boss who wants a site up and running *yesterday*.

Whatever your circumstances, as you surf the Web, it's easy to be intimidated by some of the creative, interesting, and downright amazing sites out there today, such as The Spot, a world-famous Web site that chronicles the lives of a group of Generation X'ers. You might find yourself thinking, "I could never do that," or, "It would take forever to build a site like that."

Remember, though, that few of these super-cool sites existed as little as 18 months ago, at least not in their present forms. Certainly, some of the people who put these whiz-bang sites up are true computer geniuses, but many more are just a little further along the learning curve than you. They just had a more pressing need, a little sooner than you, to try their hands at some Web site wizardry. You can get there, too, with some basic tools and some imagination. Plus, you can benefit from the wisdom of the Web pioneers, which is gathered in this book.

I'm definitely not any kind of Web über-wizard, although I do happen to know people who are. I'm just someone with the time and motivation to learn about building Web sites, and the opportunity to pass this information along to you. Take advantage of the pearls of Web wisdom that the people interviewed for this book have so generously contributed. Use the tricks and shortcuts they reveal. And let me know how it goes! You can email me at **krcma@coriolis.com**. I look forward to hearing from a whole new generation of Web-site wizards.

1

LAYING A GOOD FOUNDATION

Arnold Kling, who runs a consultancy called ASK Real Estate Information Services (http://www.homefair.com/homefair/) to help real estate companies use the Web, has come up with a list of six basic questions that he asks himself when planning a site:

1. Who is your audience?

2. What do you want to tell them? What specific content are you providing?

3. How do you want them to respond? Emotionally, with a good laugh? Commercially, with a desire to buy your product or find out more about your service? Or perhaps some other way?

4. How do you want your site to work? Which links should go where?

5. How do you want your pages to look?

6. Which tools should you use to achieve the look you want?

Kling stresses the importance of answering these questions in order, and not moving on to the next until you're satisfied that you've fully answered the current one. Many people, he says, create problems for themselves by skipping directly to step 5, or even step 6. As enticing as that might be, it seldom works well. The danger is that you'll find yourself locked into a particular look that you've invested considerable time and money in, but which does not actually suit your audience or your message.

Determining Your Audience

When you've narrowed down who you want to visit your Web site, you've made a huge step towards ensuring that it will be a success. The more specific you can be about this audience, the better; you can't possibly design a site that will fit everyone, and it's an exercise in frustration to try. Here are some specific things to consider about the visitors you're trying to attract:

@ *What browser or browsers do they use?* This is one of the most important pieces of information you can determine about your audience because so many cool Web effects are only compatible with a few browsers, usually Netscape Navigator and sometimes Microsoft's Internet Explorer. If your site is typical, you can assume that about 75 percent of your visitors will be using Netscape.

However, if it's a site geared toward consumers, you should expect more than the usual number of visitors accessing it via the commercial services: America Online, CompuServe, and Prodigy. For example, Arnold Kling's

Salary Relocation Calculator page gets almost half of its traffic from AOL and Prodigy.

◎ *What do they want?* Free stuff? News and information? Entertainment? A particular product?

◎ *What level of multimedia are they used to?* If your audience expects flashy graphics and high-quality sound effects, you'll need to plan your site accordingly. For example, the Pop Rocket site (http://www.poprocket.com) is geared primarily toward 13- to 45-year-old males who like music, humor, and computer games. Every page at the site provides one or more of these items, as you can see from the sample page in Figure 1.1.

◎ *What kind of connection do they have to the Web?* You can include a lot more Web wizardry at your site if you expect visitors with T1 connections than if you need to support mainly visitors with 14.4 modems.

◎ *How much time do they have to spend at your site?* Corporate users will want to just get whatever they came for and get on to the next task. Casual users and hobbyists will be more inclined to browse around.

◎ *How comfortable are they with the Web itself?* If you expect newbies, you'll need to provide much more help and guidance than you would if your audience is mainly experienced Web surfers.

◎ *What are their cultural backgrounds?* Too many people forget the "worldwide" part of "Worldwide Web." If you want to attract visitors from countries or backgrounds other than your own, you'll need to address their needs and preferences as you build your site. For example, if you're setting up a commercial site designed, in part, to support your Japanese customers, you'll probably want to have both English and Japanese versions of your pages. You'll also need to consider online ordering and customer-service procedures for these international visitors. You might even consider changing the content of the pages to better suit their expectations.

The answers to these questions will be mostly assumptions when you start your site design. As your site matures, you can use feedback from visitors and the statistics from usage logs to find out whether or not your assumptions were correct, and then fine-tune your site content and design based on how well you are targeting your audience.

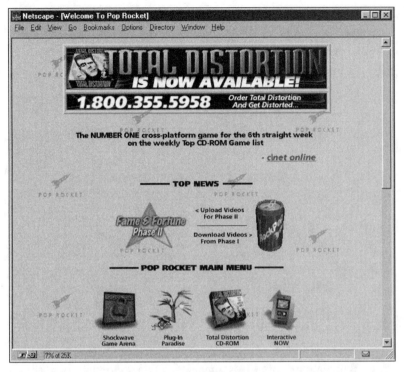

Figure 1.1   The Pop Rocket site includes plenty of high-quality multimedia because that's what its visitors want to see. On this screen the pop can spins and a special message appears in the status bar when you position the mouse on the Total Distortion graphic.

Deciding What You Want to Say

The Web, for all its glitz, glamour, and media coverage, is just another means of communication. When you make a telephone call, write a memo, or give a speech, you have a specific message in mind. The same principle applies to the Web. It sounds obvious that a Webmaster should know what he or she wants to say before putting up a site, but if you've been surfing the Web for any length of time, you've undoubtedly run into sites that had you scratching your head and wondering, "What, exactly, are they trying to say?"

I call these sites "Hello, world" pages. They typically don't do much but announce their existence with a few paragraphs of text and perhaps a graphic or two, followed by undocumented and/or out-of-date links. Figure 1.2 is one example of such a page—and in case you're wondering, I didn't make it up.

"Hello, world" pages are not going to get many visitors, so why *do* people keep putting them up? The answer is simply that Web technology is new and rela-

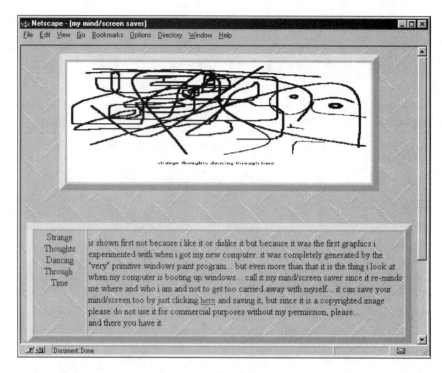

Figure 1.2   Believe it or not, this is a real Web page—in fact, there are many, many more pages like it on the Web, although they tend not to last very long. The moral: always respect a visitor's valuable bandwidth.

tively cheap, so lots of curious people with a little time on their hands are testing it out without first learning anything about it. You might remember a similar phenomenon when fax machines first became widely available and offices found themselves swamped by faxes produced by people who just wanted to see if their machines worked and what all the little buttons did.

If you have ever been involved in planning a business, you might have heard the advice that if a stranger asks what your business is, you should be able to immediately describe it in a single sentence. If you can't do that, the prevailing wisdom is that you need to sit down and refine the business plan. The same advice applies to planning Web sites. Think about your Web site; could you describe its message to a stranger clearly and succinctly? Here are a few good descriptions:

@ "My site informs a specific segment of the scientific community about my research on global warming."

- "My site tells Brady Bunch fans where to find information and products, and how to get in touch with other fans."
- "My site helps the whole Smythe clan keep in touch."
- "My site builds awareness of XYZ Corporation's line of body-piercing equipment and accessories."
- "My site teaches the ancient history of Ireland."
- "My site provides great drink recipes you can make with cough syrup."

When you read each of these, you can easily get some kind of picture of what might be at the site. For example, the Ireland site might include these pages and elements:

- A timeline presented as a clickable image map (see Chapter 5), with links to important historical figures and events.
- A quiz presented as a form linked to a CGI script (see Chapter 7).
- Pages of Celtic art.
- Audio clips from ancient Irish songs and legends (see Chapter 8).
- Annotated links to other Web sites dealing with Ireland, the Celts, and particular historical periods.

What you want to say at your site determines, to a certain extent, the amount of Web wizardry you'll need. If your site provides valuable information that's hard to get elsewhere, you won't need animated fireworks going off in the background. If, on the other hand, the basic message of your site is something like "buy this" or "hire me," you'll need to give people as many reasons as possible to visit, stay—and, perhaps most important, come back again.

Be honest with yourself about the intrinsic value of your information. For example, you might be absolutely certain that your company's new Wonder Widget is going to revolutionize the widget industry, but most other people will need some inducements to discover its importance. Games, contests, animation, and multimedia are the most common and popular ways to add value to a site.

Setting the Right Tone

Once you know who you want to reach and what you want to tell them, you need to decide how you want to say it. The key here is deciding on the response you want from the users of your site. You can think of this as the main goal of your site. If your goal is to make visitors laugh, you'll need different content than if your goal is to persuade visitors to support some political cause.

Another part of setting the tone is deciding the concept or metaphor that your site will be based on. Most successful Web sites are really digital translations of real-world (analog) ways of communicating. Here are some of these metaphors:

- A catalog or brochure
- A newsletter
- A TV commercial
- An interactive CD-ROM
- A storefront or mall
- An annual report to shareholders
- A lecture or presentation
- A slide show

Different metaphors lend themselves better to different tones. If your audience and message dictates a serious image, the annual report or lecture concept might suit your site well. If you need something more playful, think of the way a commercial or CD-ROM is put together, and how you might translate its elements into Web pages.

Creating the Site Schematic

There are two major ways to design a site: a hierarchical, top-down style, shown in Figure 1.3a, and a less-structured "web," shown in Figure 1.3b. Although it seems obvious that the web style of site design is best suited to the Worldwide Web, the top-down style is much more common, mainly because it's easier to design and maintain. With a top-down site, you assume that your visitors are doing things more or less "in order," so you don't have to make each page stand on its own. Sometimes, this is a valid assumption. In an online catalog, for example, it's logical to assume that a user starts by looking at a fairly broad range of choices on a main table-of-contents page, then goes to pages that have more specific information about the products he or she is interested in, and then either leaves the site or moves to a page that contains ordering information.

Instead of a catalog, though, suppose you wanted a site that was the Web equivalent of a shopping mall. A visitor might come into any store from any other

(a)

(b)

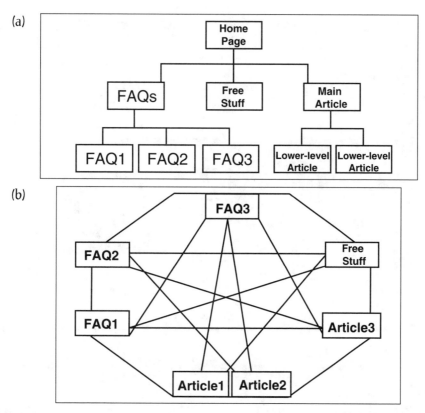

Figure 1.3 In a top-down site (a), the visitor's choices about how to move through the site are fairly limited. In a "web" site (b), the choices can be almost infinite.

store, or from the outside. There is no single "front door" where you can put all the preliminary information about things like how to navigate, how to send feedback, and how to get help. You'll have to design your site so that these things are accessible from any page.

In fact, as Web wizard Michael Sullivan puts it, "Get away from the idea that you have to have a [single] home page. Every page is a home page...you should be able to glance at any page and know what it does and how to use it." This kind of design is especially appropriate for large sites, where a visitor might have landed at a particular page because it turned up on a search list. For example, consider Figure 1.4, which shows two pages from the Discovery Channel site (http://www.discovery.com/). Either of these could be the home page for the site. In a way, they both are.

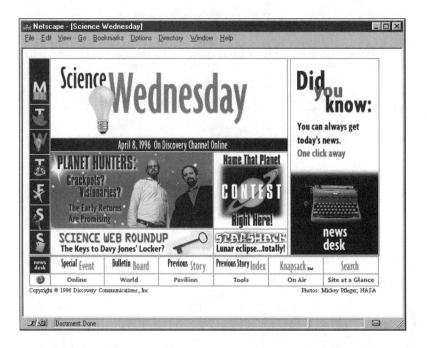

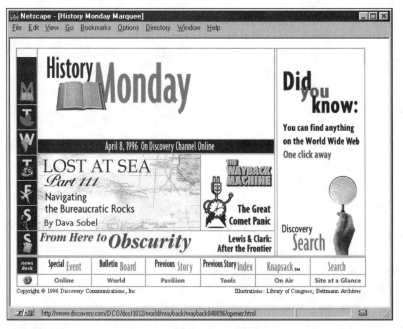

Figure 1.4   The Discovery Channel site is designed so that you can land almost anywhere and be at a "home page."

Designing a Page Prototype

Once you've got all the preliminary decisions made, you're ready to think about how you want a typical page at your site to look. This is similar to the page-design process in traditional print publishing. Here are the basic steps:

1. Start by sketching a blank area that's the size of your page—about 9 inches wide and 7 inches tall for the "live" area on a standard monitor.

2. Determine where you want the major elements, such as the links, text, and graphics, to go. Be sure to include in your plan some kind of navigational button bar and an area to hold your "signature" file. Figure 1.5 shows a sample sketch for a page that will be implemented using frames tags (Chapter 6).

3. Make some preliminary decisions about color schemes, background tiles, and graphic elements to tie your pages together. For example, how will bulleted lists look? Do you want the standard round bullet, a custom GIF such as a ball, or no bullet at all? If you're using a custom GIF, should you use different-colored versions of it for different types of items?

4. Repeat steps 1 through 3 if you need several different page prototypes for different areas of a large site.

From there, you can code one or more standard pages of HTML that will serve the same purpose as a template or style sheet in a word-processing or desktop-publishing program. The HTML page prototype helps unify the pages in your site, adds visual cues to let the visitor know where he or she is in the site, and keeps you from having to write the same code over and over again. For example, here's the HTML for the very simple page prototype shown in Figure 1.6:

```
<HTML>
<HEAD><TITLE>Page Prototype</TITLE></HEAD>
<!-- All pages at this site use the following body tag. -->
<BODY TEXT="#000000" BGCOLOR="#FFFFFF" LINK="#0000EE" VLINK="#808080"
ALINK="#FF0000" BACKGROUND="/pix/chalk.jpg">

<!-- All pages at this site have a button bar at the top. -->
<A HREF="up-one.htm"><IMG SRC="/pix/btn-back.gif" ALT="[Last Page]"></A>
<A HREF="homepage.htm"><IMG SRC="/pix/btn-home.gif" ALT="[Home]"></A>
<A HREF="next-one.htm"><IMG SRC="/pix/btn-fwd.gif" ALT="[Next Page]"></A>

<!-- Some pages may use an opening graphic here. -->
```

```
<H1><I>Main Page Heading or Graphic Here</I></H1><BR>

<H4><FONT SIZE=+1>Introductory paragraphs explaining this page go here.</_
   FONT></H4>

<!-- The content of this area will vary by page. -->
<P><BR></P>

<!-- All links should be annotated and formatted as shown here. -->
<P>
<A HREF="http://www.widget.com/instr.html">
   <IMG SRC="/pix/blubtn.gif"
    BORDER=0 HEIGHT=21 WIDTH=23 ALIGN=left>
   <FONT SIZE=+1>New ways to use your widgets</A>
Download free, illustrated, step-by-step instructions for working with _
   widgets, from basic to advanced.
   </FONT>
</P>
<P><A HREF="http://www.widget.com/order.html">
   <IMG SRC="/pix/blubtn.gif"
    BORDER=0 HEIGHT=21 WIDTH=23 ALIGN=left>
   <FONT SIZE=+1>Pricing and order information</A>
With our secure system, not only can you check prices and stock levels, you
   can even check the status of your particular order.</FONT>
</P>

<!-- All pages at this site use the following lines. -->
<HR>
<FONT SIZE=-1>
<P>Last updated ...
<BR><A HREF="mailto:webmaster@widget.com">Contact the Webmaster</A> for _
   kudos or complaints.</P>
<P><I>Copyright information ...</I></P>
</FONT>
</BODY>
</HTML>.
```

Regardless of the kind of site you're designing, your page prototype should include an area for navigational buttons. It should also include an area for a page signature—who wrote the page and how to contact him or her, when it was last updated, and basic copyright information.

If your server supports server-side includes (SSIs), you can use them to automate the process of signing and dating your pages. First, create an HTML file containing just the contact and

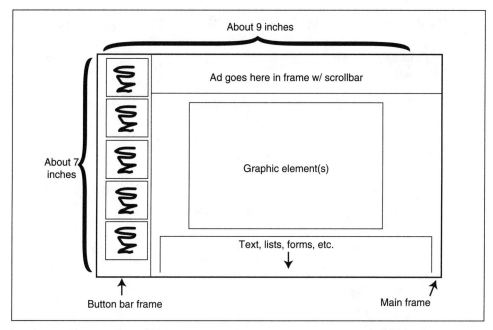

Figure 1.5 This is a typical page sketch for a casual, commercial site.

copyright information, without the normal <HEAD>..</HEAD>, <TITLE>..</TITLE>, and <BODY>..</BODY> tag pairs. Save it as sigfile.htm. Then, add these two lines to the bottom of every page:

```
Last updated: <!--#flastmod virtual=""-->
<!--#include file="sigfile.htm"-->
```

The first line is an SSI to get the date when the file was last updated. The second line is an SSI to append the contents of sigfile.htm. For more about SSIs, see Chapter 7.

Picking the Right Tools

There are dozens of different software tools you might use to create your Web site, depending on the types of wizardry you want to include. Many of the specific tools you need for various Web-related techniques are discussed in detail in the chapters that follow. For now, though, if you've followed the site-planning steps covered in this chapter so far, you're ready to start putting together your Web wizard's toolkit (kind of a mixed metaphor, I know—you might prefer to think of it as your book of spells or bag of tricks). The software collection listed

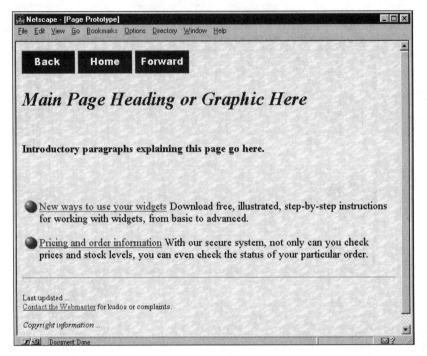

Figure 1.6   This page prototype would work well for a simple, straightforward site.

in Table 1.1 provides a good place to start. Many of these tools are available on the CD-ROM or online, either as demos or shareware.

The Web Wizards Speak: Budgeting Time and Money

One of the things that makes Web sites so attractive, especially to businesses, is that you don't have to spend massive amounts of money to have a professional-looking site that gets good traffic. On the other hand, some large companies spend hundreds of thousands of dollars annually to build and maintain their sites.

How much your particular site will cost depends on how large and fancy it needs to be to accomplish its goal, and on whether or not you intend it to be a profit source. A scholarly, text-based site or a personal home page could be built for just the cost of your time and a $20 or so monthly fee to an Internet Service Provider (ISP). Since you're reading this book, however, you presumably want to add at least a few bells and whistles to your Web pages, which will take extra time and money.

Essential Ingredients for Web Wizardry	Good to Have on Hand
An HTML editor, either stand-alone (like WebEdit†) or an add-on to a word processor	An illustration program like CorelDraw
A paint program like Paintshop Pro† (shareware) or Photoshop (commercial)	A 3D tool like Virtual HomeSpace Builder† (freeware) or 3D Studio (commercial)
Recent versions of all the browsers you intend to support	A sound editor like GoldWave† (shareware) or SoundEdit 16 (commercial)
Libraries of graphics and textures	Libraries of sounds and CGI scripts
An image-mapping utility like MapThis† (freeware)	Macromedia Director with AfterBurner for making Shockwave movies
	The Java Developer's Kit (JDK, freeware) for writing Java applets and applications
	Various special-purpose utilities such as the HTML Color Reference†, GIF Construction Set†, Mailto Formatter†, and RealAudio Encoder

Table 1.1   Here are an even dozen of the best kinds of Web-related tools to collect. The † character indicates that the software is included on the CD-ROM.

Here's what some Web wizards estimate that their commercial sites, which range from moderately fancy to eye-popping, cost:

@ Arnold Kling estimates that his site costs about $1,200 per month to maintain. He uses corporate sponsorship to defray the cost.

@ Web designer Michael Sullivan (http://www.hsdesign.com/), who markets his services to medium and large businesses, recommends that his clients budget at least $30,000 to build a Web site.

@ John L. Scott, co-owner of the Manhattan-based cybercafe Alt.coffee (http://www.altdotcoffee.com/), says both the real and virtual components of Alt.coffee—including restaurant supplies and computers for use by the cafe's customers—were capitalized for a total of $100,000. Since it has its own in-house server and T1 connection, Alt.coffee currently generates about $5,000 per month in revenues from renting Web access, in addition to the income from the cafe itself.

◎ The Pop Rockets site, which supports an independent commercial computer-game developer, has garnered rave reviews from just about every Web-site ranking service you can think of, primarily for its use of Shockwave (see Chapter 9). The site has been up and running for about a year with a total cost to date of about $40,000. According to Web wizard Kevin Krejci, "Traffic has gone up to over 30,000 hits per day. A majority of our customers bought our product, Total Distortion, after visiting the site," suggesting that the investment is worthwhile.

Before you get too upset by these figures, remember that the more time you're willing to put into your site as "sweat equity," the less money you'll need to spend. Also, for most of these Web wizards, their Web site is integral to the profit-making part of their business. Therefore, they need more expensive hardware and communications equipment than you'd need for a more casual site. Finally, like all pioneers, these Web wizards have paid a certain price for being on the cutting edge. They've spent time and money discovering— or even inventing—the tools and techniques to make the Web do what they want it to. Fortunately, they're also willing to pass this information on to others, so you can save time and money by following their examples.

Like the cost, the amount of time involved in setting up and maintaining a Web site varies dramatically from site to site. Most of the Web wizards I talked to for this book initially built their sites in the time-honored programming tradition of putting in lots of hours over a relatively short period of time. Weeks or months of 12- to 18-hour days seem to be fairly common at this stage. Once the sites are up and running, they require maintenance time—anywhere from 4 to 40 hours a week, depending on how automated the site is, how interactive it is, and, of course, how many hits it gets.

Maintenance is critical to running a successful Web site. The goal for Web wizards is not to have people visit their sites, but to have them add their URLs to the all-important bookmark list. To be worthy of a bookmark, a Web wizard has to persuade the visitor that his or her site is worth coming back to frequently. The only way to do that is to promise frequent changes and additions—and then to deliver. All of the sites highlighted in this book are continually evolving, as the Web wizards add content and experiment with new technologies. Alt.coffee, for example, started out as text, graphics, and CGI scripts, then added frames, Shockwave, and VRML (3D spaces), as you can see in Figure 1.7. Future plans for the site include streaming video and intelligent agents (also called *avatars*).

Figure 1.7 This page from Alt.coffee's Web site uses frames and VRML to appeal to high-end users.

Web Wizard's Touchstones for Site Planning

Do make sure you can state the message of your site in a single, coherent sentence.

Don't get locked into a specific look too early in a site's development. Allow the site design to evolve based on your audience, your message, and your goal rather than trying to force content into an unsuitable design.

Do spend plenty of time narrowing down the audience you're trying to reach with your site. The more details you can "flesh out" about your typical visitor, the better.

Don't forget that the less intrinsically valuable content you have at your site, the more Web wizardry you need.

Do include navigational buttons on your page prototype.

Don't skimp on maintenance time when budgeting for your site. It can make the difference between a successful site and a failure.

Do annotate and update all links to other sites that you include on your pages.

Don't rush to put up a site, only to have it full of pages that are "under construction." Visitors quickly get frustrated by clicking on links that don't go anywhere.

Do sign and date all your pages, using server-side includes to reduce the amount of coding, if possible.

11

BACKGROUNDS, BUTTONS, BARS, AND OTHERBITMAPS

Putting graphics on your Web pages is fun, relatively easy to do, and, for most Web sites, essential for attracting and keeping visitors. Most people, after all, are visually oriented, relating to things best when they can see them, not just read about them. Big-time advertising agencies have been taking advantage of this fact for a long time—why shouldn't you? However, the ever-increasing flood of new, image-filled Web pages makes it harder and harder for the images at *your* site to stand out.

Everyone on the Web has access to stock photographs and clipart. It's not enough anymore just to toss up a background or dot your pages with 3D buttons. You must choose your images with care and use them with style, or your pages will look ordinary, even if you've got GIFs filling every available inch of space. Fortunately for those of us who are somewhat artistically challenged, there's plenty of help out there—and a decent percentage of it is gathered in this chapter (if I do say so myself).

Your backgrounds, buttons, bars, and other graphics tell visitors to your site a lot about your image. Make sure the image they see is the one that you've consciously decided to project. Remember to plan what you're going to say and who you're going to say it to **before** you get too deep into how you're going to say it with pictures. Otherwise, you're liable to waste lots of time and money searching for, scanning, downloading, manipulating, and managing images that will just end up on the virtual cutting-room floor.

All You Need to Know about GIF vs. JPEG

There are literally dozens of graphic file formats in the world. Fortunately, in the Web world, you really only have to deal with two: GIF (which stands for the *graphic interchange format* and can be pronounced with either the hard or soft *g*, in case you were wondering) and JPEG (which stands for *joint photographic experts group* and is pronounced "jay-peg"). Unfortunately, even these two are enough to confuse most people.

You might have heard, for example, that the GIF format is proprietary, and that CompuServe is suing people for using it. Like most rumors, this one has a grain of truth in it, although it probably won't affect you in any way. The details are complicated and boring, unless you happen to be a copyright attorney, but they boil down to this: *software developers* are supposed to pay royalties to various patent-holders of GIF-related technology—including CompuServe, under some circumstances—if they use that technology in their products. In other words, if you're developing a word processor that will enable users to save their work as GIF files, you might have to pay. On the other hand, if your kid draws a picture that you want to post on your Web page, you're perfectly free to save it as a GIF without fear that the copyright cops will come knocking on your door.

To add to the confusion over file formats, when most people talk about using GIFs on their Web pages, they're really talking about a specific version of the GIF format, GIF89a, which supports two of the coolest and most frequently used graphic effects: transparency and interlacing. Transparent GIFs are those that appear to "float" on a Web page, while interlaced GIFs seem to quickly "fade in" onscreen. Interlacing is just a trick, really; a GIF file loads at basically the same speed whether or not it's interlaced. The only benefit to interlaced files is that they give the user something to look at while he or she waits, thus fending off the download doldrums. While the transparency technique can apply to any GIF file, interlacing is usually reserved for relatively large GIF files (at least 20K). Step-by-step instructions for making both transparent and interlaced GIFs are given later in this chapter.

The standard JPEG format doesn't support transparency or interlacing. There is a new format called Progressive JPEG that does something similar to interlacing, but it's not yet very common. Also, unlike GIF, the JPEG format is not supported by every Web browser—although the most important ones, including Netscape and Microsoft's Internet Explorer, do support it. What JPEG has in its favor is more bang for the byte. Because of the way it compresses information, the JPEG format can produce a file that's easily one-half to one-tenth the size of the same image in GIF format. At the same time, a JPEG file can provide much more detail on the colors used in the image. Information on over 16 million (also called *24 bit*) possible colors can be stored in the JPEG format, versus GIF's maximum of only 256 colors (*8 bit*).

Some people contend that, since JPEG stores more color information in much less space, you should just use JPEG all the time. However, there are at least four problems with this position. You've already read about three of them:

- JPEGs can't be made transparent.
- JPEGs can't be interlaced.
- The JPEG format is not supported by all browsers.

The fourth problem is this: to squeeze all that information into such a small amount of storage space, JPEG drops some of the less-important information about the image. This is referred to as *lossy* compression, since you lose something in the translation. Most of the time, you won't be conscious of the loss, but if you ever put a GIF and JPEG version of the same image side by side, you might notice some fuzziness around the edges of objects in the JPEG, especially if the image is a simple line drawing. On the other hand (you knew there'd be one, didn't you?), a JPEG can actually look better than a GIF, even though the GIF is much larger in file size, because the JPEG file has a much larger palette of available colors to choose from, as shown in Figure 2.1. The GIF version looks "speckled" because it doesn't have enough colors available to create the continuous tones needed in the fish's body. Also, note that the word *Fish* looks smoother in the JPEG version; the type in the GIF version has an obvious case of the jaggies.

Are you sufficiently confused yet? Not to worry. I, your faithful Web companion, have delved through many an arcane tome and spent many long nights in research to bring you the answer to the whole controversy in a single sentence:

Use the JPEG format for large images that use lots of colors and for photographs, especially photographs of people, because of the fleshtones; use the GIF format for everything else.

I know, I know: it's a run-on sentence. Nobody's perfect!

The Wizards Speak: Choosing Your Tools

Michael Sullivan, creative director of the design firm Haywood & Sullivan, has designed the Web sites of organizations such as NBC News, Stanford University, and Pilgrim New Media. His firm has had a Web site at http://www.hsdesign.com/ since the autumn of 1994. Like any good Web site, it's continually evolv-

Figure 2.1   The JPEG version of this art (the top one) looks better because it has more colors to work with.

ing, but the home page that was up when I wrote this is shown in Figure 2.2.

Bonnie Carasso, owner of Carasso Design at http://www.-carasso.com/, has had a presence on the Web even longer than Haywood & Sullivan—all the way back to November of 1993. Her clients for Web sites have included the Wimbledon Association and Vantive Corporation.

Both Carasso and Sullivan use a wide collection of hardware and software to design Web sites, but like many design firms, theirs are basically Mac shops. Both also rely on basic editors such as BBEdit (a popular shareware text editor among Mac-based Web wizards) and Notepad for their HTML coding. As Carasso says, "If you rely on HTML editors and code genera-tors, you'll never really learn what you need to know about cod-ing HTML." Sullivan has experimented with Adobe's PageMill HTML generator, but has found, at least for now, that the code it generates is "not great." In fact, his design firm is planning a series of projects for developing PageMill templates. The first ones could be out by the time you read this; check the Haywood & Sullivan home page for news.

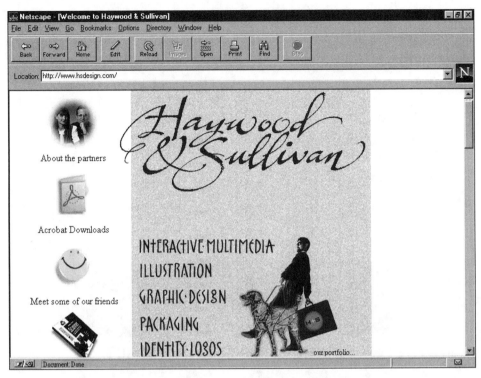

Figure 2.2 At the home page of Haywood & Sullivan, the buttons down the side are transparent GIFs. The main logo is a transparent, interlaced GIF. The rest of the display type and the man-with-dog form an image map.

For aspiring Web wizards, these two graphic experts suggest the following basic tools for creating Web art:

- Adobe's Photoshop.
- A Photoshop plug-in, such as PhotoGIF (for the Mac only) or GIF 89a Export (for PCs), to create interlaced and transparent GIFs in versions of Photoshop earlier than 3.0.5.
- Software for making image maps, such as Webmap for the Mac or MapThis for the PC (included on the CD-ROM).
- Access to a scanner.

Most Web wizards agree that these are the basic tools for good graphics, although some use Corel's PhotoPaint in place of Photoshop. For Web wizards on a tight budget, the shareware Paintshop Pro provides many of the basic functions of Photoshop, and is an inexpensive place to start exploring Web graphics.

Many graphics gurus also mention the Photoshop add-ins, especially Kai's Power Tools, for adding cool effects to Web graphics. You can find out about Kai's Power Tools and even download samples from KPT Online at http://the-tech.mit.edu/KPT/ and from MetaTools at htpp://www.hsc.com/. In addition, some designers use raytracing programs such as Corel Dream and Ray Dream Designer to create 3D and hyper-realistic effects. For example, Web wizard Morgen Sagen's logo, shown in Figure 2.3, started as simple type. He used Corel Dream to extrude it into 3D.

Figure 2.3   Morgen Sagen used Corel Dream to create this 3D logo.

Choosy Web Wizards Choose Transparent GIFs

Transparency is undoubtedly the most popular graphic effect used on Web pages. Inappropriate use of non-transparent GIFs is a sure sign of a not-ready-for-prime-time Web site, as you can see in Figure 2.4.

In order to make a successful transparent GIF, your paint program needs to be able to identify a background color that surrounds all the art. The easiest images to make transparent, then, are relatively simple ones that have well-defined borders. Icons are a good example. Consider the icon in Figure 2.5. It might seem transparent, but it really isn't. If you were to put it on a Web page witha blue background, you'd see a white box all around the icon. To make it transparent, you need to tell your paint program to replace the particular shade of white surrounding the icon with the software equivalent of clear glass. Then, when you put it on a Web page, whatever is underneath the "glass" will show through.

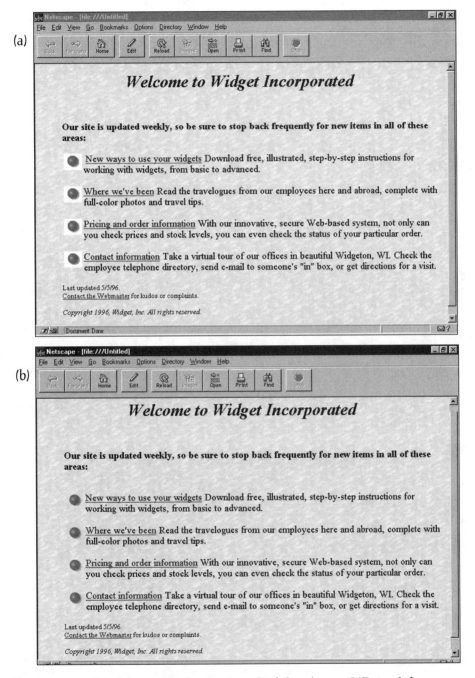

Figure 2.4   A Web page looks amateurish if the wrong GIFs are left non-transparent (a). Changing them to be transparent results in a more professional page (b).

Figure 2.5
This GIF might seem transparent, but it isn't.
If you put it on a page with a colored background,
you'd have a white block with an icon in it.

The image in Figure 2.5 is on your CD-ROM as newicon.gif. To make it transparent, open it in Paintshop Pro (also included on the CD-ROM), then go through these steps:

1. Select File|Save As to bring up the Save As dialog box in Figure 2.6.

2. Click on the Options button to bring up the GIF Transparency Options dialog box in Figure 2.7. If the Options button is unavailable, you've got the wrong file format chosen in the Save As dialog box. Make sure the List Files of Type box shows GIF - Compuserve, and the File Sub-Format box shows Version 89a. - Noninterlaced.

3. Since this is a simple graphic, Paintshop Pro will be able to find the background on its own. In the GIF Transparency Options dialog box, choose Set the Transparency Value to the Background Color, then click OK.

4. Make any changes you want to the name and location of the file, then click OK. You now have a transparent GIF.

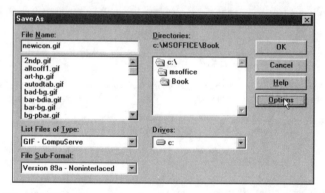

Figure 2.6 The Options button in the Save As dialog box is the key to transparent GIFs in Paintshop Pro.

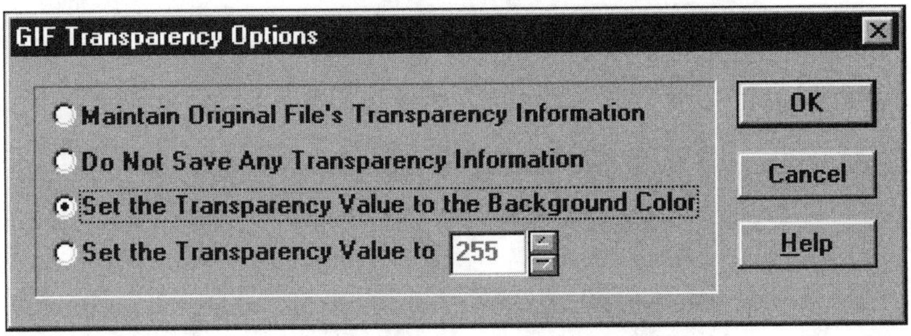

Figure 2.7   Based on the selection in the dialog box, Paintshop Pro will change whatever it sees as the background color to "clear glass."

Test your GIF on a sample page of HTML that includes a non-white background color, like this:

```
<HTML>
<HEAD>
      <TITLE>Test Transparent Gif</TITLE>
</HEAD>
<BODY BGCOLOR="FFD0A2">
<DIV ALIGN=CENTER>
      <H1>Welcome to Widget, Incorporated!</H1>
</DIV>
<BR>
<P>
<FONT SIZE=+1>
      <IMG SRC="newicon.gif" BORDER=0  HEIGHT=42 WIDTH =66
ALIGN=LEFT>
      <A HREF=
          "http://www.widget.com/dir.html">Contact information
      </A>
      Take a virtual tour of our offices in beautiful Widgeton, WI.
Check
      the employee telephone directory, send e-mail to someone's
      &quot;in&quot; box, or get directions for a visit.
</FONT>
</P>
</BODY>
</HTML>
```

If you follow these steps with your own images and the GIF is not transparent on the test Web page, Paintshop Pro hasn't been able to select the right background color. You'll have to select it manually by reopening the GIF in Paintshop Pro, selecting the eyedropper tool, and running the mouse around the background. As you do, you'll see numbers changing in a bar at the bottom of the screen. The number after the letter *I* is the color index, as shown in Figure 2.8. Make a note of

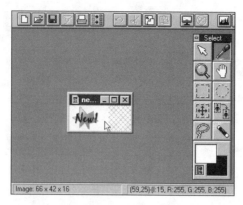

Figure 2.8   With the eyedropper tool pointing to the background, the color index at the bottom of the screen shows I:15, which is this particular shade of white.

it. Then, go back through the steps to make a transparent GIF, but in step 3, choose Set the Transparency Value from the GIF Transparency Options dialog box, and click the spinner to the color you noted, as shown in Figure 2.9.

VARYING THE STEPS

If you're using Photoshop and want a transparent GIF, first determine what version of the software you have. If it's earlier than 3.0.5, you'll need to add the GIF 89a Export plug-in (available from Adobe's Web site at http://www.adobe.com/) to your /plugins directory. When you choose GIF 89a as the file type in the Export dialog box, a box will pop up to prompt you for transparency, among other effects. The Export plug-in requires you to use layers or the Alpha channel to select a transparency color, unless you originally created the file with a transparent background color. These fairly advanced Photoshop

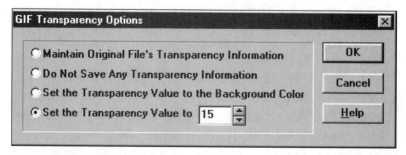

Figure 2.9   In this case, the transparency is manually set to color 15, the color noted in Figure 2.8.

functions are beyond the scope of this book, but Adobe includes detailed instructions with the plug-in as file gif89a.pdf.

Interlace

As mentioned earlier, interlaced images are GIFs that appear to "fade in" onscreen, so from the end-users' point of view, they seem to load more quickly.

To interlace a GIF in Photoshop, follow these steps:

1. If you're using a version of Photoshop earlier than 3.0.5, load the Export plugin (found at Adobe's Web site, http://www.adobe.com/) into the /plugins directory.

2. Choose File|Export|GIF89a and the GIF89a Export Options dialog box will pop up.

Just make sure the Interlace box is selected, and continue with the export.

To interlace a GIF in Paintshop Pro, do this:

1. Choose File|Save As to bring up the Save As dialog box.

2. In the File Sub-Format scrollbox, choose Version 89a-Interlaced.

3. Click OK or press Enter to save the file and close the dialog box.

That's it! You won't be able to see the interlacing effect from within your paint program. It's also impossible to show the effect of interlacing on paper. If you want to see a sample, open the transgif.htm file from the CD-ROM in your browser.

The Wizards Speak: Thinking like a Pro

When clients come to Michael Sullivan saying they just need him to design 100 unique, identifiable icons to make their site go from mediocre to great, he advises instead that they "go back to the beginning—decide what you're trying to say, and then think about how you want to say it. How many topics are there? How can you organize them? With different backgrounds? Different graphics? Identify the navigation methodology and all the graphics will fall into place."

Gil Kasparek puts it this way: "Disregard traditional technique in favor of more effective communication, but don't sacrifice aesthetics."

All Web wizards agree that the hardest part about designing graphics for the Web is that the graphics have to be so small in terms of file size. Sullivan advises, "Look at every pixel in every piece of art on your page. Ask whether it's doing work for you. If not, get rid of it."

Reduce, Resize, Reuse

To keep file sizes small and downloading fast, reduce the color depth of your GIFs as much as possible without damaging the image quality; never use a 256-color graphic when a 16-color one would do. To reduce the color depth, load the GIF in a paint program such as Photoshop or Paintshop Pro. Then, experiment with the appropriate color options in your paint program, such as Color|Decrease Color Depth (for Paintshop Pro) or Mode|Indexed Color (for Photoshop), undoing each time until you find the right compromise between image size and quality. If it's a simple line drawing, you might even be able to convert it to black-and-white (1 bit). Reducing color depth doesn't usually apply to JPEG files, since the whole reason to use a JPEG is its ability to hold lots of color information in a relatively small space.

Whether you're working with a GIF or a JPEG, crop your art tightly. Remember Michael Sullivan's advice to examine each pixel and decide if it's really necessary. Also, consider resizing or rescaling your art. Does that photograph of your company's new widget really need to be 4 inches square? A 2-inch version might be just as effective and load much faster.

Reuse graphics like backgrounds, buttons, and bars as much as possible at your site. A piece of art that's already in the Web browser's cache will appear almost instantly, so reusing the same button for all the items in all your lists on all your pages will be much faster than using different buttons on each page.

Add Some Text

Have you ever stared and stared at a blank Web page waiting for its graphics to load, without having any idea of how many images there are or how long it will take? Imagine if that page had a few paragraphs of text, which appear almost instantly. Now, you've got at least some idea of the page layout from the position of the text, and you've got something to read while the graphics load.

Even if you don't have any other text on your page, consider adding some information about the graphics down in the bottom corner where you've signed it and given the date of the last revision. (You *do* sign all of your pages, don't you?) For example, you might add a line that says "Total page size 50K; 6 GIFs, 1 image map."

Use Thumbnails

Thumbnails are really the only way to effectively present lots of large graphics from a single Web page. Remember the whole GIF versus JPEG discussion? Well, one thing I didn't get into there is that all the inline graphics used on a page (the ones with the <IMG SRC> tag) have to share the same global palette. If you've got several colorful GIFs on a Web page, for example, this can lead to some strange color shifts as your browser tries to pick the right 256 colors for that page. The loophole is to keep the full-color graphics external to the page, perhaps as JPEGs to allow for greater color depth, and just load them as needed by anchoring them with the <A HREF..> tag to small versions, the *thumbnails,* on the page itself.

Bonnie Carasso of Carasso Design uses thumbnails to good effect in presenting images from her portfolio. Each of the thumbnails shown in Figure 2.10 is no more than 5 KB, so the page loads relatively quickly even though there's lots of art on it. The thumbnails are small, relatively low-quality JPEGs that link to large, higher-quality ones, typically 40 KB each. Carasso recommends keeping all of the thumbnails on a page approximately the same size to add a feeling of continuity, "like a slideshow."

Here are the steps to create and use thumbnails like those at Carasso Design at your site:

1. Open the large version of the file in the paint program of your choice.

2. Resize the image to be about an inch to an inch-and-a-half wide (between 72 and 110 pixels), keeping it in proportion so the height is changed automatically.

3. If it's too small to be useful at this size, undo it. Crop a representative piece of the image, and just resize that.

4. To make the thumbnail load faster, reduce its color quality. For example, in Figure 2.11, the compression ratio for the thumbnail JPEG was increased from 15 to 20. (In Paintshop Pro, do this by clicking the Options

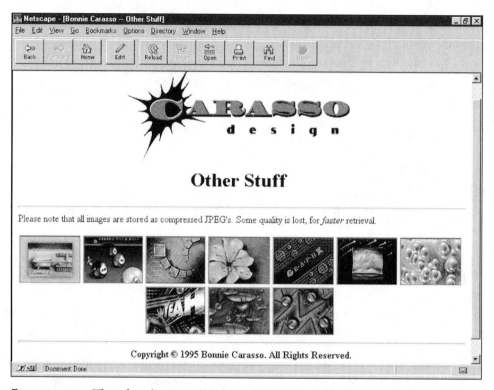

Figure 2.10 Thumbnails are really the only effective way to organize lots of high-quality graphics at a site, as this page from the Carasso Design site illustrates.

button in the Save As dialog box for the JPG file type.) Finish saving the thumbnail with a new name, so you have two versions of the same graphic.

5. In your HTML editor, create the link that will make the full-scale graphic load when a user clicks the thumbnail. For example, if the regular graphic was called fruit.jpg and the thumbnail was fruit-tn.jpg, the HTML would look something like this:

```
<A HREF="fruit.jpg"> <img src="fruit-tn.jpg" width=84 height=72></A>
```

Make Better Use of the <IMG SRC> Tag

The developers of Netscape's extensions to HTML have added several attributes to the <IMG SRC> tag that you can use to make your images more "user-friendly": WIDTH, HEIGHT, and LOWSRC. WIDTH and HEIGHT should be part of every <IMG SRC> tag at your site. These attributes tell the browser the dimensions of the graphic in pixels, so it can lay out the appropriate area and continue with the other items on the page without having to wait for the whole image to

Figure 2.11   The thumbnail, fruit-tn.jpg, is a mere 4 KB. It links to the full-color, full-size, 85 KB version.

load. They are simply ignored by browsers that don't support them, so you've got nothing to lose.

If you use the integrated HTML editor in recent versions of Netscape to write your Web pages, the dimensions of each graphic you use will automatically be added to its <IMG SRC> tag. If you use some other editor, you'll probably need to specify it yourself. Finding the dimensions of a graphic is easy; just open it up in your favorite paint program. In Paintshop Pro, the size of the current file in pixels shows up in the bottom-left corner. In Photoshop, choose Image|Image Size and change the width and height measurements from inches to pixels.

Unlike WIDTH and HEIGHT, the LOWSRC attribute should not be used in all your <IMG SRC> tags. Save it for images with large file sizes—at least 20 KB. Like interlacing, the purpose of LOWSRC is to keep visitors to your page from getting bored waiting for a large image to load. When you specify LOWSRC, Netscape puts a "preview" version of the image onscreen first—the low source—then puts up the other elements on the page. When everything else is in place on the page, Netscape goes back to "fill in" the details of the low source image, turning it into a high-quality one.

To use LOWSRC, you need to make two versions of the same image: a small, quick-loading, poor-quality one, and the regular, slow-loading, high-quality one.

You can mix JPEG and GIF file formats any way you want, perhaps using a JPEG as the high-quality image and a GIF as the low-quality one.

To make the LOWSRC image, start by opening the regular one in the paint program of your choice. Then, follow these steps:

1. Reduce the color depth down to 1, 2, 3, or 4 bits. In Paintshop Pro, do this by selecting Colors|Decrease Color Depth and choosing 2 Colors or 16 Colors. In Photoshop, choose Mode|Indexed Color Mode, then 3 or 4 bits/pixel. Remember, image quality doesn't really count here, as long as the picture is fairly recognizable.

2. If the file size of the LOWSRC version is still too big, resize or resample it to smaller dimensions with Image|Resize. Make sure to maintain the aspect ratio. On your Web page, Netscape will remap the LOWSRC image to match the dimensions of the larger, high-quality image, so don't make the height and width of LOWSRC too different from the regular image, or the LOWSRC image might seem skewed.

3. Save the LOWSRC version of the file as a GIF with a new name. To make it easy, just add an *l* onto the regular filename to designate the LOWSRC version, such as fish-l.gif.

In your HTML browser, open your Web page and add a line like this at the appropriate place:

```
<IMG SRC="fish-h.jpg" LOWSRC="fish-l.gif" WIDTH=553 HEIGHT=288>
```

The two files, fish-h.jpg and fish-l.gif, are shown in Figure 2.12. The regular JPEG version is 40 KB, while the LOWSRC version is only 5 KB.

To make coding and maintaining the HTML of your site faster, keep a reference worksheet of all the graphics you use, either on paper or on your hard disk. As you prepare each graphic in your paint program, note on the worksheet its name, file size, dimensions in pixels, and color depth. Then, when you're deep in HTML, you can just refer to this sheet for information instead of going back to the graphics themselves.

Figure 2.12   When used with the LOWSRC attribute of the <IMG SRC> tag, the black-and-white fish-l.gif file (a) will load quickly. Then, it will be gradually replaced by the full-color, high-quality fish-h.jpg version (b).

Sources of Art

I'm not the most artistically gifted person in the world, or even in my house. To paraphrase my sainted grandmother, I can barely draw a straight line with two dots and a ruler. So how does someone like myself get attractive art to use on a Web site? There are four basic options, listed here in increasing order of cost and difficulty:

- Use the public-domain and royalty-free images found on lots of archives all over the Web. This is a cheap, easy, and popular option. In fact, it's too popular. Remember, the art at your site needs to look different from the art at everyone elses' sites. One way to do this is to start with free clipart, then modify it with a paint program such as Paintshop Pro or Photoshop. A little experimenting with filters and colorizing options can yield totally new looks. Be aware, though, that modifying a piece of clipart does not negate any copyright its original creator might have.

- Draw or paint your own unique images. For simple icons and background tiles, this isn't as hard as it sounds, as you'll soon see.

- Buy the art you need, in the form of commercial clipart, stock photography, or by hiring a graphic designer. Hiring a designer, although more expensive, gives you greater control and legal rights to the art you use.

- Use a scanner. Either buy one yourself, or pay to have scans made for you.

The Wizards Speak: Scanner Tips

There are two cardinal rules for scanning material for the Web, according to graphic designers Bonnie Carasso and Michael Sullivan:

1. Get a scanner with the highest possible D-max (dynamic range, a measure of depth). Sullivan explains, "Many people think, because the Web is basically low-resolution, you don't need a good scanner." In fact, to get a scanned image with sufficient "depth" to be attractive on the Web, you need a scanner with a D-max of at least 3, according to Sullivan. Scanners that have this capability should be available for $1,200 or less by the time you read this.

2. Scan the item in at its actual size, not the size you want it to be on your Web page. Save this first scan and keep it as a reference. Then, as Carasso says, "let Photoshop do the rest"—all the enhancements, manipulation, and resizing—and save the finished product in a new file. Although, according to Carasso, "this is exactly the opposite of what all the Photoshop books I've read say," it results in better-quality scans, especially for beginners. Also, it produces an "audit trail," so if you totally mess up an image, you can go easily back to the original file and start over.

Once you've got a scanner, what do you scan? Start with flat objects, such as paper that you've crumpled and then unfolded, different types of fabrics, leaves, and, of course, photographs. When you've got the hang of it, graduate to three-dimensional objects. Everyday items like coins, watches, keys, and kitchen utensils make great scanned images, not just for the objects themselves, but for the textures they produce that can be made into backgrounds and combined with clipart.

For more information on buying and using a scanner, point your Web browser to http://www.hsdesign.com/scanning/welcome.html.

Whose Art Is It, Anyway?

One of the great things about creating your own Web graphics, either with a scanner or with a paint program, is that you don't have to worry about violating anyone else's intellectual property rights. As long as you create your art from scratch or scan common, ordinary things and not, say, the logo on a Coca-Cola can, you have total freedom to do whatever you want with your graphics. And, since you've probably gone to some trouble to create those original works of art, you'll want to specify what people can and cannot do with them by adding a link to a page of copyright or registration information, such as the one in Figure 2.13.

Of course, you should, in turn, respect the copyrights of others. It's sometimes hard to know just what these rights are, though. When you find a piece of art either at a Web site or in a software collection that you want to use, the best and safest rule of thumb is to **always** read and abide by the artist's disclaimer or copyright page. Many people assume, incorrectly, that when someone puts a collection of free images on the Web, he or she has given up all rights to them. In fact, you'll often find provisions that prohibit the use of the art at a commercial site or that require some kind of acknowledgment of the image's creator.

If you're unclear as to who owns the particular image you want to use, you might try emailing the archive's Webmaster, but don't hold your breath waiting for a response. The safest choice in this case is to heave a sigh of regret and move on to less anonymous art.

Never use a well-known logo or cartoon character at your site unless you've gotten written permission from its copyright-holder to do so. Yes, I know it seems like everyone else uses pictures of the Simpsons or Calvin & Hobbes, but you're better off avoiding them. Even if you find these images at clipart archives, be wary of them. Most are playing fast and loose with copyright, knowing that the owners are not going to prosecute every little infringement. You don't want to be the unlucky "example" case, though.

Figure 2.13 This fairly standard copyright page for clipart is from the Image Systems company, http://www.itw.com:80/~imagesys/.

The Wizards Speak: Using a Graphic Artist

The complete design of a fairly large site by a graphic professional doesn't come cheap. Michael Sullivan's design firm, for example, has consciously positioned itself toward high-end Web sites. He explains, "A Web site from our company means committing at least $30,000. That way, I know the client is serious about it, and I know that we have the budget to do a really good job. If you come in and say you've got a budget of $5,000, we can't do it; I'll refer you to a smaller agency."

What if all you need, though, is a catchy opening graphic or some navigational buttons? Prices vary widely. You can expect to pay any-where from $150 for a few buttons or icons to around $2,000 or more for a Web "corporate identity": a home page with an opening graphic (often called a *splash screen*), a coordinating set of back-grounds, buttons, bars, and maybe an image map.

When I asked Gil Kasparek of the Web design firm Up All Night Productions for his favorite graphic tips for aspiring Web wizards, one of the items he mentioned was: "If you can't handle it, hire a professional." How do you know when you can't handle it? One way is to simply compare costs. Using a professional will cost up-wards of $750 per Web page. Doing it yourself will take the cost of your time, plus, for most people, an investment in new hardware and/or software of at least a few hundred dollars, even if you use mostly shareware.

A better way to decide which graphics to create yourself and which to hand off to a professional, according to the Web wizards, is to consider the goals and audience for your site. What do people who come to your site expect to see? What do you expect to get from the site?

Despite what some software companies suggest, you can't just buy a $500 graphics program and instantly fill your Web pages with awe-inspiring artistic masterpieces. The question is, does your audience *expect* awe-inspiring graphics? If so, you'll have to either learn how to create them yourself, or hire someone to create them for you.

Don't get too discouraged by all this. There's still a lot you can do yourself with practice, the right tools, and the techniques presented in this chapter. Just keep in mind that you can always hire someone to fill in the gaps if you don't have the artistic ability or tools to meet all the expectations of your audience, your boss, or yourself.

Finding someone to create some custom art for your Web pages doesn't have to be difficult or time-consuming. There are hundreds of portfolios on the Web from graphic designers all over the world. Using a Net search service such as Alta Vista, Excite, or Yahoo!, search on terms like "graphic designer" and browse through the resulting pages. Email a few likely candidates for more information and price quotes. Remember, this is cyberspace, so there's no need to restrict yourself to designers who are geographically nearby. Using the Internet, it can be just as easy to work with someone on the opposite coast.

Backgrounds

Of all the ways to use graphics at a site, none gives more instant gratification than adding a background. With the simple addition of the BACK-GROUND attribute to the <BODY> tag, you've instantly wallpapered your entire page:

```
<BODY BACKGROUND="mytile.gif">
```

Unlike other graphic tags, with backgrounds, you don't have to worry about affecting the size or position of the other elements on your page; the background will automatically fill the entire page by repeating the specified GIF or JPEG tile over and over again. The tiles themselves are easy to come by, too. Lots of Web sites offer them free for the downloading. Try the collections at these URLs for a start:

- Jay's Background Page at http://www.columbia.edu/~jll32/bg.html
- Pattern Land at http://www.netcreations.com/patternland/
- Texture Land at http://www.eat.com/textures/

Some sites even encourage you to use the tiles directly from their servers, saving you the effort of downloading them. For example, to use one of Netscape's well-known backgrounds, you could use a line like this:

```
<BODY BACKGROUND="http://home.netscape.com/assist/net_sites/bg/water/ _
  raindrops_light.gif">
```

BANISH BAD BACKGROUNDS

It's no wonder that backgrounds are such a popular decoration on so many pages—they're free, easy to use, relatively fast to load, and can potentially add to the visual appeal of a site. Notice the use of the word *potentially*. At many Web sites, backgrounds actually detract from the look of the pages, instead of enhancing them. Take a look at the home pages in Figure 2.14, for example. Even in black-and-white and smaller than actual size, you can see that they seem amateurish. What are the Webmasters of these pages doing wrong? They're breaking one or more of these rules for backgrounds:

- *Make your backgrounds unique.* If you can't make them unique, at least make sure they're not ordinary. As you're browsing through the online collections of free background tiles, remember that many people have been there before you, and many people will be there after you. You don't want to see your carefully chosen background showing up at hundreds of other sites, do you? One provider of Web backgrounds, DiP Pixelware, has addressed this problem by only making a particular tile available for a limited number of days. Then, it's "decommissioned" and a new one is put up in its place. You can check out the current crop of tiles at http://www.algonet.se/~dip/pix-aday.htm.

◎ *Make them seamless.* Seamless backgrounds are ones where the tiles fit together so that you can't tell where one ends and the next begins. Most of the tiles that you'll find in collections on the Web are seamless, but it's always a good idea to test them on a dummy page before you use them all over your site. If you make your own tiles, you can buy add-ons for popular graphic programs to make your tiles seamless. The Seamless Welder filter in Kai's Power Tools is one well-known example. Even after you've used this tool, however, it's always best to test; if your tile has very definite edges, there's only so much a filter can do to even it out.

◎ *Make them work well with the content and image of the site.* A site devoted to the latest rock-music trends should have a very different background than an online newsletter about pension plans. Similarly, a Web page of text should have an extremely subtle background, if any, while one that's mostly large graphics and single-line links could have a bolder background.

◎ *Make sure they're really in the background.* On some professionally designed Web pages, the background isn't really a "background" at all. It serves as the central graphic element of the design, and everything else—all the text, pictures, etc.—is built around it. This is a difficult look to pull off, though, and probably is best left to the graphic professionals. For the rest of us, a background should serve the same purpose that wallpaper or carpeting usually does in a room: to set the stage, not to be the star of the show. The best backgrounds tend to blend into, well, the background. If you've ever spent several minutes browsing a page before you even noticed it *had* a background, study it carefully to pick up some tips about creating good background tiles.

(a)

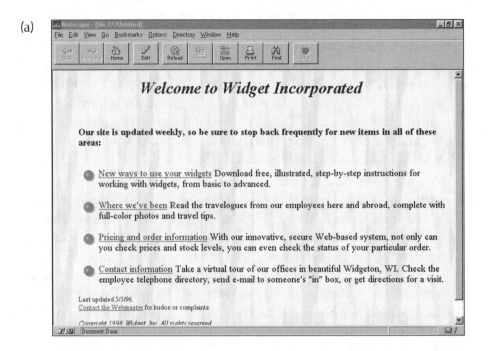

(b)

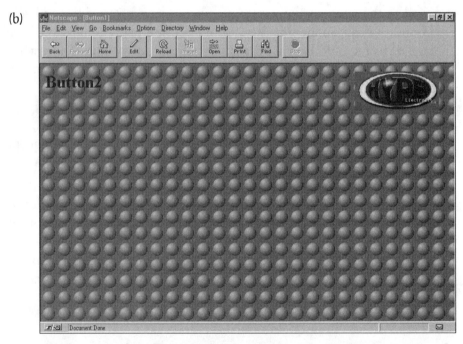

Figure 2.14 This collection of four Web pages have "problem" backgrounds: (a) too often seen at other sites, (b) too distracting and bright-colored, (c) seams showing, (d) inappropriate for the page's content.

(c)

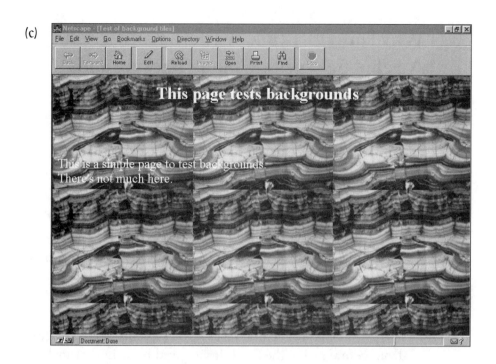

(d)

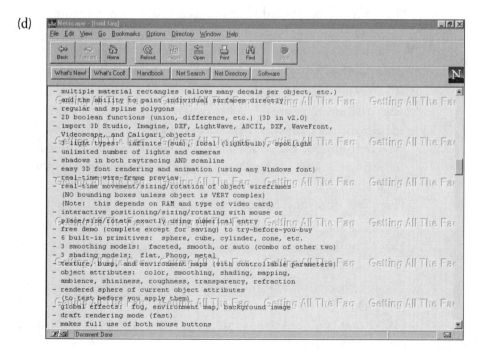

"Why Didn't I Think of That?": A Set of Seamless, Unique Backgrounds

One way to make your own seamless tiles is to use a random pattern, such as the Noise filter found in many paint programs. By varying the color schemes and amount of "noise," and by applying additional filters and other effects on the results, you can create an infinite number of unique backgrounds. Best of all (for me, anyway), you don't need any artistic ability.

Here's how to make a unique, seamless, custom tile using the Paintshop Pro shareware program (included on the CD-ROM):

1. Start in Paintshop Pro with no files open, black as the foreground color, and white as the background color.

2. Select File|New. In the dialog box that appears, set up your new file with both Width and Height equal to 100, and Image Type set to 16.7 million colors. Click OK. (You'll reduce this color depth before saving the file, but you need it for now to make all the different filters available.)

3. With the empty file onscreen, select Image|Special Filters|Add Noise. You'll get the Add Noise dialog box shown in Figure 2.15a. Keep the Random Noise option chosen, and increase the % Noise to about 25—lower for a more subtle pattern, higher for a bolder one. Click OK to get the "speckled" effect shown in Figure 2.15b.

4. Continue applying additional filters and adjusting colors to further customize your tile. When you're finished, reduce the color depth by selecting Colors|Decrease Color Depth. Remember, you're trying for the smallest possible file size without drastically effecting the look of the tile. For this example, the options shown in Figure 2.16 should work well. If you don't like the results, however, just undo and try something else.

5. Save the file as a GIF version 89a, non-interlaced, with Do Not Save Any Transparency Information chosen from the Option button. I called this file noise.gif.

6. Test the background using the BACKGROUND attribute of the <BODY> tag in a very basic HTML file, such as Figure 2.17. Note that you need to have at least some text in your file in order for the background to appear.

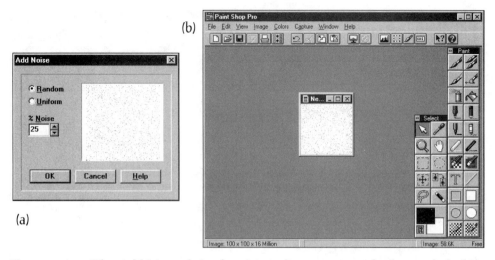

Figure 2.15   The Add Noise dialog box (a) produces an instant background tile (b).

Varying the Steps

Once you've got this technique down, you can quickly produce lots of unique, seamless tiles by changing background and foreground colors, combining the filters in different ways, and varying the brightness, contrast, hue, saturation, and other color properties. (Remember, in order for all of the image-enhancement options to be available in Paintshop Pro, the image needs to be 24-bit. After reopening a file that you've already saved as a GIF, go to the Colors menu and choose Increase Color depth, then 16 Million Colors.) If you have Photoshop, you have even more options for applying noise and conrolling the results.

Figure 2.18 shows just a few of the possibilities for creating new tiles based on the basic noise.gif tile (all included on the CD-ROM as noise1.gif through noise4.gif):

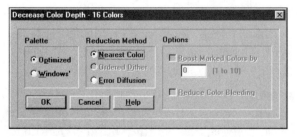

Figure 2.16   The Decrease Color Depth dialog box is set at 16 colors, optimized palette, Nearest Color reduction method.

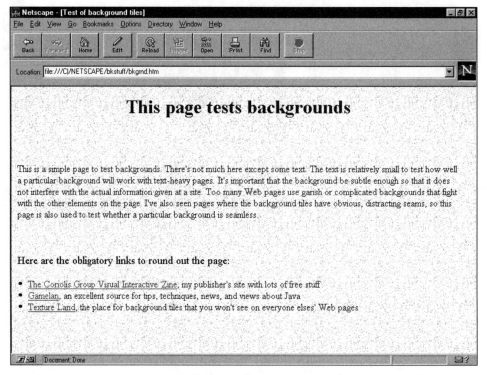

Figure 2.17 This basic page of HTML tests the noise.gif background tile.

@ To get the "pebbled" look in Figure 2.18a, start by applying the Emboss filter to noise.gif. Then, convert the results to grayscale using the Gray Scale option from the Colors or Mode menu. To lighten the results, choose the Adjust option from the Colors menu, then choose Brightness/Contrast from the resulting submenu, and increase the brightness to 45%.

@ For the "parchment" look in Figure 2.18b, apply the Mosaic filter to noise.gif. Then, to make the results yellowish-brown, choose Colorize from the Colors menu. In the Colorize dialog box, set Hue equal to 30.

@ To get the "blue paper" look in Figure 2.18c, use Colors|Histogram Functions|Stretch on noise.gif. Turn the results blue by setting Hue equal to 140.

@ I'm not sure why anyone would want the tile in Figure 2.18d, but I included it to show how far from the original you can get without much effort. It's just the basic noise.gif file with the Find Edges filter applied.

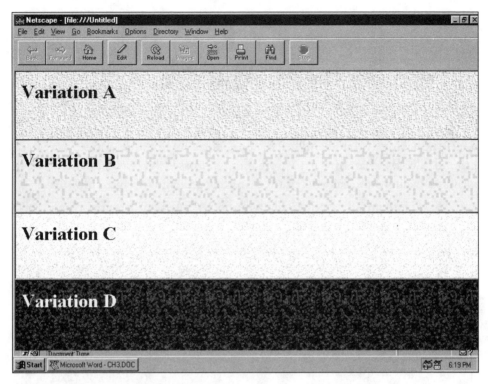

Figure 2.18   Here are four variations on the noise.gif theme: (a) pebbled, (b) parchment, (c) blue paper, (d) wild worms.

Coping with a "Problem" Tile

As you collect background tiles from online sources, clipart collections, and your own experiments, you'll probably find ones that you can't use as-is. Typically, these problem tiles are too busy, too intensely colored, or both. Should you banish them forever from your Web pages? Not necessarily. With a little work and imagination, they can be part of Web pages that you'll be proud to call your own.

A Ghosted Background

One way to deal with a tile that attracts too much attention to itself is to fade it. This technique, usually called *ghosting*, involves converting the colors of the tile to very light grays. Ghosting is especially useful as a way to turn logos and words into suitable background images. For example, consider the logo in Figure 2.19. It's a graphic called nasaworm.gif that you can download from ftp://explorer.arc.nasa.gov/pub/SPACE/LOGOS/.

Figure 2.19   The original NASA logo is fairly large and bright red.

The original logo is large and bright red, definitely not appropriate for a background tile. By changing it to a smaller, embossed, ghosted image, it works well as a background, as you can see on the test page in Figure 2.20.

Here are the steps to change the NASA logo into a ghosted, embossed tile in Paintshop Pro:

1. Open the nasaworm.gif file. It comes in as 490 pixels wide, 123 pixels tall, and 256 colors. The graphic comes right up to the edge of the canvas, which means if it were tiled, the images would run together. To keep this from happening, resize the canvas using Image|Resize Canvas. Change the width to 520 and the height to 175.

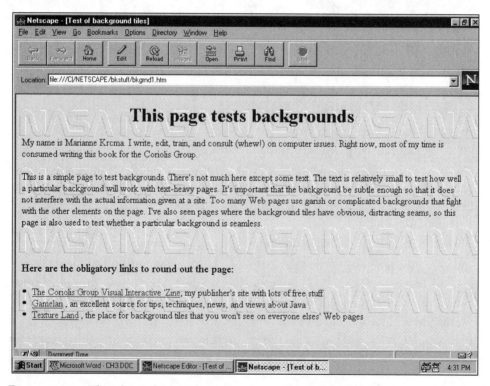

Figure 2.20   The ghosted NASA tile works well on a test Web page.

2. Convert the image to grayscale by choosing Colors|Gray Scale.

3. Apply the emboss filter by choosing Image|Special Filters| Emboss|Apply. This step isn't absolutely necessary for creating ghosted images, but it looks cool and, for more complicated images, it tends to reduce the number of grays involved, which makes editing the palette (step 5) easier.

4. To "ghost" the embossed logo, choose Adjust from the Colors menu. Choose Brightness/Contrast from the resulting submenu, and set the brightness to 40%.

5. The drop-shadow behind the letters is still too dark. Increasing the brightness any further, though, would wash out the rest of the image too much. (This is less of a problem if you use Photoshop as your paint program because it gives better control over the highlights and shadows.) Instead, customize the palette by manually editing just that color. Start by clicking on the eyedropper tool in the Select toolbox. Then, zoom in to somewhere on the shadow and click the tip of the eyedropper on the shadow, as shown in Figure 2.21. The

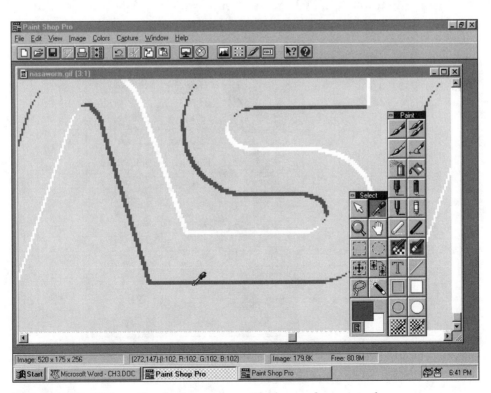

Figure 2.21   Pick up the shadow color with the eyedropper tool.

foreground color in the Select toolbox changes to match the color you clicked on.

6. Double-click on the foreground color in the Select toolbox to bring up the Color Palette dialog box shown in Figure 2.22.

7. Double-click on the selected color, which has a box around it. In this case, it's color 102. You'll see the dialog box in Figure 2.23. Click farther up the spectrum on the right side of the box to change the shadow to a lighter gray. For this example, setting the red, green, and blue values to about 187 is a good choice. Click OK to work your way out of the dialog boxes and back to the main screen.

8. The image is now ghosted, but you're not done yet. The file size is still too big. One way to reduce it is to make the graphic physically smaller. It would be a good idea to shrink this logo even if you weren't concerned with file size; otherwise, the tile would be too big to repeat across the screen enough to show the background effect. Choose Image|Resample, which is similar to Resize, but tends to keep things in better proportion. Change the width to a custom size of 175. Make sure Maintain Aspect Ratio is turned on, so the height will take care of itself.

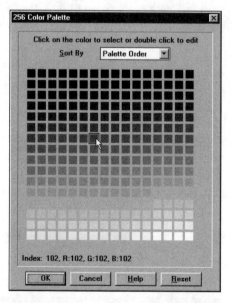

Figure 2.22 The Color Palette dialog box has the shadow color, 102, selected.

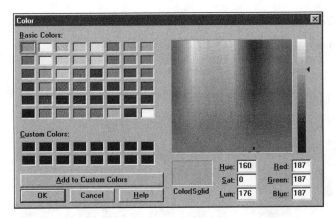

Figure 2.23   The Color dialog box has a new, lighter gray selected.

9. As a last step to further decrease the file size, reduce the color depth to 16 (Colors|Decrease Color Depth|16 Colors). Save the file as a non-interlaced GIF with no transparency.

A Vertical Column Down the Side of Your Page

Another versatile way to use a tile that you like, but don't want to stretch all the way across the screen, is to put it in a vertical column running down the right side of the screen. Gil Kasparek's Up All Night Productions Web site (http://www.alnight.com) puts this trick to excellent use, as you can see in Figure 2.24. A "single-column" background gives tremendous flexibility in terms of what graphics you can use as backgrounds, as well as helping divide the page into grids like those commonly used in traditional, paper-based page layout. For example, Kasparek uses the column created by his background to hold the navigational buttons, while the rest of the page holds the content.

There are several ways to create the effect of a vertical column of art running down the side of your page. For this first try, start with an existing tile that you like. Unlike the other background techniques discussed so far, your tiles don't have to be subtle at all here, so if you've had your eye on that purple plaid tile, here's where you can use it. The tile for this step-by-step procedure is yet another variation on the Noise filter tile discussed

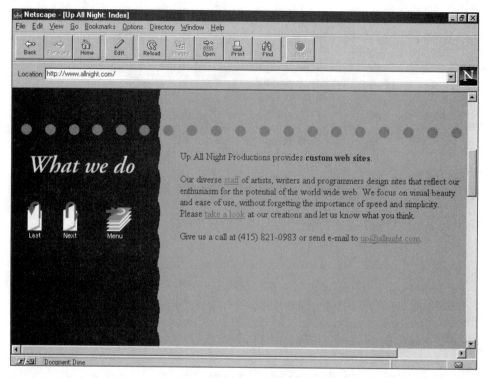

Figure 2.24 At this page from Up All Night Production's Web site, the background creates a two-column grid. Navigational buttons and major headings appear in the left "column," text appears in the right.

earlier in this chapter. This one, called noise5.gif on the CD-ROM, was made in Paintshop Pro by first applying 20% random noise to a 100-by-100-pixel black background, then applying the Mosaic filter with a block width of 2, increasing the brightness 20%, colorizing to hue 140, and decreasing the color depth to 16 colors. The result is the tile in Figure 2.25. Even in black-and-white, you can see that it is too dark and detailed to make a good background the normal way. In color, it looks like a close-up of some dark-blue mineral, as you can see by opening it up from the CD-ROM into the paint program of your choice.

To use the tile in Figure 2.25 as a background, follow these steps:

1. Open the tile in the paint program of your choice.
2. Make a note of the size and color depth of the image; you'll need these measurements later. In Paintshop Pro, this appears in the lower-left cor-

Figure 2.25   The noise5.gif will be the basis of the vertical-column background.

ner of the screen, as shown in Figure 2.26. The noise5.gif tile is 100x100x16. The first number is the width (in pixels), the second is the height, and the third is the number of colors in its palette.

 Many of the measurements in popular paint programs are in pixels. The number of pixels per inch varies on different computer monitors set at different resolutions, but as a rough rule of thumb, estimate about 72 pixels per inch. Using a tile that's 100 pixels wide, then, means you'll end up with a border about an inch-and-a-third wide running down the left side of the screen.

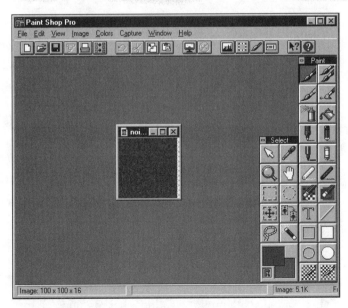

Figure 2.26   The noise5.gif tile is opened in Paintshop Pro. Note the dimensions of the tile in the lower-left corner of the screen.

3. Click the Copy tool or choose Edit|Copy from the menus. You don't need to select anything before copying because you want to copy the entire image.

4. Close the file. If you're prompted to save changes, select No.

5. Now you're ready to create a new tile that incorporates the one you just copied. Click the New tool or choose File|New from the menus. You should see the New Image dialog box, where you can specify the width, height, and color depth of the new file.

6. Set the image width to 1,024, so the tile you create will be wide enough to cover just about any screen. This is important; otherwise, the tile might repeat across the screen, creating the undesirable effect shown in Figure 2.27. Some sites instruct users to set their browser screens to a specific width to avoid this, but it's better for you to take care of it in your design than to ask the user to compensate for it later. Set the image height equal

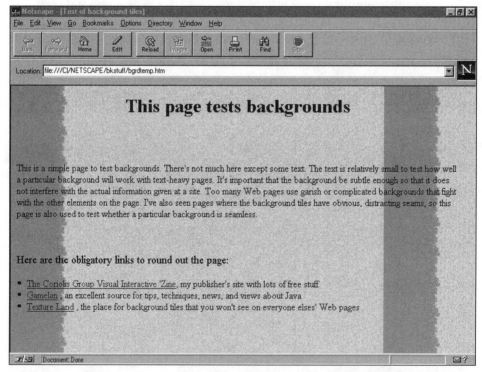

Figure 2.27   This is a failed attempt at creating a background column. It probably looked okay on the creator's monitor, but the tile is too narrow for this monitor, so it repeats.

to the height of the original image, as noted in step 3. (For this example, that's 100.) Increase the image type, if necessary, to match the color depth of the original image, also noted in step 3.

7. Click OK or press Enter, and a very short, wide new file appears on screen.

8. Select Edit|Paste|As New Selection. The tile you copied will appear, and you'll be able to drag it around inside the new file. Move it to the far left side of the file and click to drop it.

9. Make any changes you want to the art: colorize it, increase the color depth and apply a filter, paste another copy of the original tile next to the one you already have to make a wider column, etc.

10. Before saving the finished file, experiment with reducing it to 16 colors (4 bits). In Paintshop Pro, select Colors|Decrease Color Depth|16 Colors. If it looks acceptable at 16 colors, you'll have drastically reduced the size of the finished tile, something visitors to your site who have slow modems will appreciate. If it looks absolutely unacceptable at 16 colors, click the Undo button or select Edit|Undo to change it back to 256 colors.

11. Save the file in GIF89a, non-interlaced format, with no transparency. The example file is called col-blu.gif on the CD-ROM.

12. To test the background, use the <BODY BACKGROUND=> tag in a simple HTML file such as this one:

```
<HTML>
<HEAD>
<TITLE>Minerals home page</TITLE>
</HEAD>
<BODY BACKGROUND="col-blu.gif">
<CENTER>
<H1>The Rocks and Minerals Site</H1>
<H2>A site devoted to the beauty of rocks and minerals</H2>
<BR>
<P>Add a whole bunch of text, links, and other cool stuff here.</P>
<BR>
<ADDRESS>You can reach me by e-mail at: <A
HREF="mailto:rocky@mine1.com"> rocky@mine1.com</A></ADDRESS>
</CENTER>
</BODY>
</HTML>
```

13. Save the file as col-test.htm (or col-test.html, depending on the tool you're using to create the page). To preview the results, use the function of your Web browser that opens local files. With Netscape Navigator, select File|Open File in Browser and choose col-test.htm to produce the page shown in Figure 2.28.

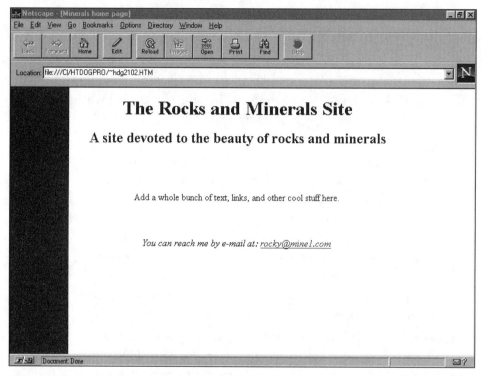

Figure 2.28   The finished sample page works well with the column background.

You might have noticed in step 12 that I centered everything on the col-test.htm sample Web page. This brings up an important point to remember when using a single-column background: place your text carefully to avoid having it "disappear" into the art on the left side of the page. You'll probably want to center the text, indent it with multiple <UL> tags, and/or put it in a table.

VARYING THE STEPS

Although it does place some restrictions on the way you can use text on the page, this kind of background greatly increases your options for usable tiles, and, of course, it looks cool. Once you get the procedure down, you can easily make new tiles from scratch this way—no artistic talent necessary. In fact, some of the most elegant backgrounds you'll see on the Web involve very simple adaptations of this technique. Try these with your favorite paint program:

◎ Start with a 1,024-by-50-pixel file with a black foreground and white background. Create a filled-in black box on the left side of the file, as high as the file itself (50 pixels) and about 1/2 inches (108 pixels) wide. Before saving the file, decrease it to an indexed color depth of 2 colors (1 bit). This results in an extremely small file that still makes an attractive, understated background, as shown in Figure 2.29a.

◎ Reopen the black-and-white file created in the previous suggestion. Switch the foreground and background colors to white-on-black. Choose the airbrush or spraycan tool. Paint freehand with this tool along the edge of the black box, applying more white on the very edge and less as you move into the box, to make the black and white portions of the tile appear to fade into each other, as shown in Figure 2.29b.

◎ With no files open, set the foreground to a dark or intense color and the background to a light shade of the same or a complementary color. Create a new 1,024-by-50-pixel file. Using the pencil or color-marker tool, draw a wavy vertical line all the way down the file, about 144 pixels (2 inches) in from the

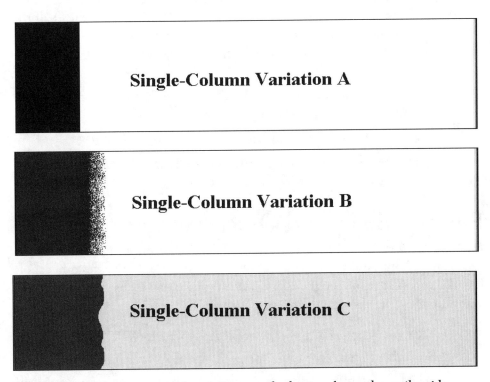

Single-Column Variation A

Single-Column Variation B

Single-Column Variation C

Figure 2.29 Here are several variations on the basic column-down-the-side background.

left side. If you're using Photoshop, select the area to the left of the line with the Magic Wand. Next, choose the flood fill tool or Edit|Fill, and click anywhere to the left of the line you drew. You should end up with a background similar to the one in Figure 2.29c. With this method of creating tiles—or in fact any method that involves freehand drawing—be sure to test carefully for seams. You might need to tweak the top or bottom of the line you made so that it blends seamlessly as a background.

Trimming Seams in Photoshop

If your tile is "seamy" and doesn't produce a continuous, smooth image when used as a background, Web wizard Bonnie Carasso suggests trying this Photoshop trick to fix it:

1. Open the file. If it's a GIF, select Mode|RGB color to make the filters available.

2. Note the width and height in pixels using Image|Image Size.

3. Select Filter|Other|Offset. In the Offset dialog box, fill in Horizontal with half the width from step 2 and Vertical with half the height. Make sure Wraparound is selected in Undefined Areas. Click OK. Photoshop will "fold the edges" of the image into the middle, so the "seamy" part is in the center.

4. Use one or more of the Smudge, Lighten, Blur, and Rubber Stamp tools to even out the center of the tile.

5. Save the new tile and test it out on a sample Web page.

This technique works best when the seams are not too pronounced and the tile pattern is fairly abstract.

Buttons, Balls, and Other Icons

Many of the Web wizard tips and techniques about backgrounds apply to buttons as well. You can make lots of unique icons using the filters and other tools found in popular paint programs, or you can download GIFs from one of the many archives that provide them, such as these:

- CERN image index at http://www3.org/hypertext/WWW/Icons
- Icon Tools at http://www.halcyon.com/gened/Icons/icons.html
- Psyched Up Graphics at http://www.econ.chs.dk/people/nagemal/psyched/

"Why Didn't I Think of That?": "Fake" Buttons

You can create custom "graphic" buttons right from within Netscape's version of HTML, without any drawing or painting at all, using either form tags or table tags. Tables and forms are discussed in detail in later chapters. For now, here's the relevant HTML code to produce Figure 2.30:

```
<HTML>
<HEAD>
<TITLE> Button samples </TITLE>
</HEAD>
<BODY>
<H3>

Here are two shortcuts to create beveled buttons without any drawing
or painting.<BR>
Both of these methods work best when you just need a single button
on a page.

</H3>

<P>The first way is to use forms, which produces a button like _
   this:</P>
<!--Substitute your own link in the ACTION and your own button text

_
   in the VALUE-->
<FORM
      METHOD=LINK ACTION="http://nowhere.com/homepage.htm">
      <INPUT TYPE="SUBMIT" VALUE="Home">
</FORM>

<P>The second way is to use the Netscape BORDER attribute with the _
   standard table tags, like this:</P>
<!--Substitute your own link in the A HREF tag-->
```

AN EASY BEVELED BUTTON IN PHOTOSHOP

Using table and form tags to make beveled buttons is slick, but has some major limitations, mostly because each form will be placed on a line by itself and tables with more than one button won't have the right beveled effect. It's a good idea, therefore, to know how to make a more "traditional" beveled button.

Here's a quick way to make a beveled button in Photoshop:

1. In a blank, "scratch" file, use the Marquee tool to select a rectangle about the size of the button you want.

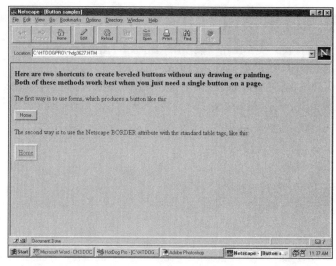

Figure 2.30 The first button is actually a single item form. The second one in this screen is actually a mini-table.

2. Change the foreground color so that the red, green, and blue values each equal about 187, which produces a neutral gray.

3. Fill the selected rectangle with the foreground color.

4. Choose Filter|Stylize|Emboss. Keeping the angle at 135, set the height to 9 pixels and the amount to 50%. Click OK.

5. Crop, reduce color depth to 4 bits, and save the button. Voilà! Instant beveled button.

6. The finished button should look like the first one in Figure 2.31.

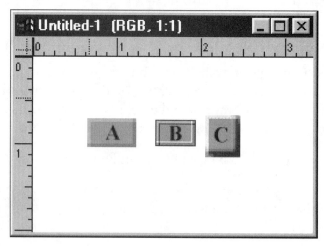

Fig 2.31 Each of these three buttons was made in less than a minute using Photoshop.

Varying the Steps

There are all sorts of variations on making a basic button. For example, if you stroke the rectangle selected in step 1 with black before going on to step 2, you get a stylized button like the second one in Figure 2.31. Or, if you substitute applying a linear gradient using bright foreground and background colors for step 2, you get a jewel-like effect, like the third button in Figure 2.31.

"Why Didn't I Think of That?": Three Methods to Make a 3D ball

Every Web wizard worth his or her wand contains a large collection of 3D balls in assorted sizes, colors, and textures to use as the basis for lists, navigational buttons, logos, and bars. The obvious way to start building your collection, of course, is to "swipe" from public-domain archives. Another, more elegant way is to surf on over to Patrick Hennessey's very useful and clever Interactive Graphics Renderer at http://www.eece.ksu.edu/IGR/.

From the main screen of this Web-based C program, shown in Figure 2.32, you can fill out a form that creates a custom 3D ball, bar, or other icon for you. The steps given at the site are pretty straightforward, so I won't go into the details here. Note, however, that the license agreement specifies that the graphics be used only for personal and not-for-profit purposes.

The Pixelsite company promises an even more elaborate version of this idea at http://www.pixelsight.com:80/PS/pixelsite.html. It wasn't completely ready at the time I visited, but it shows a lot of potential for making buttons and balls with all kinds of special effects—beveling, 3D, metallic looks, etc.—just by filling out an online form.

A third way to get 3D balls involves making them yourself using Photoshop or some similar high-end paint program. (Paintshop Pro won't work for this because it doesn't have the necessary filters.) This example also includes an easy way to make a drop-shadow, a very popular effect that adds to the 3D look. If you don't want a drop-shadow, skip steps 4 through 7:

1. Start in a new file about 4x3 inches, with Content set to Transparent.

2. Change the Marquee tool from a rectangle to a circle by double-clicking on it and choosing Elliptical from the shape list in the

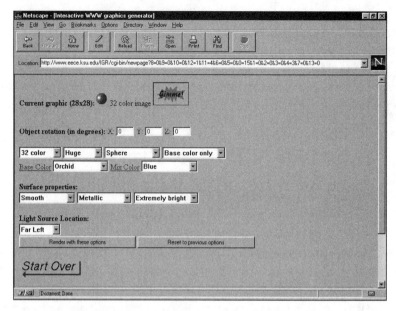

Figure 2.32 Patrick Hennessey's Interactive Graphics Renderer produces an endless supply of 3D balls and bars.

dialog box that appears (Adobe calls these dialog boxes "palettes"), as shown in Figure 2.33.

3. Hold down the Shift key while clicking and dragging with the Marquee tool until the circle is about the right size for your 3D ball.

4. Change the foreground color to a dark gray (about 80 red, green, and blue).

5. Fill the circle with the gray foreground color as the basis for your shadow.

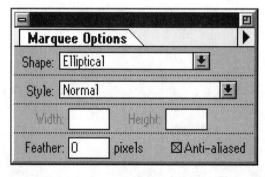

Figure 2.33 Photoshop's Marquee palette with Elliptical as the selected shape.

6. Copy the gray circle selection to the clipboard, so you can paste it back after you're finished making the shadow.

7. Select Filter|Blur|Gaussian. In the resulting dialog box, set the blur to about 3 pixels. This will soften the shadow.

8. Now you're ready to work on the ball itself. Choose Edit|Paste, then the Magic Wand, and drag the pasted circle up and to the left a few pixels.

9. Change the foreground color to white and the background color to whatever you want your ball to be. Fairly intense colors work well. (Yes, I said to change the *background* to the color of the finished ball. This will work.)

10. Select the Gradient tool. In the palette that appears, set the options to Radial gradient, Foreground to Background, Midpoint all the way down to 13%, and Radial Offset to about 10%, as shown in Figure 2.34a.

11. In the selected circle, drag from about the 10 o'clock position to about 5 o'clock, as shown in Figure 2.34b.

12. (**Optional**) To increase the sense of depth, especially if you're not using a drop-shadow, change the foreground color to a dark gray, choose the airbrush tool and low pressure (about 4%), and run over the lower-right corner of the ball with your mouse. You should see a subtle shadow appear. If it's too big, undo it, reduce the brush size and/or decrease the pressure, and try again.

13. Crop tightly, experiment with reducing the color depth, and export the finished ball (Figure 2.34c) to a transparent, non-interlaced GIF.

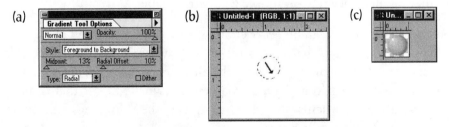

Figure 2.34   With the Gradient palette set up to change a circle into a ball (a), drag diagonally across the circle (b) to complete the 3D effect (c).

Here's a shortcut method of creating a drop-shadow for balls, buttons, and similar shapes in Photoshop:

1. Using the Marquee tool, click and drag the mouse to create a circle or rectangle the size of the ball or button you want to make.

2. Copy that empty area to the clipboard.

3. Fill the (still selected) circle or rectangle with gray and apply a Gaussian blur to make the shadow.

4. Paste the empty area back on, move it up and to the left, and fill it to make whatever image you want.

5. This works well whenever you're making simple geometric shapes for use on your Web pages. It's not an "official" way—it doesn't involve layers, masks, or channels—but it's easy and it does the job.

Bars

Use graphic bars sparingly at your Web site. Ask yourself if empty space would serve just as well as a bar to break up the elements on a page. Having too many bars on a page looks choppy, increases the download time, and could mean that you've got too much stuff on the page. Maybe it would be better to separate the information into several linked pages instead of a single long one broken by bars.

It's especially tricky to use bars with a graphical background. Whatever graphic you use for the bars needs to complement the background while being distinct from it. The background and bars at the home page of Up All Night Productions, discussed earlier in this chapter and shown in Figure 2.24, work well together because they rely on simple geometric shapes.

You don't have to draw an object over and over to create the kind of bar shown in Figure 2.24. In fact, thanks to a bit of Web wizardry with fonts, you don't even have to draw it once; instead, rely on a *type ornament* such as those in Windows' Wingdings font. A type ornament is a small graphic that is mapped to a keystroke in a particular font. For example, in the Wingdings font, typing a lowercase *u* produces a diamond.

A Nontraditional Bar

Follow these steps to create a bar of diamonds similar to the bar of dots at Up All Night Productions Web site:

1. Start up Windows' character map, found in the Accessories group, and browse through the fonts until you find Wingdings or some other font that includes type ornaments. Make note of the keystroke for the ornament you want to use, *u* in this case. Close the character map.

2. In your favorite paint program, start with a new file about 600 pixels wide and 100 high. (In Photoshop, set the Contents to Transparent.)

3. Set the foreground to some primary color, such as bright blue, which is color 41 in my default 256-color palette (R:0, G:51, B:255).

4. Choose the text tool and click anywhere in the empty file. In the dialog box that appears, choose Wingdings as the font, Regular as the style, and 24 as the size. In the text box, repeatedly type the keystroke you noted in step 1. For the bar of diamonds, type *u* 16 times.

5. Click OK or press Enter, then position the bar wherever you want it in the file, and click to place it.

6. Crop the file as small as possible, reduce it to 16 colors (4 bits) and save it as a transparent GIF.

7. When you test your bar on a sample page of HTML, you should end up with something like Figure 2.35.

"Why Didn't I Think of That?": A Disappearing Splash Screen

Suppose you want visitors to your site to see an initial, flashy screen with a big graphic and/or a pithy quote before they enter your "real" site. How do you do this without having them go to the

Figure 2.35 The bar of diamonds is tested on a sample Web page.

effort of clicking on a link? Well, as with most things on the Web, there are several possible ways. I'm going to show you the quick and easy way here. (Surprised?) This technique is based on the use of the <META> tag, which was added in HTML 2.0. <META> has several uses, including the ability to wait for a specific amount of time before automatically switching to a particular page of HTML—exactly what you need to produce the effect of a disappearing splash screen.

Here's the HTML for a sample "splash page" that creates this effect:

```
<HTML>
<HEAD>
    <TITLE>This Month's Splash Screen</TITLE>
    <META HTTP-EQUIV="refresh" CONTENT="15; URL=realhome.htm">
</HEAD>
<BODY BGCOLOR="#000000" TEXT="#ffffff" LINK="#ff0000"
VLINK="#b7b7b7">
<IMG SRC="jpegs/biglogo.jpg" ALT="my logo" HEIGHT="300" WIDTH="400"
>
</BODY>
</HTML>
```

Basically, this code just creates a Web page that presents the image biglogo.jpg on a black background. The <META> line counts to 15 seconds after this page is displayed, then automatically tells the browser to move on to the realhome.htm page.

To use this at your own site, just make a splash page with the <META> tag at the top, substituting whatever number of seconds you want for 15 and whatever page you want to link to for realhome.htm. As always, be sure to test this; you don't want visitors waiting too long on your "doorstep," but you also want to give them sufficient time to appreciate your splash screen in all its graphic glory.

Animated GIFs

There are many ways to add movement to your site. Most of the advanced methods discussed in other chapters of this book, such as the use of Shockwave, Java, or VRML, involve a considerable investment in time, resources, or both. If all you want is a simple bouncing ball or spinning star to add a little life to a page, though, there's a fast, simple, fun, and relatively unexploited technique: GIF animation. All you need is a little creativity and two pieces of software: the paint

program of your choice to make the GIFs and a utility such as Steve Rimmer's
GIF Construction Set (included on the CD-ROM) to put them together.

> Unfortunately, Netscape is the only browser that can handle
> GIF animation at this point. Any other browser will ignore
> the animation instructions and just display the first GIF in your
> animation. So, if you expect that your site will have more than
> it's share of visitors without Netscape, make sure the first GIF
> in your series looks okay on its own.

You're actually making the Web equivalent of those flip-books you probably
played with as a kid. The first step, then, is thinking up a series of graphics that
will "flip" well without taking up much overhead in terms of file size. Many
good GIF animations consist of variations of a single image. You might, for
example, have a ball change colors, a balloon float up and down, or a star appear
to zoom in, starting small and rapidly growing bigger. You'll want at least four or
five individual, transparent GIFs to form a smooth animation sequence.

Take a look at the series of GIFs in Figure 2.36. I created the first one, wow.gif,
freehand in Paintshop Pro. Then I resized it smaller and smaller, saving each resized
version as wow1.gif, wow2.gif, etc. All six of these little icons are on the CD-ROM.

1. Once you have your GIFs and have installed the GIF Construction Set,
   you're ready to put together your animation. Here are the steps to make
   an animation out of the "wow" series of GIFs:

2. Start the GIF Construction Set and choose File|New. You shoul d see a
   screen like the one in Figure 2.37.

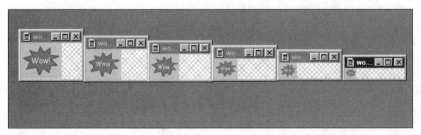

Figure 2.36   This series of GIFs will make a starburst animation.

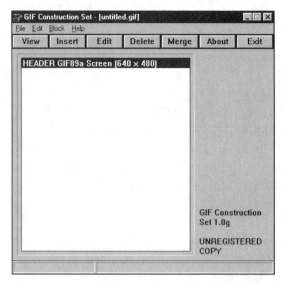

Figure 2.37 Here is the first screen of a new animation using the GIF Construction Set.

3. There are two main types of items, or *blocks*, that you're going to put in this new file: image blocks and control blocks. The easiest way to handle this is to put all the image blocks in first, then go back and add the control blocks. Click the Insert button and choose Image from the menu that comes up. You'll get the standard Open dialog box. Choose the first GIF in your animation sequence from this dialog box. For this example, choose wow1.gif, the smallest of the starbursts. Click OK to insert it. You'll probably see a dialog box like the one in Figure 2.38, asking what to do with the color palette. Since this is the first image, make it the global palette by

Figure 2.38 This dialog box handles the color differences among GIFs in an animation.

choosing "Remap this image as the global palette" and clicking OK. Notice that the block you insert is added below the currently selected block; this is true throughout the GIF Construction Set. Click Insert|Image again to add the next GIF, wow2.gif. This time, accept the default choice, "Dither this image to the local palette."

4. Repeat step 3 for wow3.gif, wow4.gif, wow5.gif and wow.gif. You should end up with a file like the one in Figure 2.39.

5. Now you're ready to add the control blocks. Each control block affects the image below it, so start by clicking on the very first line in the file, then click Insert|Control to add a control block above the first image block. With the control block highlighted, click Edit. You'll see a dialog box like the one in Figure 2.40.

6. In the dialog box, turn on the Transparent Color flag. You'll need to pick the transparency color by clicking on the eyedropper button. The screen changes to show the GIF by itself in the upper-left corner, as shown in Figure 2.41. Click with the eyedropper on the GIF's background. The dialog box appears again, with the transparency color you selected. For this example, it should be light gray, color 247 in my palette. (Your number might be different.) Since you want the animation to run quickly, set the Delay flag to 1, which means each GIF in the series will appear onscreen for one-hundredth of a second. Change the Remove By flag to Background to wipe the old GIF off before the new one appears in the animation.

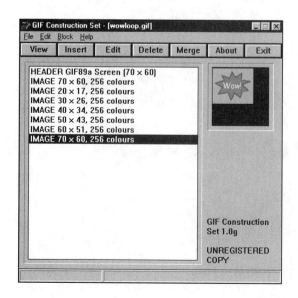

Figure 2.39 All of the image blocks are now in place for the starburst animation.

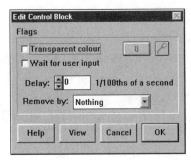

Figure 2.40   This dialog box controls how the image appears.

7. Repeat step 6 for the other images. To save time, just copy and paste the control block from step 6, above each of the other image blocks.

8. Now you need to decide whether or not you want to play the GIF in a continuous loop. Either option has a drawback. If you don't loop your animation, the user might miss it completely, especially if it's at the bottom of a multiple-screen Web page. However, if you loop it continuously, the page will seem to never finish loading, as the loop is loaded over and over again by Netscape. The best compromise in this example is to loop it for a specific period—say, 10 or 15 times. To do this, click on the first line of the file, and choose Insert|Loop. Click Edit to bring up the Edit Loop Block dialog box in Figure 2.42. Set the number of iterations to 10 and click OK.

Figure 2.41   The GIF is in the far-left corner of the screen.

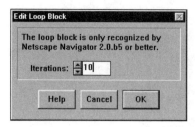

Figure 2.42 The Edit Loop Block dialog box lets you determine how many times your animation will play.

9. Before saving the file, you need to properly size the "screen" on which your animation will play: as wide as the widest image in your file and as tall as the tallest. Once again, click on the first line of the file. The click Edit to bring up the Edit Header dialog box in Figure 2.43. For this example, set the width to 70 and the depth (height) to 60. Save the file as wowloop.gif and close the GIF Construction Set.

10. Test your animation by creating a simple Web page like the one in Figure 2.44 and viewing it with Netscape. Here's the HTML:

```
<HTML>
<HEAD><TITLE>Amazing Ants</TITLE>
</HEAD>
<BODY BGCOLOR="#62FF00" TEXT="#000000" LINK="#FF3578"
VLINK="#009A00" ALINK="#FFFFFF">
<BASEFONT SIZE=4>
<H1><CENTER>It's amazing what a little ant can do!</CENTER></H1>
<HR WIDTH=25%>
<H2>Here are just two amazing facts about our friend the ant:</H2>
<BR>
<IMG ALIGN=left SRC="wowloop.gif" HEIGHT=60 WIDTH=70>Did you know _
   an ant can carry 10 times its own body weight for distances up to
   _
   10 yards? That's like a person carrying a car for a mile!!<BR>
<BR>
<BR>
<IMG ALIGN=left SRC="wowloop.gif" HEIGHT=60 WIDTH=70>In some countries,
fried or chocolate-covered ants are a popular snack. They're eaten like we
eat popcorn!<BR>
<BR>
<HR WIDTH=25%>
<H2>Find out more:</H2>
<UL>
<LI><A HREF="http://antsrus.com/trivia.htm">Ants R Us Terrific Trivia
Page</A>
<LI><A HREF="http://asu.edu/history.html">Famous Ants in History</A>
</UL>
</BODY>
</HTML>
```

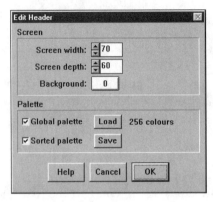

Figure 2.43 This Edit Header dialog box shows the correct width and depth for the starburst animation.

 For more information on animated GIFs and to see a gallery of what other Web wizards have done with this technique, check out Royal Frazier's GIF 89a Animation Page at http://member.aol.com/royalf/gifanim.htm. To download free animated GIFs that you can use at your site, surf on over to the MicroMovie MiniMultiplex's Animated Icons page at http://www.teleport.com/~cooler/MMMM/Icons/index.html.

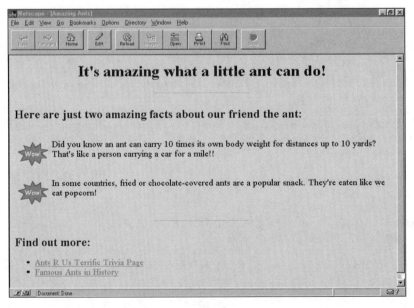

Figure 2.44 This simple Web page tests the wowloop.gif animation.

Web Wizard's Touchstones for Graphics

Do spend time experimenting with the filters and special effects in your paint program to discover weird and wonderful ways to work with graphics.

Don't be bound by the traditional graphic elements on a Web page. But tons don't have to be squares or circles; bars don't have to be narrow rectangles.

Do consider investing in a good scanner with a D-max of at least 3.

Don't try to scan an item in at the size you want it on your Web page. Instead, scan it at its original size and resize it in your paint program.

Do keep a Web graphic worksheet that tracks the file size, location, image dimensions, color depth, and any special effects for each image you use on your pages.

Don't cover your page with busy background tiles. If you want to use a detailed tile, ghost it or put it in a single column down your page.

Do work to make every graphic at your site load as quickly as possible. Always use the HEIGHT and WIDTH attributes of the <IMG SRC> tag, and whenever appropriate, use cropping, reduced color depths, interlacing, LOWSRC, and thumbnails.

Don't use a GIF where a JPEG would work better, and vice versa.

Do experiment with animated GIFs. If nothing else, it's good practice for more sophisticated animation techniques to come.

Don't publish graphics at your site without testing them first for transparency, seamlessness, appropriate colors, and reasonable speed.

III

A FEW WORDS ABOUT WORDS

It's tempting to think of text as the least-important and least-interesting part of designing your Web site. After all, reading and writing are things you've been doing most of your life. You know how they work already. If you're like most aspiring Web wizards, you're eager to explore new forms of communication that you're not as familiar with. Your thought processes might go something like this:

"Well, I'll get the splash screen set up first. It'll be really cool, with animation and sound. Then, I've got to figure out what kind of background to put up—I've already got some great 3D buttons that I've been wanting to use, so the background should work with them. I know I want a few image maps; maybe I should use frames, too? Oh, and of course I'll have to write some stuff, but that's the easy part. I'll do that later, when I know how much space I'll have left to fill."

It's easy to think like this, but it's wrong. Inevitably, the best and most useful sites are those that provide original content, and at least at this point in the evolution of the Web, that content is primarily text. True, there are some great sites whose main purpose is to deliver sound, especially the pages of music stores like the Internet Underground Music Archive (http://www.iuma.com/) and bands like Please (http://www.please.com/), but even these are really text-driven. How do you decide what audio clip you want to hear? By reading about it. And the more information you're given in the text, the better; bandwidth (which indicates the speed at which data is transmitted) is still much too narrow and expensive to waste downloading sound and video that you have no interest in.

For navigational purposes, some sites try to minimize text by substituting image maps—instead of just reading about your choices, you see a graphic that provides visual clues about the pages you can jump to. Image maps like the one in Figure 3.1 can certainly be fun and visually interesting, but they're tricky to use, both for the Web page designer and the end user. You've got to have an image that downloads fairly quickly and takes up the least possible space on the server, while being sufficiently large and detailed so that the user will be able to navigate around it without becoming frustrated (more on this in Chapter 5). Even if you decide that image maps are the perfect way to organize your site, you'll probably still end up adding a written list of the links that your image map contains, for the benefit of users whose browsers don't support image maps.

Eventually, interactive virtual-reality techniques like those in VRML will greatly reduce the use of text at Web sites. Web wizards are already busy figuring out how to make this jump in Web design from 2D to 3D, as you'll see later in this

Figure 3.1 At Web sites like this one, image maps (covered in Chapter 5) can effectively substitute for some text. Too often, though, the image-map graphic is far from being worth a thousand words—except in terms of downloading time!

book. A few years from now, perhaps, you might be in an online record store, browsing through a virtual bin of albums by your favorite band. When you pick up an album that interests you, a "store clerk" might appear to tell you about its contents. If you're interested, the "clerk" will play a sample for you.

It's easy to dream up many similarly enticing scenarios, but for now, the technology—especially in terms of bandwidth—just can't keep up with people's imagination and creativity. If you had the choice between finding an album the virtual-reality way but had to wait 10 minutes or more just for the music store to initially appear, or reading equally informative reviews in a traditional online catalog that appears in about 10 seconds, which would you choose? Well, you might choose the virtual-reality version once or twice, just for the novelty, but you'd probably find yourself returning to the traditional, text-based model when you really wanted information.

Finding Text to Fill Your Site

At this point, you might be thinking, "It's easy for *her* to keep going on and on about how I've got to come up with interesting text for my site. *She* doesn't have to come up with it!" Well, I *do* know what a challenge it can be to provide original content (I became acutely aware of it while writing this book!), but if you look carefully at what you think about, discuss, and do every day, you'll find more than enough ideas. Then, it's just a matter of doing a little research and experimentation to fill in the details.

You probably already have word-processed files full of potentially interesting text for the relatively small segment of the Web population who are likely visitors for your site. If your Web site supports your business, look at the information you provide to current customers, employees, board members, and salespeople. Much of the information in those catalogs, brochures, memos, newsletters, and press releases could be adapted for the Web.

If your site is for personal use, you might have to dig a little deeper. How about the journal you kept on your cross-country camping trip? The stories your third-grader wrote at school? The genealogical information you've been gathering? The notes you've jotted about your favorite wines or take-out places? All of these, and much more, could be adapted to provide fodder for your Web pages.

The word *adapted* is key here. Writing for online media is not quite the same as writing for print media. The tone of writing on the Web tends to be more informal, personal, and opinionated than other forms of written communication.

I don't know why that is, exactly—it would make a good sociological study for someone, which would in turn make excellent content for a Web page—but it's true. I suspect that the Web itself is largely a recreational medium. Many people access the Web primarily with a desire to explore, discover, and have fun. Most people on the Web are there with enjoyment and discovery in mind; they're not looking for the same no-nonsense stuff that's found in trade journals. With that in mind, the company brochure you've decided to put on your site probably should not just be uploaded "as is." Trim the corporate-speak and any obvious "sell." Add some anecdotes and quotes. Don't appear to be taking yourself too seriously.

In the true spirit of the Web, give information away at your site that would otherwise cost people time or money. Many companies and other Web site owners are discovering that the Web, even when it doesn't provide a great way to *sell* products and services, still is a great way to *advertise and market* those products and services. Ragu, for example, has garnered lots of positive publicity from the somewhat tongue-in-cheek Italian lessons, recipes, travel tips, and other goodies it offers at http://www.eat.com/index.html. Again, you probably already have similar information at hand; it just needs to be collected and formatted for the Web.

Remember, your text doesn't have to be brilliant or earth-shaking, it just has to be interesting enough to cause people to spend a few minutes of their lives at your site. It doesn't have to be interesting to everybody, just to a reasonable percentage of the people you're trying to reach. (If you don't know who you're trying to reach, you might want to go back to Chapter 1 and read about planning your site.)

"Why Didn't I Think of That?": Instant Content

Do you have a sales force that travels all over the country or the world? If so, write up their war stories, complaints, and tips about hotels, restaurants, and local customs, and add some relevant links. Now you've got an instant Web-based travel guide. Update it as the salespeople visit new places so that you can integrate it with your industry's calendar of major events. If the blowout industry-wide convention is next month in Las Vegas, add some timely advice from people in your company who've been there before, and re-member to include some links—maybe to a virtual casino?

If you're in a technical field or have a specialized hobby, you un-doubtedly had to master the jargon of your specialty. It would be a good idea to jot some of the more obscure terms down, convert your writing to HTML, and add some links and perhaps a few audiovisuals. *Voilà*—you've got a dictionary that other experts and wannabes in your field will find quite handy.

The possibilities for adding valuable information to your site are endless. Spend a few hours brainstorming, and you'll probably come up with enough ideas to keep your site full of text for months to come. To get you started, here are a few more suggestions for information to put on your Web pages:

- Macros and templates that someone in your organization has written for the word-processing or spreadsheet programs you use.

- Candid reviews of movies you've seen, books you've read, albums you've heard, or computer games you've played, with links to the sources if they're online.

- A calendar of events for your industry or special interest, with relevant links.

- Motivational and training material used by your sales force, customer-service, or technical support staff—as long as it doesn't give away any competitive advantages, of course.

- A directory of people and organizations relevant to your specialty—with names, descriptions, online addresses, and (with permission) street addresses and telephone numbers.

The Wizards Speak: Making Text-Based Sites Work

According to one Web wizard, most Web sites are at least 60% text. So, your site will probably have at least as much text as it does audiovisuals. Maybe your site will even be entirely text-based, except for an opening graphic and maybe a few buttons. A text-based site is not a bad thing, nor does it have to be boring for the user. Like any other method of communication, it has advantages and disadvantages.

The advantages of a text-based site include these:

- Relatively low maintenance.
- Fast delivery of information to users.
- Will look basically the same with all browsers.
- Low cost.
- Easy to change whenever necessary.

The main disadvantages of a text-based site are that it:

@ Must provide highly valuable to attract and keep users' attention.

@ Needs special attention to navigation, especially if the site is large.

@ Might look "old-fashioned" to some Web users.

Remember, the more intrinsically valuable information you have at your site, the less "glitz" you need. Still, there are many ways of delivering text to the user, some more successful than others. Consider traditional print media like books and magazines. As you thumb through the chapters and articles, you get an immediate, subconscious feel for the material—whether it's heavy or light, old-fashioned or cutting-edge, fluff or substance. Even without pictures to give you hints, you know these things. The publisher's use of fonts, whitespace (the places on the page that don't have any text, such as the margins), subheadings, lists, and other design devices tell you about the content, even if you're not consciously aware of it.

Michael Sullivan, the creative director of the design firm Haywood & Sullivan (http://www.hsdesign.com), calls this the "Information Design Technique." Sullivan considers it essential to translate this concept from the printed page to the Web page. As he says, "Users should be able to glance at a page on your Web site and know what it's for, just like you can glance at an index in a book and know it's an index without reading it."

Take a look at the Web pages in Figure 3.2. They all depend primarily on text, but each has its own distinctive look. At the same time, they all have certain design elements in common that make them helpful and interesting to the user:

@ Good use of whitespace.

@ Good use of type, within the restrictions imposed by HTML.

@ Short paragraphs interspersed with headings and lists whenever appropriate.

@ Navigational help.

@ Logical organization.

@ Annotated links that are integrated into the text.

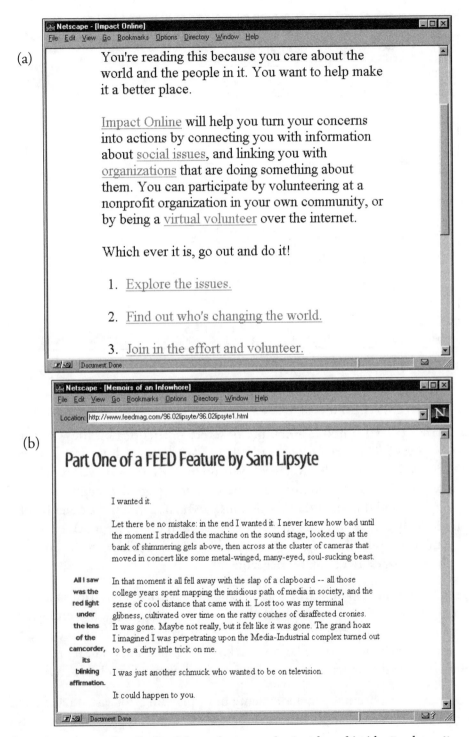

Figure 3.2a, 3.2b Each of these three popular text-based Web sites have its own style.

(c)

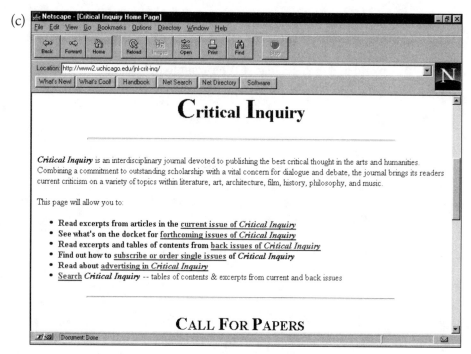

Figure 3.2c Each of these three popular text-based Web sites have its own style.

Use Whitespace and Fonts Well

It's true that HTML imposes some pretty severe restrictions on the way you design your text, which traditional publishers don't have to deal with. For example, except in the extended Microsoft version, HTML doesn't even provide a decent way to control the left and right margins on a page (although there are ways to get around this and other restrictions, as you'll see). On the other hand, if you suddenly decide you hate the look of your Web pages, it's much easier to change them — especially if they're text-based—than it would be to fix and reprint physical pages in a book or magazine.

To get a feel for the importance of interspersing normal paragraphs with subheadings and lists, sometimes called "display lines" in print publishing, flip through a nonfiction book or magazine, preferably one that doesn't have a lot of pictures. How often are the paragraphs separated by various kinds of display lines? The more informal and modern the content, the more lists and headings you'll probably see.

It's even more important to include plenty of display lines for visual relief and easy reading onscreen than it is on paper. The resolution of type on the screen is much lower than on paper, typically 72 dpi onscreen versus 1270 dpi or better from a typesetter, making eyestrain a real concern. Also, there are more distractions onscreen than on paper, including the blinking cursor, the mouse pointer, and the browser itself. Finally, the distance from the eyes to the monitor is usually much greater than from the eyes to a piece of printed material.

I'm not going to get into the various ways to translate display lines into HTML code here. The relevant tags, such as <H1>, <OL>, and <UL>, are pretty straightforward and are very well documented in lots of other reference material, as well as in many HTML editors. Just remember: whenever you can get away with using lists and headings instead of run-on paragraphs at your site, do it. Visitors to your site will appreciate it.

The fact that monitors are generally not well-suited for reading large amounts of text affects your site in other ways, as well. Keep your paragraphs short and your type relatively large. Again, think of a printed page. It's usually longer than it is wide (portrait orientation, for all you desktop-publishing mavens). Most computer screens, however, are set up exactly the opposite way. This means much longer line-lengths than people are used to reading, especially if the type is small. For psychological as well as physical comfort, aim for an onscreen line-length of about 80 characters, unless the paragraph is very short.

When you put text online, forget what you learned in grammar school about how a paragraph should have at least four sentences. On the Web, typical paragraphs should have *at most* four sentences. Otherwise, your screen ends up looking "dark" and intimidating from all the type that's on it.

How do you control line-length when HTML has no built-in margin codes? The easiest way is simply to insert
 (break) codes at the appropriate places in your text. This makes text a big pain to edit, though, as anyone who's ever pressed the Enter key at the end of every line in a word-processed document knows. Another way is to use the <PRE>..</PRE> tags, which makes text appear exactly as you typed it in terms of spaces and line breaks, like this:

```
<HTML>
<TITLE>Preamble to the Constitution</TITLE>
<H2>Preamble to the Constitution of the United States of America</H2>
<HR>
<PRE>

    <STRONG><BIG>We, the people of the United States of America,</BIG></ -
  STRONG>
```

```
           in order to form a more perfect union, establish justice,
           insure domestic tranquillity, provide for the common defense,
           promote the general welfare and secure the blessings of liberty
           to ourselves and our posterity, do ordain and establish
           this Constitution for the United States of America.

</PRE>
<HR>
Can you recite this without singing the Schoolhouse Rock song?
Me neither.
</HTML>
```

The results are in Figure 3.3. Notice that the text within the <PRE>..</PRE> tags is in a typewriter-style Courier font, while the stuff outside is in a normal, proportional, Times-like font. It's hard to make that mix of fonts look good. Also, according to HTML purists, you're limited in what codes you should use within the <PRE>..</PRE> tags, for reasons I'm not going to get into here. For example, <STRONG> would be okay, but <H1> wouldn't. You might be thinking, "If it looks okay in all the major browsers, what difference does it make whether I use <H1> inside or outside the <PRE>?" Well, you've got a valid point, and it is your site, after all, to construct however you want. I don't want to get in trouble with the HTML police, though, so you didn't hear it from me.

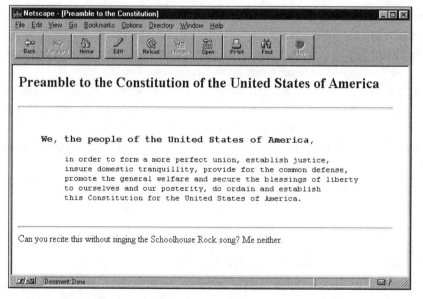

Figure 3.3 The effect of the <PRE>..</PRE> tags is to have text formatted exactly the same as it was typed in.

Why bother with <PRE>..</PRE> at all, when there are so many other ways to control the look and placement of text at your site? There are at least three situations where it makes sense:

- You want a Courier-style font for design purposes. Press releases, for example, are traditionally presented in this type-written look.

- You're fond of ASCII art and want to show some off. ASCII art uses only the keyboard characters to form pictures—similar to the concept of emoticons ("smilies"), but taken to a much higher level. You can check out the definitive gallery of ASCII art at Scarecrow's WWW Link, http://miso.wwa.com/~boba/scarecrow1.html.

- You're presenting computer listings, such as the contents of batch files or CGI scripts, at your site. Not only will the <PRE>..</PRE> tags set these listings off in their traditional font, the tags will also keep all the often-essential indentations in the code looking just like the programmer intended.

A third way to control the words on a line is to use a larger-than-normal font size. People who use Microsoft's Internet Explorer to visit your site can do this for themselves from the browser. For Netscape folks, you can use the <BASEFONT SIZE=..> tag, where <BASEFONT SIZE=3> is the default of about 12-point type and <BASEFONT SIZE=4> will give you about 14-point type. Be careful to set your base font to a reasonable size; probably 3 or 4. If you make it too big, peoples' eyes will tend to see the individual letters instead of the words, as in Figure 3.4, which uses <BASEFONT SIZE=6>. Plus, the text will overpower the headings. Of course, it's hard to get the full effect of this screen here, since it's been reduced to fit the page, but trust me: the text is too big.

Setting the base font with <BASEFONT SIZE=4>, though, doesn't affect text that you've set as headings using <H1>, <H2>, and so on. If you want to increase the size of your headings as well, you'll have to do each one individually, adding tags like <FONT=+1>, <FONT=+2>, and so on to make the headings stay in proportion to your base text. For example, if your base font is 4, the following line would make a level-2 heading appear in font 6:

```
<H2><FONT=+2>This is a pretty big heading</FONT></H2>
```

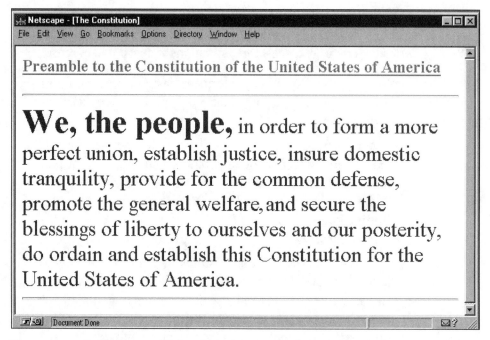

Figure 3.4   On this page, the base font is set too high (to 6) for comfortable reading.

Remember that <FONT=2> is not the same as <FONT=+2>. The first tag is an absolute size, while the second one is relative to the base font. The largest font size available is 7 (roughly equivalent to 36 points), so if you're using a base font of 4, the tags <FONT=+3> and <FONT=+4> will have the same result, setting the text to 7. Figure 3.5 shows how this works on a page that has no <BASEFONT SIZE=..> tag, so the default base size of 3 is used.

Even if you decide not to change the font size of large parts of your text, you might still want to use to make the first letter of each paragraph, major section, or page larger. You can do this with the <FONT=>..</FONT> pair of tags. This creates an effect similar to the drop-cap in traditional print publishing. It's used partly for decoration, and partly to help people visually separate the material into reasonable chunks. Here's the line that produces the drop-cap effect shown in Figure 3.6:

```
<FONT=+2>I</FONT>t <FONT=+2>W</FONT>as a <FONT=+2>D</FONT>ark and -
   <FONT=+2>S</FONT>tormy <FONT=+2>N</FONT>ight...
```

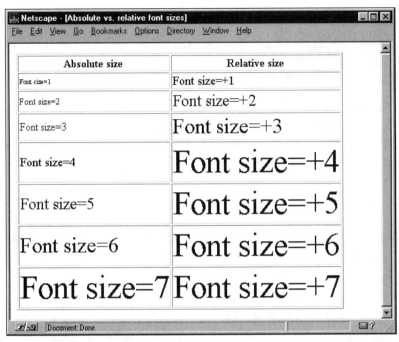

Absolute size	Relative size
Font size=1	Font size=+1
Font size=2	Font size=+2
Font size=3	Font size=+3
Font size=4	Font size=+4
Font size=5	Font size=+5
Font size=6	Font size=+6
Font size=7	Font size=+7

Figure 3.5   This chart shows absolute and relative font sizes based on the default font size, which is 3.

Think carefully about using the drop-cap effect with text that's serving as a link. The bigger first character will push the line under it lower than the line for the rest of the words. It ends up not only looking awkward, but causing unnecessary confusion, since the larger letter with the offset underline looks like it has some special importance. After all, that's often how "hot keys" are indicated in GUI-based software. I've known people who, upon seeing a screen like the one in Figure 3.7, would try to use the keystrokes Alt-B or Option-B to activate the "Business" link.

Some people object to the use of <BASEFONT SIZE=..> and <FONT=..> for ideological reasons. Basically, they say that there are other, better ways to add emphasis to your text. I agree. However, I'm not suggesting using these tags to make your words go up and down on a page for emphasis, but rather to make your pages more easily readable on browsers that support these tags. Still, be

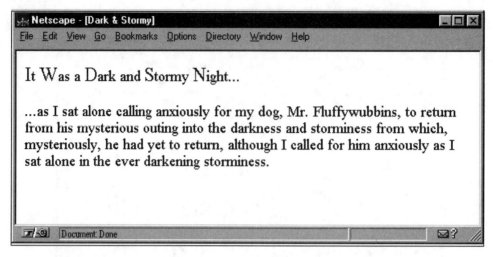

Figure 3.6   You can use <FONT> to produce a text effect similar to the drop-cap in print publishing.

aware that using <BASEFONT SIZE=..> and <FONT=..> extensively at your site might mean opening yourself up to rather pointed email from certain, um, extremely observant types.

Probably the best way to control margins and how text is positioned on a page is to put all of it in a giant table, as discussed in Chapter 4.

A quick and easy way to control the left-indent of a paragraph is to use nested <UL>..</UL> or <DL>..</DL> tag pairs. Each one will push the paragraph over about a half-inch from the left, so you can just keep surrounding your paragraph with them until it's over far enough. For example, this bit of HTML indents the paragraph about an inch and a half:

```
<ul>
<ul>
<ul>
<p>My name is Marianne Krcma. I write, edit, train, and
consult _
  (whew!)
```

on computer issues. Right now, most of my time is consumed

writing this
book for the Coriolis Group.</p>
</ul>
</ul>
</ul>
This tip works best with normal paragraphs of text.

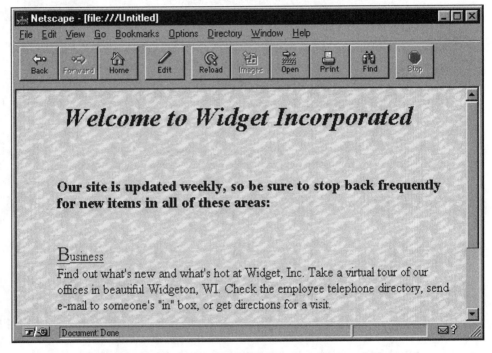

Figure 3.7. Some people might mistakenly think the B in Business could be used like a hot key.

Make Navigating as Easy as Possible

Don't put everything on one extremely long page, separated by <HR>s (horizontal rules, which create the ubiquitous shaded line, as shown in Figure 3.8). Instead, limit each page to a few screens. Most Web wizards recommend one to four screens per page, depending on the content.

An exception to that rule, however, sometimes applies for all-text pages. If you're presenting a fairly long piece of continuous text at your site, say an article in a scholarly e-zine, breaking it into several pages doesn't make a lot of sense. In this case, it's easier for the reader who's engrossed in the content to just click the scrollbar or press the PageDown key than to find the navigational link that will take him or her to the next page, click on that link, and wait for the page to load.

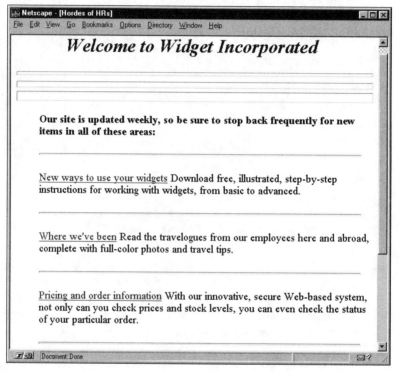

Figure 3.8 This text-based page goes pretty heavy on the <HR>s.

Navigational Links: Don't Leave Home without Them

Add links at the bottom of every page, using text, graphic buttons or, preferably, both. Whenever applicable, the page should have links that enable the user to go back to the previous page and forward to the next one. In addition, *every* page after the home page should have a link that takes the user directly up to the home page. There's nothing more frustrating than having to page back manually to home from, say, the tenth page of a site, just because the page designer forgot to include simple links.

Figure 3.9 shows simple text-based navigational links on a sample page. Here's the relevant HTML code from that page:

```
<BODY>
| <A HREF="home.htm">Home Page</A> |
<A HREF="trivia.htm">Next Page</A> |
<A HREF="files.htm">Free Stuff</A> |
<A HREF="help.htm"> Help and FAQs</A> |
<H1>A Basic Text Page</H1>
```

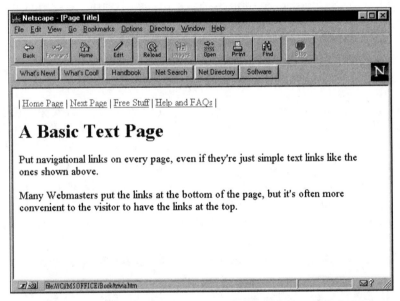

Figure 3.9   Always include links so the visitor doesn't feel stranded on a page.

The vertical bars that help to visually separate the links are made by typing the pipe symbol, |. On most keyboards, you can get it by pressing Shift-Backslash.

"CLICK HERE" CAUSES CRITICISM

Speaking of links, avoid having the words "click here" serve as a link anywhere at your site. It interrupts the flow of reading, and it's seldom necessary. Instead, just make a link out of the actual phrase that "click here" would refer to. Most people will realize that, if the words "my dog" are in blue and underlined while everything else is in black and not underlined, "my dog" is a link.

While we're on the subject, avoid underlining text that is not a link. You'll confuse and frustrate users whose browsers or monitors don't show color. Yes, they should update their hardware and software, but that's another issue.

Color Your Worldwide Web Site

One of the worst possible color combinations for reading text is black type on a medium-gray background. The color values are too close, making it hard for the eye to distinguish the type from the background. And yet, that's the default setup that Netscape, in its infinite wisdom, chose for Navigator. Actually, there is a certain logic to the choice: the "neutrality" of medium gray makes it a good background for graphics, even though it rots for text. Fortunately, you can change it with the <BGCOLOR> attribute of the <BODY> tag. Most of the time, you can't just say <BODY BGCOLOR="sky blue">; you have to use the hexadecimal equivalent of the color you want, where #000000 is black, #FFFFFF is white, and all the other colors fall somewhere in between.

Sounds like a great, big pain, doesn't it? Well, it would be, except that many HTML editors come equipped to handle the conversion from an actual color to a hex code for you. For example, Figure 3.10 shows the way that Ken Nesbitt's WebEdit, a shareware HTML editor included on the CD-ROM, handles this. If your editor doesn't include a feature for setting the color, you can use a stand-alone program to do the translation, such as the freeware HTML Color Reference, also included on the CD-ROM. There are even Web sites that will help

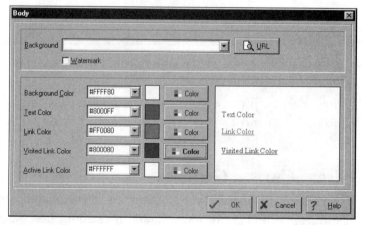

Figure 3.10 WebEdit uses this dialog box to help you set up your color scheme.

you pick the color combinations for your pages. One of my favorites is The Color Table of Way Grooviness at http://nwlink.com/~catanza/colors.html, partly because of its elegant simplicity and partly because of its cool name.

> Both Netscape and Internet Explorer, starting with their 2.0 releases, recognize some normal color names in addition to the hexadecimal values. The names that you can confidently use are ones like "black," "white," "red," "green," "blue," "yellow," "purple," and "gray." For the exact names of more specific colors, see the color-name table in Chapter 10.

Changing Colors with the HTML Color Reference

Suppose that you want to set the background of your text-based site to a very light blue using the HTML Color Reference. The first screen you'll see upon starting up the program is shown in Figure 3.11. To change the background color, follow these steps:

1. Make sure Background is selected in the Color Control area of the dialog box. If it isn't, click its radio button.

2. Drag the slider bars for red, green, and blue to the left and right. You'll see the background color in the preview box change. Also, note the different values that appear in the boxes just to the right of the slider bars. These RGB values can range from 0 to 255.

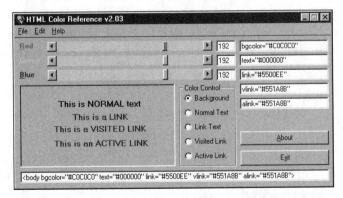

Figure 3.11   With the stand-alone HTML Color Reference program, you can experiment with all kinds of color schemes and have it do the hexadecimal conversion for you.

Zero means to use none of the particular color, 255 means to use it at "full strength."

3. For a very light blue, drag the blue slider bar all the way to the right (255). Drag the red and green slider bars almost to the right, about 240 each. The hexadecimal equivalent of this color is #F0F0FF, as shown in the bgcolor box. Figure 3.12 shows this setup.

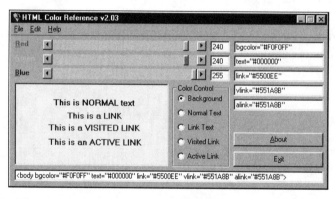

Figure 3.12 These settings in the HTML Color Reference produce a very light blue background.

4. If you want, change the colors for the other text elements as well. For example, you might keep normal text set to black and link text set to blue, but change visited links to medium gray by setting all three colors to a value of 150, and change active links to white by setting all three colors to 255. (An active link is the one you're currently clicking on when you choose a link with your Web browser. In this example, a link will turn white very briefly to show users that the browser has accepted their input.)

5. Now you need to send your results to the Web page you're working on. Click and drag across the line of HTML code at the bottom of the dialog box to select it, as shown in Figure 3.13.

6. Select Edit/Copy from the menu.

7. Open the relevant HTML page in the editor of your choice, and paste the line from the HTML Color Reference in place of the existing <BODY> tag.

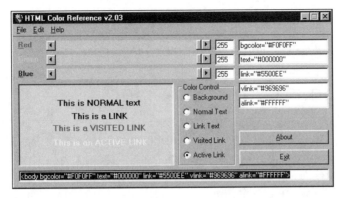

Figure 3.13   The line of code selected will be copied and pasted into a page of HTML.

The Wizards Speak: Color Schemes that Work

Thanks to programs like Web Edit and the HTML Color Reference, it's fun and relatively easy to play around with color at your Web site. But what colors should you choose? As with most things in the Web world, there aren't many hard and fast rules, but here's what most Web wizards say:

◎ If your site is predominantly text, use a white or very light back ground with black or very dark text.

◎ If your site is predominantly graphics, the default gray is okay, but many people prefer black, since it makes graphics seem to float in space.

◎ Avoid very bright background colors, such as hot pink, for a text-based site. If users spend any amount of time staring at a hot-pink screen, it will seem to vibrate or pulse—not a comfortable sensation.

◎ Make sure all of the colors you use complement each other. For example, if you've set your background to dark green, your dark-blue links might be nearly impossible to see.

You can probably find great-looking sites where one or more of these guidelines is turned totally upside-down. These guidelines are like the rules of grammar: if they're broken by masters, the results can somehow turn out to be great. Remember, though, that these people spent a long time learning the rules before they experimented with breaking them. For most of us, it's best to start fairly conservative—at least when it comes to color schemes.

Check Your Choice of Colors

When you test your page with a Web browser, the colors should look more or less like they did in the preview. They might not be exactly what you expected; that's normal. It usually takes some experimenting to find the color combination that works best for a particular site. While you're testing and experimenting, it's a good idea to check how the colors would appear on various monitors. Unless you happen to have several monitors handy, you'll have to manually set your computer display to a different resolution or palette, restart the computer if necessary, and reload the Web page. For example, if you have an SVGA monitor that's normally set for 16-bit color with a palette of 64,000 colors, reset it to VGA, which shows only 256 colors.

How does your page look? You might find that a perfect eggshell beige is now just white, or a cool forest green now appears black. That's how your page will look to someone who's viewing the Web via VGA. As long as everything is still readable and the colors aren't clashing wildly, it's fine.

Another way that users might cancel out all your hard work at devising a color scheme is to set their own predefined colors from the browser. Netscape and Internet Explorer both allow this; it's a popular option for Web surfers who've had their retinas burned once too often by some Webmonster's garish color combination. Realize, then, that you can't count on color to convey your message—some of the visitors to your site will be unable or unwilling to see it. Still, for those who can (and they're the majority), color is an easy way to dress up your text without adding much overhead in terms of file size or download time.

Starting in the HTML extensions for Netscape 2.0, you can also change the color of just certain text on a page by surrounding it with the <FONT COLOR=..> and </FONT> tags. For example, the following line of HTML would turn the selected text light orange, regardless of what text color was specified in the <BODY> tag:

```
<FONT COLOR="#FFD0A2">This is text of a different color.</
FONT>
```

Beware of <BLINK>

One final note on using text effectively at your Web site: Don't use the <BLINK> tag unless you want to get lots of email from disgruntled visitors to your site. Yes, it does attract attention, but so does a disabled car on the highway. Except in a few very unusual cases, this tag is unnecessary at best and maddening at worst.

So far, I've only seen one place on the Web where I thought <BLINK> was used appropriately: a particular page of Terminal X, a very well-designed unofficial site at http://www.neosoft.com/sworks/xfiles/xfiles.html devoted to the television show "The X Files." After you've chosen the "multimedia" link at the Terminal X splash screen, you see the screen in Figure 3.14. It's set up to make your computer seem to have accessed a top-secret government system, with the word "Proceed" blinking in red to indicate that you've cleared security.

If you can think up some similarly innovative use of <BLINK>, give it a try. Otherwise, avoid it like Cancer Man himself. (That's an inside X Files joke; sorry!)

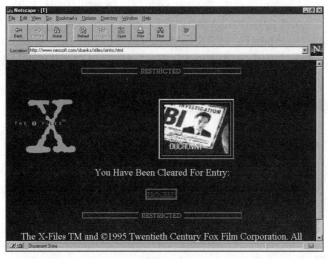

Figure 3.14   The word "Proceed" blinks on the virtual security panel at the Terminal X site, just as it might on a real government computer.

Web Wizard's Touchstones for Text

Do consider using a slightly larger-than-normal base font and/or a drop-cap effect with the <BASEFONT SIZE=..> and <FONT=..> tags.

Don't use too many <HR>s, or your page will start to look chopped up.

Do use plenty of navigational links, even if they're just the words "Previous," "Home," and "Next."

Don't make your lines or paragraphs too long, especially if your site is text-intensive.

Do use headings and lists as alternatives to run-on text whenever you can.

Don't use the words "click here" as a link.

Do make sure there's enough contrast between the information on your page and the background. Set the colors of a text-intensive page to black or dark-colored text on a white or very light-colored background.

Don't use very bright colors for either the background or normal text on text-intensive pages.

Do make sure the colors you choose complement each other and look good on both VGA and SVGA monitors.

Don't rely on colors to convey information about your site—not everyone will see them like you do.

Do let visitors know if your site is best viewed in the colors you've set.

Don't use blinking text.

Do adapt the written material you already have to suit the tone of the Web. In your writing, stress informality, candidness, and the concept of free information.

IV
TABLES

Tables are an important part of every Web wizard's bag of tricks. Table tags address many of the shortcomings of HTML for formatting text and graphics. Of course, they're also great for holding the kind of data that you would normally put in spreadsheet programs like Lotus 1-2-3 and Microsoft Excel.

Tables That Hold Spreadsheet Information

When most people think of computer-generated tables, they think of spreadsheets with rows and columns that define cells. The cells typically hold data and the answers to math problems. HTML's table tags can be used to create exactly that kind of a table, among other things. Unlike a real spreadsheet program, an HTML-based table has no way to do "number crunching" on its own, although some Web wizards have added limited math abilities to the tables on their pages with add-ons such as Java scripts.

Figure 4.1 shows a typical example of a table that presents spreadsheet-type information. Here's the HTML that creates the table:

```
<TABLE BORDER>
<CAPTION><H2>California Cabernets</H2></CAPTION>
<TR>
   <TH>Producer</TH>
   <TH>Name</TH>
   <TH>Vintage</TH>
   <TH>Rating</TH>
   <TH>Bottle Price (Retail)</TH>
   <TH>Stock (Cases)</TH>
</TR>
<TR>
   <TD>Caymus</TD>
   <TD>Napa Valley</TD>
   <TD>91</TD>
   <TD>90</TD>
   <TD>$24</TD>
   <TD>0.5</TD></TR>
<TR>
   <TD>Chateau Montelena</TD>
   <TD>Calistoga Cuvee</TD>
   <TD>91</TD>
   <TD>92</TD>
   <TD>$40</TD>
   <TD>2</TD>
</TR>
<TR>
   <TD>Laurel Glen</TD>
   <TD>Terra Rosa North Coast</TD>
```

```
  <TD>92</TD>
  <TD>89</TD>
  <TD>$9</TD>
  <TD>6</TD>
</TR>
<TR>
  <TD>Robert Mondavi</TD>
  <TD>Woodbridge</TD>
  <TD>92</TD>
  <TD>83</TD>
  <TD>$6</TD>
  <TD>8</TD>
</TR>
<TR>
  <TD>Stag's Leap</TD>
  <TD>SLV</TD>
  <TD>90</TD>
  <TD>90</TD>
  <TD>$30</TD>
  <TD>3</TD>
</TR>
</TABLE>
```

Like all tables on the Web, this ones starts with the <TABLE> tag and ends with a closing </TABLE>. In between, each row is specified with <TR>..</TR>. Within the rows, each individual cell is created with a <TH>..</TH> or <TD>..</TD> pair . (The *TH* stands for "table heading," and the *TD* stands for "table data.")

There are lots of other tags and attributes you might see in tables, such as <CAPTION> for the first line of a table, or <COLSPAN> and <ROWSPAN> to have certain cells take up more than their default amount of space in the table. However, <TABLE>..</TABLE>, <TR>..</TR>, and <TD>..</TD> are the constant, basic elements.

Suppose you want to help yourself and other people remember which browsers support which Web features, and you've decided to put up a Web page that summarizes the current situation. To keep it from getting too complicated, you're sticking to the browsers that you know pretty well: Netscape, Internet Explorer, and CompuServe's version of Mosaic. You decide that a table would be the logical way to organize the information. Here's how to create it:

1. Start by figuring out how the table should be organized. In other words, what goes in the rows, and what goes in the columns? Since the horizontal space across the screen (where the columns appear) is

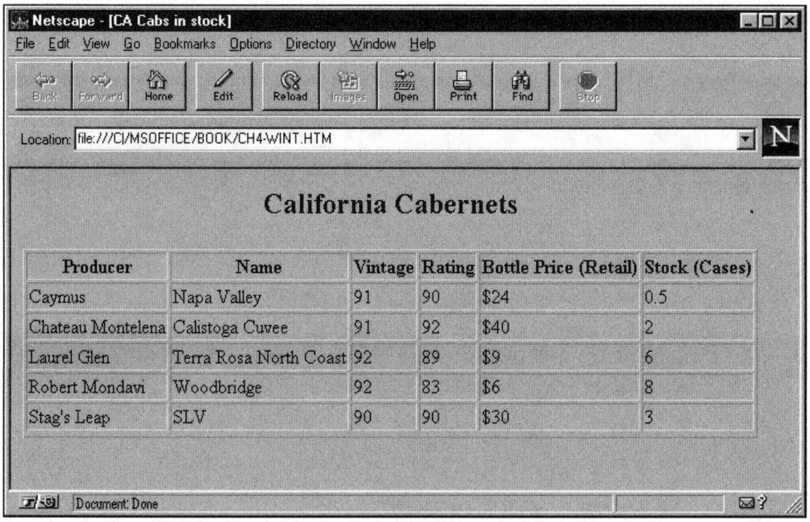

Figure 4.1   This table could just as easily be in a spreadsheet as on a Web page.

more limited than the vertical space (where the rows appear), it makes sense to put whatever there's fewer of in the columns. In this step-by-step example, there are only three browsers, but there might eventually be dozens of features, so the browser names should go across the top of the table, and the features should go down the side.

You're going to start with five features, or rows, in your table. The browser names as headings across the top add a sixth row, so you've got a six-row-by-four-column table. For more complicated tables, it helps to sketch things out, but since this one is pretty basic, you're ready now to just dive right into coding.

2. Many HTML editors will create a skeleton table for you; all you have to do is indicate the number of rows and columns, and any other elements you want. For this example, though, assume that you don't have access to these shortcuts, so you need to code by hand. Here's the HTML for the table so far, shown in Figure 4.2:

```
<TABLE BORDER>
<TR><TH></TH><TH>CompuServe's Mosaic</TH><TH>Internet Ex-
plorer</TH><TH>Netscape Navigator</TH></TR>
<TR><TD></TD><TD></TD><TD></TD><TD></TD></TR>
<TR><TD></TD><TD></TD><TD></TD><TD></TD></TR>
<TR><TD></TD><TD></TD><TD></TD><TD></TD></TR>
<TR><TD></TD><TD></TD><TD></TD><TD></TD></TR>
<TR><TD></TD><TD></TD><TD></TD><TD></TD></TR>
</TABLE>
```

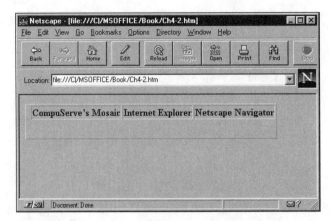

Figure 4.2 Here's the "skeleton" of the 6x4 Web Browser Comparison table.

It looks strange now, but it will look better as the rows and columns automatically resize themselves to accommodate the content you add. The BORDER attribute of <TABLE> helps to show where the cells begin and end.

3. Now you're ready to fill in the individual cells (<TD>..</TD> pairs) in each row. You can put pretty much anything you want in the cells: text, graphics, sounds, links, forms—even embedded tables. For this example, it's just text, so the first row would look something like this:

```
<TR ALIGN=CENTER>
  <TD ALIGN=LEFT><EM>Tables</EM></TD>
  <TD>No</TD>
  <TD>Yes</TD>
  <TD>Yes</TD>
</TR>
```

The ALIGN=CENTER attribute, as you've probably guessed, centers each item in a row within its cell, except for the first cell in this example, where it's overridden by the ALIGN=LEFT attribute in <TD>.

4. Repeat step 3 with the other rows, until you've got a table like Figure 4.3.

5. Once you've created the basic table, there are lots of ways to enhance it. One way is to add some "air" around the cells with the CELLPADDING attribute of <TABLE>. Another thing you'll

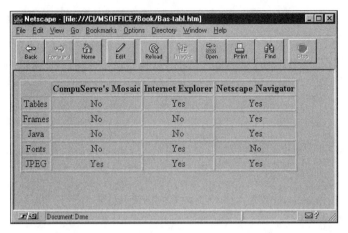

Figure 4.3   All of the data is in. Now it's time to dress it up.

probably want to do is add a level <H1> or <H2> heading above the table. You can use the <CAPTION>..</CAPTION> tag pair to add it across the top of the table. Finally, center the entire table by surrounding it with <CENTER>..</CENTER>. Here's the HTML for the finished sample page, shown in Figure 4.4:

```
<HTML>
<TITLE>A Browser Comparison Table</TITLE>
<BODY>
<CENTER>
<TABLE CELLPADDING=10 BORDER>
<CAPTION><H2>Web Browser Comparison</H2></CAPTION>
<TR>
  <TH></TH>
  <TH>CompuServe's Mosaic</TH>
  <TH>Internet Explorer</TH>
  <TH>Netscape Navigator</TH>
</TR>
<TR ALIGN=CENTER>
  <TD ALIGN=LEFT><EM>Tables</EM></TD>
  <TD>No</TD>
  <TD>Yes</TD>
  <TD>Yes</TD>
</TR>
<TR ALIGN=CENTER>
  <TD ALIGN=LEFT><EM>Frames</EM></TD>
  <TD>No</TD>
  <TD>No</TD>
  <TD>Yes</TD>
</TR>
<TR ALIGN=CENTER>
  <TD ALIGN=LEFT><EM>Java</EM></TD>
```

```
            <TD>No</TD>
            <TD>No</TD>
            <TD>Yes</TD>
        </TR>
        <TR ALIGN=CENTER>
          <TD ALIGN=LEFT><EM>Fonts</EM></TD>
          <TD>No</TD>
          <TD>Yes</TD>
          <TD>No</TD>
        </TR>
        <TR ALIGN=CENTER>
          <TD ALIGN=LEFT><EM>JPEG</EM></TD>
          <TD>Yes</TD>
          <TD>Yes</TD>
          <TD>Yes</TD>
        </TR>
        </TABLE>
        </CENTER>
        </BODY>
        </HTML>
```

VARYING THE STEPS

There are lots of other special attributes and formatting options you could add to the table, including these:

@ You might want to "stack" the headings so the columns aren't so wide. To do this, just add the <BR> tag between the words in the <TH> cells, like this:

```
<TH>CompuServe's<BR>Mosaic</TH>
```

The table will automatically adjust so that each column is only as big as the longest word or phrase in it, plus any cell spacing or padding you've added.

@ If you want to force a particular column to be wider than its default, add the WIDTH=.. attribute either in the <TH> tag or any one of the <TD> tags for the column. The number for WIDTH can be in pixels or percent. Many Web wizards prefer percent, although at the moment, Netscape is the only browser that supports percentage widths. For example, you might decide that the first column in the browser comparison table is too narrow relative to the rest of the table. This modification will change that (in Netscape only), as you can see in Figure 4.5:

```
<TD ALIGN=LEFT WIDTH=25%><EM>Tables</EM></TD>
```

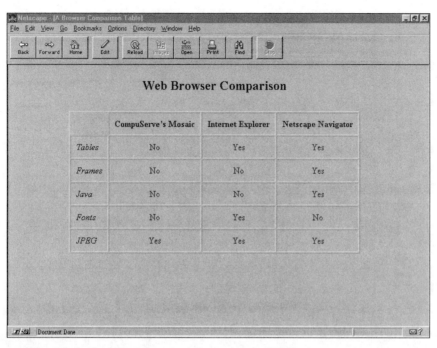

Figure 4.4   The finished Web Browser Comparison table.

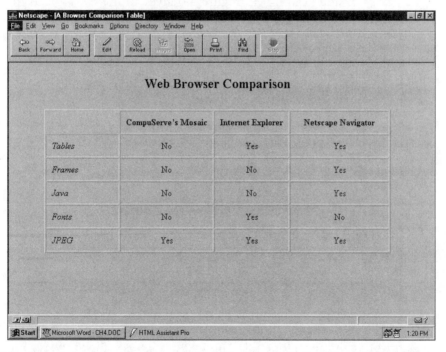

Figure 4.5   The first column has been widened to take up 25% of the table's width.

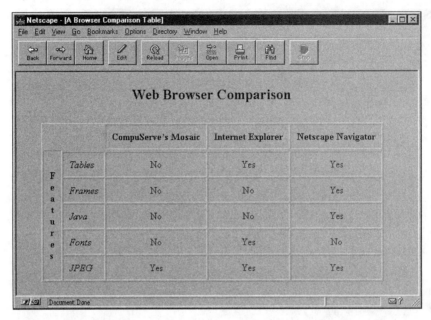

Figure 4.6   The word "Features" acts as a row heading for the table.

The "side heading" in Figure 4.6 gives a different look to the table, helping the table stand out. To create the side heading, you'll need to first indicate to the browser that you've got another column. The easiest way to do this is to change the first <TH> in the HTML of the browser comparison table to <TH COLSPAN=2>. Then, add the following HTML after the row of headings:

```
<TR>
  <TD ROWSPAN=6 ALIGN=CENTER>
<STRONG>F<br>e<br>a<br>t<br>u<br>r<br>e<br>s</STRONG></TD>
</TR>
```

"Why Didn't I Think of That?": Changing a Table's Rules

If you've worked with tables in spreadsheets or other programs, you've probably noticed one of the major limitations of formatting tables on the Web: there's no easy way to add rules (lines) to just certain rows or columns. Hopefully, this will change as some of the recommendations for tables in HTML 3.0 start showing up in the major browsers. Specifically, the proposed RULES=.. and FRAME=.. attributes of <TABLE> would give you much more control over where and how rules are placed on your tables. To find out more about the proposed changes to tables and other elements in HTML 3.0, check the list of updates and status reports at http://www.w3.org/pub/WWW/TR/.

For now, though, all you've got is the standard BORDER attribute, which is an all-or-nothing way of adding rules to a table. Either you've got a box around every single cell in your table, or you don't have any rules at all. This is one of those limitations of HTML that really takes some creative Web wizardry to get around, but it can be done.

Suppose that you want to end up with the table in Figure 4.7, which has a horizontal rule under the headings and a vertical one between the first and second columns. Here's how you could create it in Netscape:

1. Remove any BORDER attribute from the table, so you don't have any rules at all.

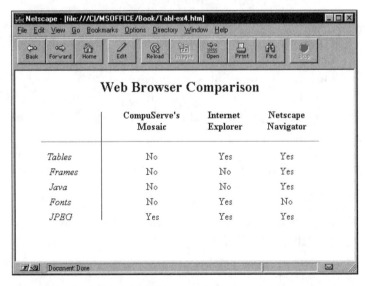

Figure 4.7   With a little bit of Web wizardry, you can get greater control over how rules (lines) look in your tables.

2. The horizontal rule is easier to make than the vertical one, so let's start by adding a row between the headings and the rest of the table to hold the horizontal rule. This row will need to span the entire table, so you'll need to set it to COLSPAN=5 (the four regular columns plus one extra for the vertical rule that you'll add soon). The only thing in the new row is a short, wide <HR>, which creates the horizontal rule. Setting the size of <HR> to 1 makes a nice thin line, instead of the usual thick one. Exactly how wide to make the <HR> will take some trial-and-error. After a few attempts, you should end up with a line of HTML like this, inserted after the last <TH>..</TH> tag pair:

```
<TR><TD COLSPAN=5><HR SIZE=1 WIDTH=400></TD></TR>
```

3. Now you need to tackle the vertical line. Unfortunately, you can't use <HR> here to get a thin line. You'd need something like <HR WIDTH=1 SIZE=250>, but SIZE can only have a maximum value of 100 in the <HR> tag, to which it defaults if you try using a higher number. Instead, open your paint program and create a very small, black GIF (one or two pixels square). Call it blackdot.gif and save it as non-transparent.

4. Back in the HTML, add a new <TH>..</TH> pair between the existing first and second headings to hold the blackdot.gif. This new heading should have a ROWSPAN of 7 (six normal rows plus the one that holds the horizontal rule), and VALIGN equal to BOTTOM. In the new heading, put in an <IMG SRC> tag for blackdot.gif, with a width of 1 and a height set by trial-and-error, like this:

```
<TH ROWSPAN=7 VALIGN=BOTTOM><IMG SRC="blackdot.gif" WIDTH=1 _
    HEIGHT=225></TH>
```

5. As a finishing touch, put a little whitespace around the cells with the CELLPADDING=5 attribute to <TABLE>.

Here's the complete HTML for the page:

```
<HTML>
    <TITLE></TITLE>
    <BODY BGCOLOR="#FFFFFF">
    <CENTER>
    <TABLE CELLPADDING=5>
    <CAPTION><H2>Web Browser Comparison</H2></CAPTION>
    <TR>
      <TH></TH>
      <TH ROWSPAN=7 VALIGN=BOTTOM><IMG SRC="blackdot.gif" WIDTH=1
    HEIGHT=225></TH>
      <TH>CompuServe's<BR>Mosaic</TH>
      <TH>Internet<BR>Explorer</TH>
      <TH>Netscape<BR> Navigator</TH>
    </TR>
    <TR>
      <TD COLSPAN=5><HR SIZE=1 WIDTH=400></TD>
    </TR>
    <TR ALIGN=CENTER>
      <TD ALIGN=LEFT><EM>Tables</EM></TD>
      <TD>No</TD><TD>Yes</TD><TD>Yes</TD>
    </TR>
    <TR ALIGN=CENTER>
      <TD ALIGN=LEFT><EM>Frames</EM></TD>
      <TD>No</TD><TD>No</TD><TD>Yes</TD>
    </TR>
    <TR ALIGN=CENTER>
      <TD ALIGN=LEFT><EM>Java</EM></TD>
      <TD>No</TD><TD>No</TD><TD>Yes</TD>
    </TR>
    <TR ALIGN=CENTER>
      <TD ALIGN=LEFT><EM>Fonts</EM></TD>
      <TD>No</TD><TD>Yes</TD><TD>No</TD>
    </TR>
    <TR ALIGN=CENTER>
      <TD ALIGN=LEFT><EM>JPEG</EM></TD>
      <TD>Yes</TD><TD>Yes</TD><TD>Yes</TD>
</TR>
</TABLE>
</CENTER>
</BODY>
</HTML>
```

As always, be sure to test your tables in other major browsers. In this case, visitors who use Internet Explorer will see a table that's not quite as attractive, as shown in Figure 4.8.

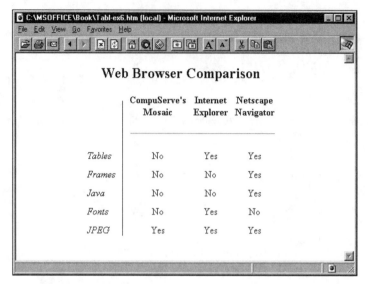

Figure 4.8 Because of the way Internet Explorer handles space between cells and the WIDTH attribute, the table doesn't look quite as good, but it's still perfectly usable.

If you already have tables that you've made with a spreadsheet program, you don't need to manually re-create them in HTML. Several freeware utilities that you can download from the Web will do the conversion for you. Probably the best-known is xl2html.xls, an Excel spreadsheet macro included on the CD-ROM. Another one to try is xl2web.exe, which you can download from http://www.baarns.com. Most spreadsheet-to-HTML conversion utilities are designed for Excel spreadsheets; Lotus 1-2-3 users might need to first export their tables to Excel format.

The Wizards Speak: Sizing Tables

One of the most tedious things about working with tables is trying to set the right column (<TD>) widths. You take a stab at the proper width: 250 pixels? No, that's too small—maybe 300? No, now it's too big—how about 275? This process can go on for what seems like hours.

Not surprisingly, Web wizards have a few tricks for minimizing the trial-and-error of sizing tables. Michael Herrick, whose Matterform Media company (htttp://www.matterform.com) has designed the Web sites of Booz-Allen & Hamilton and the New Mexico Department of Tourism, among others, summarizes table-sizing this way: "I prefer to set the overall width of the table in the table tag. For example, <TABLE WIDTH=468> give you a table 6.5 inches wide [assuming a screen resolution of 72 pixels per inch]. Then, use percentages in the <TD> tags. So, if you have a row of four cells, you can just set each to <TD WIDTH=25%>."

Of course, it is certainly possible to have good-looking tables onscreen that are wider than 6.5 inches, and there will be times when you'll want them. However, setting the table width to 468 pixels is a very convenient starting place for laying out your screen because it gives you about the same line length as you would get on a piece of paper with standard, one-inch margins. (The paper is 8.5 inches wide, minus two inches for the left and right margins.) This helps ensure that your table-based Web pages will be formatted properly when they're printed out. It also helps if you're converting word-processed documents into Web pages, since the "margins" are basically the same. And, it keeps your tables within Netscape's default "live area" of 470 pixels.

If you do need tables that are wider than 468 pixels, remember that the average user's monitor has a viewable image width of about 9 inches. Therefore, you should try very hard to keep your tables within 640 pixels.

Tables That Control the Flow of Text

Using tables to simulate margins and text columns is not really very hard to do. Like a lot of other things about Web design, however, it does require some fairly careful planning, plus a certain amount of experimenting to get things just right.

Figure 4.9 shows a good use of table tags to create margins on a simple but elegant page of text from Impact Online (http://www.webcom.com/~iol/), a Web-based volunteer organization. All the text shown in Figure 4.9 is inside a very simple, one-row, one-cell table that defines the text margins. The table, in

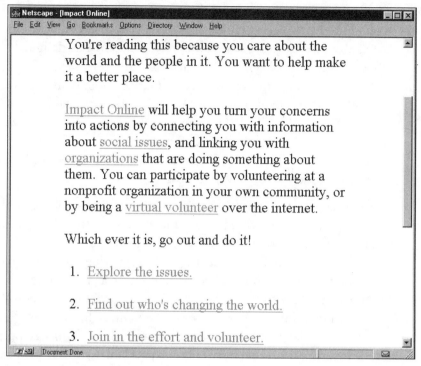

Figure 4.9 The text on this page from Impact Online is formatted with very simple table tags.

turn, is within a pair of <CENTER>..</CENTER> tags. Here's the skeleton HTML for the table:

```
<CENTER>
<TABLE WIDTH=490 BORDER=0>
<TR>
<TD><FONT SIZE=5>All the content goes here...</FONT></TD>
</TR>
</TABLE>
</CENTER>
```

The Web wizards who created the Software Engineering Institute's site (http://www.sei.cmu.edu/) also relied on table tags to format text. This time, the table code creates a three-column text layout, shown in Figure 4.10.

 Suppose that you're in charge of putting your organization's newsletter on the Web. You want it to have a basic three-column format, plus a masthead and a few graphical elements, like the sketch in Figure 4.11.

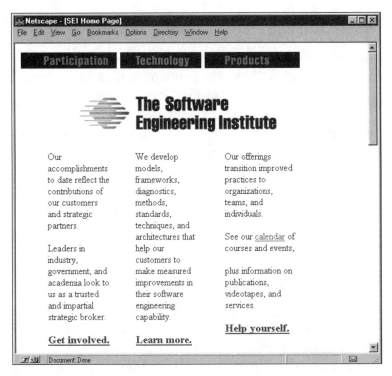

Figure 4.10   Table tags put the contents of this page in a three-column layout.

Figure 4.11   Drawing a sketch helps you figure out the "skeleton" HTML code for the table.

1. Working from the sketch, you figure out how many rows and columns you'll need in your table. Next, you need to decide the overall width. The standard width of 468 is a little small for a table with so much text, so you decide to stretch it to 576, or about 8 inches wide.

2. For the masthead, you have two choices: you could keep it outside the table altogether and just use alignment and sizing tags to position it over the table, or you could make it the first row of the table with a COLSPAN attribute. You decide to keep it outside the table for maximum flexibility. That leaves you with a table that is one row and three columns big. The graphic in the lower-right corner of the table, though, spans two columns. This is where things start to get interesting.

3. Unlike the tables you might design in, say, a desktop-publishing program, you can't layer table elements in HTML (at least, not yet), so you can't put the graphic "on top" of the three columns of text. Basically, that would mean trying to make the text block into a polygon that looks like a sideways *L*, as shown in Figure 4.12. That's not allowed; you have to think in terms of squares and rectangles when creating tables in HTML.

What you've really got here, then, are two tables: a main one and an embedded one. The main one has one row and two cells. The first cell is the normal first column of text. The second cell holds the embedded table. The embedded table is a 2-by-2 matrix, equaling four cells. The first cell in the embedded table is the second column of text, and the second cell is the last column of text. The second row in the embedded table holds the graphic, which spans both cells using the <COLSPAN=2> tag. Complicated? Figure 4.13 will help you visualize the relationship.

4. Now that you've got a layout that works, turning it into HTML is the easy part. Here's the skeleton table code, with a few comments added to make it easier to follow:

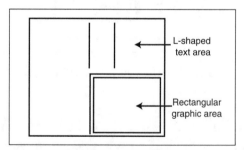

L-shaped
text area

Rectangular
graphic area

Figure 4.12   This sort of table layout is not allowed.

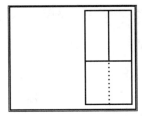

Figure 4.13   This is the layout you'll need to turn into HTML.

```
<TABLE WIDTH=576>
<TR>
<!--here's the first column of text-->
<TD WIDTH=33% VALIGN=TOP>A whole bunch of text.</TD>
<TD VALIGN=TOP WIDTH=67%>
<!--start embedded table in the second cell-->
  <TABLE CELLPADDING=5>
  <TR>
<!--here's the second column of text-->
    <TD VALIGN=TOP WIDTH=50%>More text.</TD>
<!--here's the third column of text-->
    <TD VALIGN=TOP WIDTH=50%>Still more text.</TD>
  </TR>
<!--here's the graphic spanning the second and third columns
of text-->
  <TR>
    <TD COLSPAN=2><IMG SRC="somepic.jpg"></TD>
  </TR>
</TABLE>
<!--end embedded table-->
</TR>
</TABLE>
```

5. With some content added to the rows and cells, you'll get a Web page like the one in Figure 4.14a. Whether or not that's the final version of the table depends on how picky you are about text alignment. See how the first column of text starts slightly higher than the other two? That's because the extra space for borders is pushing the embedded table farther down, since it has, in effect, two top borders, as you can see in Figure 4.14b.

   Unfortunately, even with every possible spacing attribute set to zero, the columns still won't align vertically. The only way to handle this problem is to put the first column of text in an embedded table, too. And since I'm pretty picky about this kind of stuff, that's what I've done in Figure 4.15. Here's the complete HTML

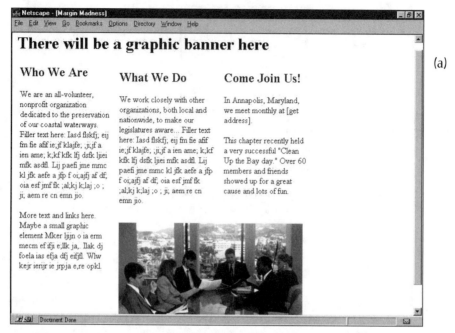

Figure 4.14a　Here's the table with some content added.

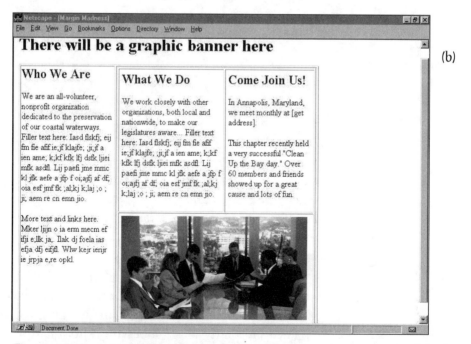

Figure 4.14b　Here's the table with borders turned on so you can see the table structures.

for this page (minus the meaningless filler text that I made by typing random letters):

```
<HTML>
<HEAD><TITLE>Margin Madness</TITLE></HEAD>
<BODY BGCOLOR="#FFFFFF">
<H1>There will be a graphic banner here</H1>
<TABLE WIDTH=576>
<TR>
<TD WIDTH=33% VALIGN=TOP>
<TABLE CELLPADDING=5>
<TR><TD>
<H2>Who We Are</H2>
<P>We are an all-volunteer, nonprofit organization dedicated _
   to the preservation of our coastal waterways. Filler text
here.</P>
<P>More text and links here. Maybe a small graphic element. _
   More filler text.</P>
</TD></TR>
</TABLE>
</TD>
<TD WIDTH=67% VALIGN=TOP>
<TABLE CELLPADDING=5>
<TR>
<TD VALIGN=TOP WIDTH=50%>
<H2>What We Do</H2>
<P>We work closely with other organizations, both local and
nationwide,
to make our legislatures aware... Filler text here.</P>
</TD>
<TD VALIGN=TOP WIDTH=50%>
<H2>Come Join Us!</H2>
<P>In Annapolis, Maryland, we meet monthly at [get address].</
P>
<P> This chapter recently held a very successful &quot;Clean Up
_
   the Bay day.&quot; Over 60 members and friends showed up for
a
   great cause and lots of fun.</P>
</TD>
</TR>
<TR><TD COLSPAN=2><IMG SRC="mugshot.jpg" VSPACE=0 HSPACE=0
BORDER=0 WIDTH=357 HEIGHT=192 ALIGN=TOP></TD></TR>
</TABLE>
</TR>
</TABLE>
</BODY>
</HTML>
```

This is a pretty complex example of using table tags to control text. If you followed through the step-by-step and got the finished table looking about right, congratulations! You're well on your way to becoming a Web tables wizard.

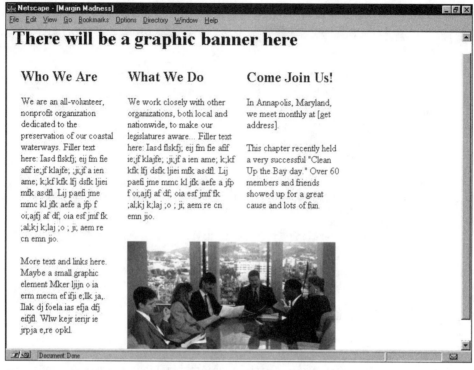

Figure 4.15 Thanks to some wizardly HTML, the final version of the Web-based newsletter is formatted very much like the original sketch.

Tables That Hold Navigational Buttons

Table tags are great for holding and formatting the navigational buttons that, as a good and faithful aspiring Web wizard, you undoubtedly have on every Web page at your site. The button bar at the bottom of Figure 4.16 is a fairly typical example of this kind of table. This table has just one row (one set of <TR>..</TR> tags) and five data cells (five <TD>..</TD> pairs).

That's right; I said "one row." You could design this table with two rows, one for the GIFs and one for the text, but it would require several lines of unnecessary HTML code—and you probably get plenty of practice typing as it is.

Each cell in a table is like a mini-page; it can hold as many different graphics, links, or paragraphs of text, as you want it to. You can visually break up these elements in a cell just like you would on a page. In this example, putting a <BR> tag between each GIF and its text pushes the text down to the next line in the

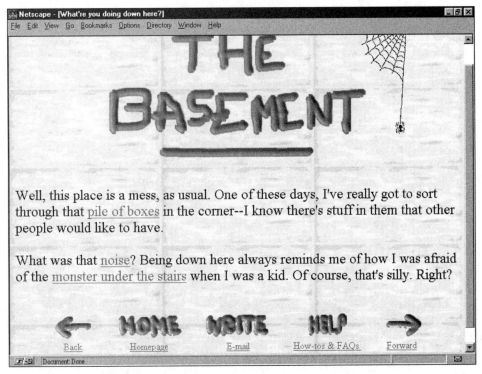

Figure 4.16   The button bar at the bottom of this page is a simple table.

cell. To get the GIFs and text links to line up the way they should in the cells of the row, you can use <TR ALIGN=CENTER>.

Here's the HTML that makes this page:

```
<HTML>
<HEAD>
<TITLE>What're you doing down here?</TITLE>
</HEAD>
<BODY BACKGROUND="grwall1.gif" BGCOLOR="#EFEFEF" LINK="808000"
VLINK="#COCOCO" ALINK="#COCOCO">
<CENTER><IMG SRC="baselogo.gif" WIDTH=600 HEIGHT=250></CENTER>
<BASEFONT SIZE=5>
<P>Well, this place is a mess, as usual. One of these days, I've really _
   got to sort through that <A HREF="http://made-up.com/freestuf.html">pile
   of boxes</A> in the corner--I know there's stuff in them that other
   people would like to have.
</P>
```

```
<P>What was that <A HREF="http://made-up.com/growl.wav">noise</A>? _
   Being down here always reminds me of how I was afraid of the <A
   HREF="http://made-up.com/monster.html">monster under the stairs</A> when
   I was a kid. Of course, that's silly. Right?</P>
<CENTER>
<TABLE CELLPADDING=15 CELLSPACING=0>
<TR ALIGN=CENTER>
   <TD><A HREF="http://made-up.com/upstairs.html">
       <IMG BORDER=0 SRC="grafti-1.gif" WIDTH=78 HEIGHT=50>
       <BR>Back</A>
   </TD>
   <TD><A HREF="http://made-up.com/homepage.html">
       <IMG SRC="grafti-2.gif" WIDTH=119 HEIGHT=50 BORDER=0>
       <BR>Homepage</A>
   </TD>
   <TD><A HREF="mailto:webcritter@made-up.com">
       <IMG SRC="grafti-3.gif" WIDTH=121 HEIGHT=50 BORDER=0>
       <BR>E-mail</A>
   </TD>
   <TD><A HREF="http://made-up.com/help.html">
       <IMG SRC="grafti-4.gif" WIDTH=78 HEIGHT=50 BORDER=0>
       <BR>How-tos &amp; FAQs </A>
   </TD>
   <TD><A HREF="http://made-up.com/stories.html">
       <IMG SRC="grafti-5.gif" WIDTH=80 HEIGHT=50 BORDER=0>
       <BR>Forward</A></TD>
</TR>
</TABLE>
</CENTER>
</BODY>
</HTML>
```

The custom wallpaper, grwall1.gif, is included on the CD-ROM. The buttons are also included on the CD-ROM as GIFs grafti-1.gif through grafti-5.gif. They started as one continuous bar, shown in Figure 4.17, which I made by writing freehand with the Airbrush tool in Paintshop Pro, then applying the Emboss filter, changing the results to grayscale, and filling the background with a neutral gray (R:187, G:187, B:187). I then selected each button individually, copied and pasted it as a new image, and saved it as a transparent GIF.

Notice that in Figure 4.17 the buttons were originally pretty close together. Putting them in a table gives you control to space them out in any way you want with the CELLSPACING, CELLPADDING, and ALIGN attributes. Table tags also make it easy to add visual cues to button bars that tell the user which page he or she is on. For example, on the home page itself, instead of using this line of HTML to make the "Home" table cell:

```
<TD><A HREF="http://made-up.com/homepage.html">
    <IMG SRC="grafti-2.gif" WIDTH=119 HEIGHT=50 BORDER=0>
    <BR>Homepage</A>
  </TD>
```

you could use this:

```
<TD><IMG SRC="homegray.gif" WIDTH=119 HEIGHT=50 BORDER=0>
    <BR>Homepage</A>
  </TD>
```

By removing the link and substituting a grayed-out version of the usual button, you've made it easier to see which page is current. To make the grayed-out version of the button, just open it in whatever paint program you prefer, convert it to grayscale if necessary, and increase its rightness by about 30%.

Figure 4.17   The buttons started out as all part of the same GIF file.

 Do you ever get confused about the difference between CELLSPACING and CELLPADDING? Figure 4.18 shows two versions of the "Basement" page button bar, with table borders turned on so you can see better what's going on. The first table has CELLPADDING=15 and CELLSPACING=0. The second one has CELLPADDING=0 and CELL-SPACING=15. Notice that the first table is considerably wider than the second one. That's because CELLPADDING is cumulative, so there's actually 30 pixels of space between adjoining cells. CELLSPACING, on the other hand, is absolute: there's 15 pixels of space between each cell instead of all around each cell.

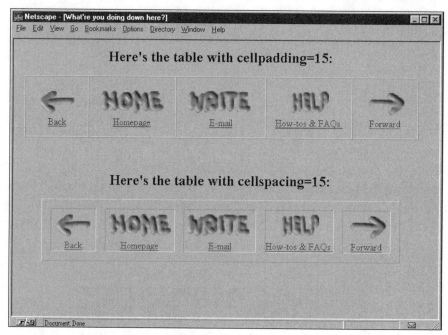

Figure 4.18 Notice the difference in table width between CELLPADDING and CELLSPACING.

The Wizards Speak:
Tables Versus Image Maps

As you wander the Web looking for cool uses of tables that control graphics, you'll probably come upon many sites that look like great examples of good table technique. When you look at their source code, though, you'll find that some of the things you thought were tables were actually image maps. In other places, you'll see what you think are attractive image maps, only to find that they are cleverly done tables (see Figure 4.19).

How do Web wizards decide when to use an image map and when to use a table? It used to be that if you didn't have access to the cgi-bin on your server, image maps weren't an option; you'd have to use tables to organize your graphics because image maps needed CGI scripts to interpret the user's mouse clicks. This problem with image maps has

Figure 4.19   Can you guess which is the table and which is the image map? Sometimes it's hard to tell without looking at the source. (The top one is the table.)

been reduced by the USEMAP attribute of <IMG SRC>, which both Netscape and Internet Explorer began supporting in their 2.0 version. (You'll find more about this in the next chapter.)

With CGI access no longer the deciding factor, choosing between a table and an image map becomes a little more complex. Web wizard Michael Herrick uses both tables and image maps for button bars. Sometimes, he even mixes table- and image-map-based button bars on the same Web page. Herrick advises that tables are the best choice when one of the buttons in the bar changes from page to page, such as when you want to "gray out" the current page's button. He explains, "We use separate images [in a table] at the tops of the InterArt pages because the images change depending on the page that is active, and it is better to download one small image in a group than an entire new banner. But we use an image map at the bottom of the pages, because that graphic never changes."

Also, tables are supported by more browsers than image maps are—and tables still show some kind of links even in browsers that don't support them, where an image map would just be invisible. If you need to support older or text-based browsers, it's relatively easy to add text to a table, either by adding a row of text links or by using the ALT attribute of the <IMG SRC> tag. It can be virtually impossible to add understandable text links to image maps, however.

A Button Bar down the Side of the Screen

When you've got a background that creates a single vertical column down the left side of your screen, like the one on the Up All Night Productions page in Figure 4.20, you've got a natural place to put your navigational buttons. To get everything to line up the way it should on your background, use table tags.

The Web page in Figure 4.21 uses this idea. Here are the steps to create it:

1. Collect or create the icons/buttons you want to use. The ones shown here are from the Corel Gallery, so they're not included on the CD-ROM, but you can find lots of freeware GIFs at sites all over the Web. (Chapter 2 gives more information on finding and making Web graphics.) Using a paint program such as Paintshop Pro or Photoshop, make the buttons transparent if they aren't already. Also, resize them so they're all about the same size. In this example, the largest GIF is the phone at 100 pixels high by 80 pixels wide, and the smallest is the mailbox at 50 by 80 pixels.

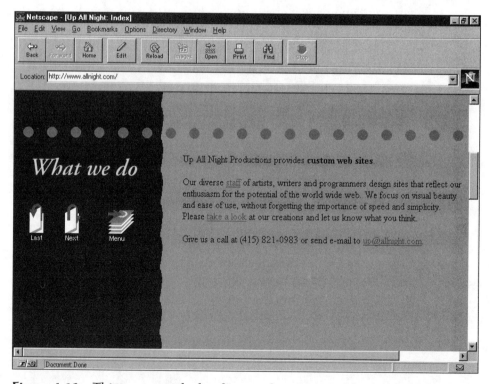

Figure 4.20   This page puts the headings and navigational buttons in the column created by the background.

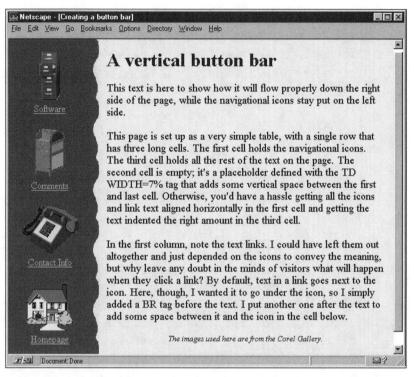

Figure 4.21 Using the background to divide the page into two columns is an easy, elegant trick with table tags.

2. Sketch out your table layout. When you do this, remember that a single table cell enclosed within a pair of <TD>..</TD> tags can hold as much stuff as you want it to, from a single line to several screens' worth. So, instead of putting each button in its own cell on different rows, you can put them all in just one cell, as shown in Figure 4.22.

Figure 4.22 The table sketch shows that a simple 1-row, 2-cell table will do, since each cell can hold more than one item.

3. Start coding the page in your HTML editor or word processor. As you can see in Figure 4.23, the first draft of the table definitely isn't perfect. Like many other things in Web page design, tables often take some trial and error to get right. Here's the HTML for the first draft:

```
<HTML>
<HEAD>
    <TITLE>Creating a button bar</TITLE>
</HEAD>
<BODY TEXT="#000000" BGCOLOR="#FFFFFF" LINK="#00FF00"
VLINK="#0000EE" ALINK="#FF0000" BACKGROUND="bg-gbar.gif">

<TABLE BORDER>
<TR>
  <TD ALIGN=CENTER>
    <A HREF="files.html">
      <IMG SRC="file.gif" VSPACE=5 HSPACE=15 BORDER=0
      HEIGHT=80 WIDTH=50><BR>Software
    </A>
    <A HREF="mailto:me@isp.net">
      <IMG SRC="mailbox.gif" VSPACE=5 BORDER=0
      HEIGHT=80 WIDTH=70><BR>Comments
    </A>
    <A HREF="contact.html">
      <IMG SRC="phone08.gif" VSPACE=5 BORDER=0
      HEIGHT=80 WIDTH=100><BR>Contact Info
    </A>
<A HREF="home.html">
      <IMG SRC="home.gif" VSPACE=5 BORDER=0
      HEIGHT=80 WIDTH=95><BR>Homepage
    </A>
  </TD>
  <TD ALIGN=LEFT VALIGN=TOP>
    <H1>A vertical button bar</H1>
    <FONT SIZE=+1><P>This text is here to show how it will flow
    properly down the right side of the page, while the _
    navigational icons stay put on the left side.</P>
  </TD>
</TR>
</TABLE>
</BODY>
</HTML>
```

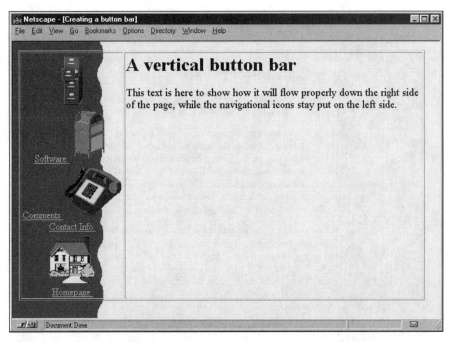

Figure 4.23   This first draft looks pretty bad, but it's an easy fix.

Whenever you're tweaking a table to get it to look right, include the BORDER attribute of the <TABLE> tag so you can easily see where cells begin and end. When everything is correctly set up, remove the BORDER attribute.

4.   The main problem with the table as it is right now is that the text links in the left column aren't lining up under their buttons like they're supposed to. Because they're sticking out all over the place, the first column is also too wide, so the buttons aren't staying within the left background area. There's an easy fix for this: just put each whole link inside a <P>..</P> pair, like this:.

```
<P><A HREF="files.html"><IMG SRC="file.gif" VSPACE=5 HSPACE=15
BORDER=0 HEIGHT=80 WIDTH=50><BR>Software</P>
```

By making it a paragraph, a Web browser will keep everything in the link together onscreen, as shown in Figure 4.24.

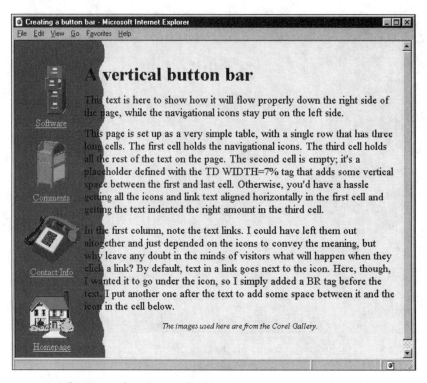

Figure 4.24   This second version is better.

5. "But wait," you say, "now the first column's too narrow." What an observant apprentice Web wizard you are! Again, the fix is easy. Just add an empty column between the other two to space them out, using the WIDTH attribute of the <TD> tag. Note, though, that this attribute is not supported by other browsers like Internet Explorer. There, your table will still look a little "off" unless you actually create a blank, transparent GIF file of the appropriate size and put it in the new cell you made. For this example, assume people are using Netscape, so the line to add after the first <TD>..</TD> pair is something like this:

```
<TD WIDTH=7%></TD>
```

The 7% means that this column should take up seven percent of the total width. It's just a guess, but a good one in this case. Once you remove the BORDER attribute from the <TABLE> tag, you've got the Web page you wanted back in Figure 4.21.

Here's the complete HTML for this page:

```
<HTML>
<HEAD>
   <TITLE>Creating a button bar</TITLE>
</HEAD>
<BODY TEXT="#000000" BGCOLOR="#FFFFFF" LINK="#00FF00" VLINK="#0000EE"
  ALINK="#FF0000" BACKGROUND="bg-gbar.gif">

<TABLE>
<TR>
  <TD ALIGN=CENTER>
    <P><A HREF="files.html">
      <IMG SRC="file.gif" VSPACE=5 HSPACE=15 BORDER=0
       HEIGHT=80 WIDTH=50><BR>Software
    </A></P>
    <P><A HREF="mailto:me@isp.net">
      <IMG SRC="mailbox.gif" VSPACE=5 BORDER=0
       HEIGHT=80 WIDTH=70><BR>Comments
    </A></P>
    <P><A HREF="contact.html">
      <IMG SRC="phone08.gif" VSPACE=5 BORDER=0
       HEIGHT=80 WIDTH=100><BR>Contact Info
    </A></P>
    <P><A HREF="home.html">
      <IMG SRC="home.gif" VSPACE=5 BORDER=0
       HEIGHT=80 WIDTH=95><BR>Homepage
    </A></P>
  </TD>
  <TD WIDTH=7%></TD>
<TD ALIGN=LEFT VALIGN=TOP>
<H1>A vertical button bar</H1>
<FONT SIZE=+1>
<P>This text is here to show how it will flow properly down the right _
  side of the page, while the navigational icons stay put on the left
  side.</P>
<P>This page is set up as a very simple table, with a single row that _
  has three long cells. The first cell holds the navigational icons. The
  third cell holds all the rest of the text on the page. The second cell is
  empty; it's a placeholder defined with the TD WIDTH=7% tag that adds some
  vertical space between the first and last cell. Otherwise, you'd have a
  hassle getting all the icons and link text aligned horizontally in the
  first cell and getting the text indented the right amount in the third
  cell.</P>
<P>In the first column, note the text links. I could have left them _
  out altogether and just depended on the icons to convey the meaning, but
  why leave any doubt in the minds of visitors what will happen when they
  click a link? By default, text in a link goes next to the icon. Here,
  though, I wanted it to go under the icon, so I simply added P../P tags
  around each link.</P>
```

```
<CENTER><FONT SIZE=-1><em>The images used here are from the Corel _
  Gallery.</FONT></CENTER>

</TD>
</TR>
</TABLE>
</BODY>
</HTML>
```

"Why Didn't I Think of That?": You Might Not Need Special Tags at All

If you just want a set of simple navigational icons parading in horizontal rows across the top or bottom of your page, you might not need to bother with table tags at all. Remember that all the major graphical Web browsers, by default, place as many images as they can on a single line, one right after another, and then start a new line. Most of the time, you're trying to avoid this look by using all kinds of attributes and tricks, but a button bar is one case where you might be able to take the easy way out and just let Netscape, Internet Explorer, or Mosaic do its thing. For example, the "table" of buttons in Figure 4.25 was made with these very basic HTML tags:

```
<A HREF="http://nowhere.com/lastp.htm"><IMG SRC="btn-back.gif"
ALT="[Last Page]"></A>
<A HREF="http://nowhere.com/homepage.htm"><IMG SRC="btn-home.gif"
ALT="[Home]"></A>
<A HREF="http://nowhere.com/nextp.htm"><IMG SRC="btn-fwd.gif"
ALT="[Next Page]"></A>
```

The background color of the buttons happens to be a particular shade of royal blue (R:0, G:0, B:156) that blends very nicely with the default blue border that Netscape places around links, so I left the borders alone. Otherwise, I would have simply added the BORDER=0 attribute to each of the <IMG SRC> tags.

The two-by-two "table" that holds the four links on the fictional home page in Figure 4.26 is a slightly more advanced variation on this idea. First, each link was created as a GIF in Paintshop Pro by starting with an empty file, 150 pixels wide and 50 pixels high, adding the words with the Text tool, and applying the Median filter (Image|Special Filters|Median) to get the subtly blurred, softened look.

Figure 4.25   A simple set of navigational buttons doesn't need a table.

Then, the links were lined up in a tabular format using this HTML to make the page:

```
<HTML>
<HEAD>
<TITLE>Another Figure 4.26. The navigational links on this page _
   are set up without any table tags."untable"</TITLE>
</HEAD>
<BODY bgcolor="#FFFFFF">
<CENTER>
<PRE>
<FONT SIZE=5> Welcome, weary pilgrim. You've found...</FONT>
<FONT SIZE=7><strong>Shareware Nirvana</strong></FONT>
(Need to add intro paragraph and a few graphics here. _
   Go for exotic/psychedelic look.)
</PRE>
<BR>
<A HREF="http://nowhere.com/freeware.htm">
   <IMG SRC="icon-fre.gif" ALT="[Freeware]" WIDTH=150 HEIGHT=50
BORDER=0>
</A>
<A HREF="http://nowhere.com/prs.htm">
   <IMG SRC="icon-new.gif" ALT="[News]" WIDTH=150 HEIGHT=50 BORDER=0>
</A>
<BR>
<A HREF="http://nowhere.com/about-us.htm">
   <IMG SRC="icon-abt.gif" ALT="[About Us]" WIDTH=150 HEIGHT=50
BORDER=0>
</A>
<A HREF="mailto:webmaster@nowhere.com">
   <IMG SRC="icon-fdb.gif" ALT="[Feedback]" WIDTH=150 HEIGHT=50
```

Figure 4.26   The navigational links on this page are set up without any table tags.

```
BORDER=0>
</A>
</CENTER>
</BODY>
</HTML>
```

The <CENTER>..</CENTER> tag pair pushes everything to the middle. The <BR> tag after the first two buttons pushes the next two buttons, still centered, to the line below, completing the table effect.

"Fake" tables like these work best if all the images are a consistent size. If they aren't, you can try forcing them into alignment with the WIDTH and HEIGHT attributes of <IMG SRC>. Just make sure they don't end up looking skewed—unless that's the look you're going for. Also, when using this trick, be aware that there will be narrow spaces between the buttons where the background will show through. To make these spaces invisible, use icons with transparent backgrounds for your buttons or make your buttons' background the same color as the page's background.

That row of navigational buttons stretching all the way across the screen might look great on your 17" monitor, but baffling on a smaller screen, where one or two will wrap, seeming isolated on the line below the others. If you're working on a larger-than-normal monitor (at the moment, a 15" monitor is typical), be sure to resize your browser to get an idea of how your pages look at other widths. To keep a row of buttons or icons all on the same line regardless of the monitor width, surround them with the <NOBR>..</NOBR> tag pair—or put them in a table.

Tables That Work Like Image Maps

Take a look at the Discovery Channel home page in Figure 4.27. It looks like an image map and acts like an image map, so it must be an image map, right? Not in this case. The Web wizards at the Discovery Channel cleverly used table tags to get the effect of an image map without its limitations.

By using tables, you increase the portability of your pages and increase the number of Web browsers that will show something usable where the links should be, even if it's not in the format you intended. Also, in the case of the Discovery Channel, many of the items that make up the individual cells of the table are thumbnails of graphics that already existed; it wouldn't have made sense to try to combine them into one large, continuous image just to accommodate an image map. Finally, the cell that provides the current date could not have gone in the middle of an image map, since it must be constantly updated.

Using tables in place of image maps is basically a work-around, however. Like all work-arounds, it has some definite drawbacks. There are two main ones:

1. Different browsers implement table tags in different ways. Or, to put it less delicately, tables that look great in Netscape might look anywhere from slightly strange to downright awful in Microsoft's Internet Explorer, and vice versa, especially if a visitor to your site is using an older version of Explorer (prior to version 2.0). How much of an issue this is at your site depends on your audience and your own attitudes about browser wars. At one extreme, you

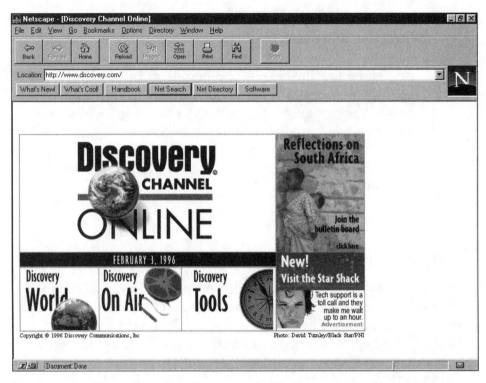

Figure 4.27 This page makes clever use of tables to create an effect similar to an image map.

can create different versions of your tables for different browsers, as needed. At the other, you can just add one of those handy little "best viewed with Netscape" icons to your page and let the tables fall where they may.

2. When using tables as imitation image maps, you have to use some imagination to come up with a result that looks like a coherent image, while staying within basic "building block" shapes—squares and rectangles stacked on top of and beside each other. In fact, the Discovery Channel home page is actually a combination of three tables, as shown in Figure 4.28.

Here's the relevant HTML that produces the tables on the Discovery Channel's home page (the indentations are mine, to make it easier to follow here):

```
<TABLE BORDER=1 CELLPADDING=0 CELLSPACING=0>
<TR>
<TD COLSPAN=3 VALIGN=top ALIGN=center WIDTH=442 HEIGHT=190>
   <A HREF="/DCO/doc/1012/masthead.html">
```

```
      <IMG BORDER=0 SRC="/DCO/doc/1012/onlineheader.gif"
      alt="Discovery Channel Online">
      </A>
</TD><BR>


<TD ROWSPAN=3 VALIGN=top  WIDTH=150 HEIGHT=319 ALIGN=top>
      <TABLE BORDER=0 CELLPADDING=0 CELLSPACING=0>
      <TR>
          <TD Align=left ALIGN=bottom WIDTH=149 HEIGHT=321>
          <A HREF="/cgi-bin/to-bbs?people.cry">
            <IMG VALIGN=BOTTOM BORDER=0 WIDTH=149 HEIGHT=196
            SRC="/DCO/doc/1012/online_buttons/southafrica.gif"
            alt="Reflections on South Africa"><br>
          </A>
          <A HREF="/DCO/doc/1012/world/science/science.html">
            <IMG BORDER=0 WIDTH=149 HEIGHT=63
            SRC="/DCO/doc/1012/online_buttons/smstar.gif"
            alt="The Star Shack">
          </A>
          <A HREF="/cgi-bin/ref/www.austin.ibm.com/pspinfor/
  drkdc4.htm">
            <IMG valign=bottom BORDER=0 WIDTH=149 HEIGHT=63
            SRC="/DCO/doc/1012/world/science/sp/ibm/galleryhome/
  dc4.gif"
            alt="IBM Ad">
          </A><BR>
          </TD>
      </TR>
      </TABLE>

</TD>
</TR>


<TR>
<TD ALIGN=right HEIGHT=23 COLSPAN=3 VALIGN=top WIDTH=441>
   <IMG width = 441 height = 23 BORDER = 0
   SRC="/cgi-bin/daybanner?online"><BR>
</TD>
</TR><BR>
<TR>
<TD ALIGN=RIGHT VALIGN=TOP WIDTH=136 HEIGHT=104>
   <A HREF = "/DCO/doc/1012/world/world.html">
     <IMG width=135 height=104 BORDER=0
     SRC = "/DCO/doc/1012/globe.gif"
     alt="Discovery World">
   </A><BR>
</TD>

<TD ALIGN=RIGHT VALIGN=TOP WIDTH=141 HEIGHT=104>
   <A HREF = "/DCO/doc/1012/on_air/on_air.html">
     <IMG width=140 height=104 BORDER=0
     SRC = "/DCO/doc/1012/reel.gif"
     alt="Discovery On Air">
   </A><BR>
```

```
</TD>

<TD ALIGN=RIGHT VALIGN=TOP WIDTH=160 HEIGHT=104>
   <A HREF = "/DCO/doc/1012/tools/tools.html">
     <IMG width=140 height=104 BORDER=0 align=right
     SRC = "/DCO/doc/1012/compass.gif"
     alt="Discovery Tools">
   </A><BR>
</TD>
</TR>
</TABLE>

<TABLE BORDER=0 CELLPADDING=0 CELLSPACING=0>
<TR>
<TD WIDTH=289 valign=top>
  <FONT SIZE=1>Copyright & copy 1996 Discovery Communications, Inc
</TD>
<TD ALIGN=RIGHT WIDTH=303>
  <FONT SIZE=1>Photo: David Turnley/Black Star/PNI</FONT>
</TD>
</TR>
</TABLE>
```

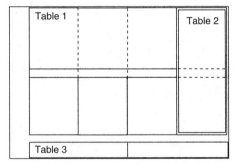

Figure 4.28   This is how the tables that make up Figure 4.27 come together.

The code in the first two sets of <TABLE>..</TABLE> tags might seem pretty complicated. Basically, though, this code sets up a 3-row by 4-column table, with a "sub-table" in column 4. The Webmaster had to do some pretty tricky coding to get each of the elements in the table a particular size and position. If you were a little less picky about sizing, you could get away with a much simpler scheme. Among other things, you could do away with the sub-table altogether.

Creating an Imitation Image Map

There's a little town in Lancaster County, Pennsylvania named Blue Ball. Like many towns in that part of PA, a lot of its economic health depends on tourism generated by being in "Amish country." Blue Ball also has the special tourist draw of being on a route from the town of Intercourse to the town of Paradise. (No kidding—you can look it up.)

Your reputation as a powerful Web wizard has reached even this small town, and the tourist bureau has hired you to create a Web site promoting Blue Ball. The central navigational element for the site is to be a ball (blue, of course) with links printed on it in a contrasting color (red), like the one in Figure 4.29. You've decided not to use an image map because the tourist bureau wants maximum portability and browser-independence for the site; they want as many people using as many different browsers as possible to be able to view it, and they want to be able to freely move it to different ISPs running different servers, including ones that don't give them access to the cgi-bin. Also, an image map would be harder for non-wizards to maintain as links change—and you can't stay in Blue Ball forever, since your Web wizardry is needed elsewhere.

 You decide to whip up an imitation image map. First, you need to create the quadrants of the ball using Photoshop. (Paintshop Pro is not a good choice here because it doesn't provide an easy way to measure and line up the quadrants). Then you'll use table tags to put them together on the Web page.

Figure 4.29 On the sample Web page shown here, users click on quadrants of the ball to navigate through the site.

Here are the steps:

1. Create the graphic using the steps in Chapter 2 for creating a 3D ball in Photoshop, or load the graphic from the CD-ROM (balldone.gif). Note that it's not a transparent GIF at this point. If it were transparent, cutting up and re-piecing the quadrants would be harder because Photoshop wouldn't take into account the transparent background of each quadrant, so you'd end up working with odd-sized rectangles instead of equal squares.

2. You're going to divide the ball up into four equal quadrants, and save each one in its own file. Make sure the rulers are turned on so you can see exactly where each quadrant begins and ends (Window|Show Rulers). For even more precise information, make sure the Info palette is turned on (Window|Palettes|Show Info).

3. To create the first quadrant, drag the rectangular Marquee tool from the 1/2-inch points on both the vertical and horizontal rulers to the 21/2-inch points, so you have a 2-inch square like in Figure 4.30. Check the Info palette to make sure your selection begins precisely at the 1/2-inch points and ends precisely at the 21/2-inch points. It's important to be precise in your selecting; otherwise, you'll have gaps in the finished image where the quadrants aren't the same size.

4. Select Edit|Copy, then File|New. Photoshop will suggest a file that's just the right size for the piece of the ball in the clipboard, so click OK.

5. Select Edit|Paste, and you've got the upper-left corner of the ball in a file by itself. Export it to a transparent GIF called quad1.gif.

If you have trouble getting the transparency right for the GIFs in Photoshop, just export them without worrying about transparency. Then, open the files in Paintshop Pro, WebImage, or some other shareware or freeware that creates transparent GIFs and do it there.

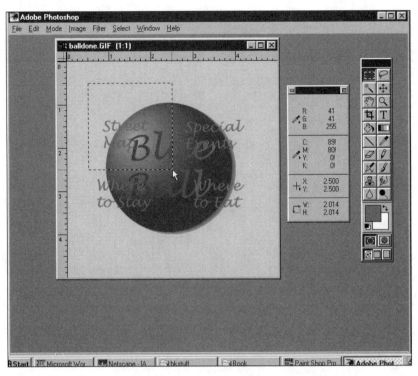

Figure 4.30 The first 2-inch quadrant of the ball is selected.

6. Repeat steps 3 through 5 for the other three quadrants of the ball, exporting each one to a separate GIF. Make quad2.gif the upper-right corner, quad3.gif the lower-left, and quad4.gif the lower right.

7. Now you're ready to create the table itself, which is a simple one with two rows (<TR>..</TR>) and two cells in each row (<TD>..</TD>). The basic thing to remember at this point is that any attribute that would add space anywhere in the table, such as BORDER, CELLPADDING, CELLSPACING, HSPACE, and VSPACE, must be set to zero. Also, as always, include the HEIGHT and WIDTH attributes in the <IMG SRC> tags. Here's the HTML that creates the table.

```
<HTML>
 <HEAD><TITLE>An Imitation Image Map</TITLE>
 </HEAD>
```

```
<BODY BGCOLOR="#FFFFFF" TEXT="#000000" LINK="#0000FF"
VLINK="#AA0000" ALINK="#FFFFFF">
    <CENTER>
<TABLE CELLPADDING=0 CELLSPACING=0 BORDER=0>
    <TR>
    <TD><A HREF="http://blueball.com/map.htm">
        <IMG SRC="quad1.gif" ALT="Street Map"
         HSPACE=0 VSPACE=0 WIDTH=145 HEIGHT=145 BORDER=0>
         </A>
    </TD>
        <TD><A HREF="http://blueball.com/calendar.htm">
         <IMG SRC="quad2.gif" ALT="Calendar of Events"
         HSPACE=0 VSPACE=0 WIDTH=145 HEIGHT=145 BORDER=0>
         </A>
    </TD>
    </TR>
    <TR>
    <TD><A HREF="http://blueball.com/stay.html">
        <IMG SRC="quad3.gif" ALT="Where to Stay"
         HSPACE=0 VSPACE=0 WIDTH=145 HEIGHT=145 BORDER=0>
         </A>
    </TD>
        <TD><A HREF="http://blueball.com/eat.html">
         <IMG SRC="quad4.gif" ALT="Where to Eat"
         HSPACE=0 VSPACE=0  WIDTH=145 HEIGHT=145 BORDER=0>
    </A>
    </TD>
    </TR>
</TABLE></CENTER>
</BODY>
</HTML>
```

The four sections of the ball are nice and seamless. If they weren't, you could try tweaking the alignment of each cell and/or image in the table, or experimenting with different WIDTH and HEIGHT values. Blue Ball's tourist bureau is very pleased with the results, especially because you've done such a good job setting up a table that is navigable from many different browsers. Figure 4.31 shows that the table looks great in Netscape, and it also looks good in Internet Explorer. Thanks to the use of ALT, it would even appear as a table if images were turned off.

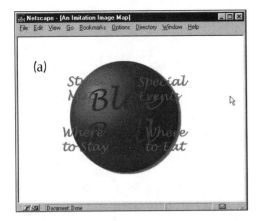 

Figure 4.31   The "Blue Ball" table works not just in Netscape (a), but also in Internet Explorer (b).

Turning a circular image like the blue ball into a table is more challenging than working with rectangular images because the parts of the circle have to fit together perfectly within the rectangular cells of the table. For an easier imitation image map, think in terms of discrete, transparent, rectangular images like stamps, calendars, the tiles in a mosaic, and the squares in a quilt. (There's that Amish theme again!)

Web Wizard's Touchstones for Tables

Do check your tables carefully in the major browsers you expect visitors to use, such as Netscape, Internet Navigator, and the more common versions of Mosaic. Make sure the tables are at least usable, even if they're not perfectly formatted in all the browsers.

Don't set the BORDER attribute of <TABLE> to a large number (say, five or higher). Such highly beveled borders draw attention away from the information you're presenting in the table.

Do make a sketch of your table to visualize its squares and rectangles, especially if you're formatting something fairly complicated, like a newsletter.

Don't use tables for button bars if you can accomplish the same thing with just the aligned <A HREF> and <IMG SRC> tags.

Do remember that a single cell in a table can hold more than one piece of information.

Don't panic if a table you've coded looks bizarre the first time you test it. Often, all it needs is a simple fix like adding a missing </TD> or changing a ROWSPAN to a COLSPAN.

Do make sure all your <TABLE>, <TH>, <TR>, and <TD> tags have closing </TD>, </TR>, </TH>, and </TABLE> tags, and that they're in the right order.

Don't set your table widths to values higher than most people's monitors can accommodate. Try to stay within 640 pixels.

Do remember the <CAPTION>..</CAPTION> pair of tags for a heading that you want to automatically stretch across the width of a table.

V

IMAGE MAPS:
YOU CAN
GET THERE
FROM HERE

You can do a lot of Web building with just the elements discussed so far in this book: graphics, text, and tables. To be a genuine Web wizard, though, you have to understand how to use the more advanced Web building blocks, even if you don't actually use them at every site. When you have access to the whole bag of tricks, you can make a better choice about which particular bit of wizardry to pull out in a specific situation.

Image maps are probably the most common bit of advanced wizardry you'll see as you surf the Web. They're really not hard to make, once you've got the tools you need. At professionally designed sites, image maps like the one in Figure 5.1 typically provide the central navigational device for linking dozens or even hundreds of pages together.

Figure 5.1 The retro Internet Underground Music Archive (http://www. iuma.com) relies almost completely on image maps to guide visitors through its pages.

Before you make a map, you need to decide whether you want server-side image mapping, client-side image mapping, or both. Server-side mapping is the traditional way. It requires a special CGI script on the server, which processes a user's mouse clicks on the map. Client-side image mapping (sometimes abbreviated *CSIM*) is newer and easier, since it relies strictly on HTML. However, at this point, it's only supported by Netscape Navigator and Internet Explorer.

The Coolness of Client-Side Cartography

It seems to me that standard (server-side) image maps are much more complicated than they should be. All you want to do, after all, is tell the browser that when a user clicks on a particular place in an image, the browser should load a particular page. Why should that require a CGI script and separate calls to the server?

Apparently, lots of Web wizards also think there should be an easier way to create image maps, because there have been several proposals to the standards committees working on HTML 3.0 for client-side image mapping. With CSIM, everything the browser needs to interpret the image map is right in the HTML file, so it doesn't need to go back to the server for information. One suggested implementation of this technique involves the proposed <FIG> tag, which would effectively replace <IMG SRC> for most things, and do lots of things that <IMG SRC> can't, including allow client-side image maps.

The bad news is that the future of <FIG> looks doubtful at the moment. The good news is that high-end browsers like Netscape and Internet Explorer have stopped waiting for <FIG>. They've gone ahead and implemented an alternative version of client-side image mapping with a special attribute of <IMG SRC> called USEMAP.

With USEMAP, the coordinates of the image map are incorporated somewhere on the same page of HTML that holds the <IMG SRC>—kind of like a subroutine in a typical computer program. The image map HTML is usually at the top or bottom of the page, set off by a comment line for easier maintenance, and surrounded by the <MAP>..</MAP> tag pair. When Netscape or Internet Explorer detects the USEMAP attribute, it looks on the page for the <MAP> tag that starts the map "subroutine" and handles the user's clicks according to the hot spots identified there.

Browsers that don't support USEMAP just ignore everything in the <MAP>..</MAP> tags. This is where USEMAP gets even cooler: it's one of the first elements of HTML to support backwards compatibility. (The <NOFRAMES> tag, discussed in the next chapter, is the other.) Backwards compatibility means you can have the best of both worlds: you can use client-side image mapping for up-to-date Web browsers, and still have a traditional, server-side image map available for older and less robust browsers. It also means a little more work, since you're creating and managing two versions of the same image map, but it's worth it if you expect, say, half your visitors to use Netscape (which allows client-side mapping) while the other half uses America Online (which does not). Web wizard Michael Herrick sums up the issue of backwards compatibility this way:

"USEMAP is much better than ISMAP, but you basically still have to do both. You want people to be able to get around your site, and that's impossible if you only have USEMAP and they can't see it. I don't worry too much about supporting text browsers like Lynx that can't use graphics at all. I have to draw the line somewhere—I always say I don't support stone tablets either—but I do need to support *anyone* who can use image maps, no matter what kind of browser they have."

Tools for Map Making

To create a client-side image map, you need these tools and pieces of information:

- The complete URLs of the pages you want to map
- An appropriate graphic to be mapped
- An image-mapping utility

To create a server-side image map, you need all that, plus

- "Read" access to the cgi-bin directory on your server
- The name of the image-map CGI script on your server (probably either *imagemap* or *htimage*)

AN IMAGINATIVE IMAGE

A great image map starts with a great metaphor, a graphic that clearly symbolizes how your site is organized. When you make an image map, your goal is to come up with a graphic that makes it as easy as possible for users to figure out that what they're seeing is a map, and intuitively have an idea of how to use it. Most users like to have some idea of where a particular link is taking them, and a good image map provides this information.

The best metaphors come right from the theme of a Web site. Because they're so well-conceived, they seem obvious. You find yourself looking at such a map and thinking, "Well, of course that's the graphic to use there." Like all great artists, however, the Web wizards just make it look easy. Behind the scenes, that simple image map probably took a lot of thought and several drafts to get just right.

The image maps that Web wizard Steve Jenkins uses at the Windows95.Com Shareware site (http://www.windows95.com/) are a perfect example of elegant simplicity, as you can see from the example in Figure 5.2. What more obvious way is there to organize Windows 95 shareware than as icons in a Windows 95 window? Not only is this metaphor easy to use, it's also easy to maintain. The hot spots are basic rectangles, and they can be changed by simply adding, moving, or deleting particular icons in the "window."

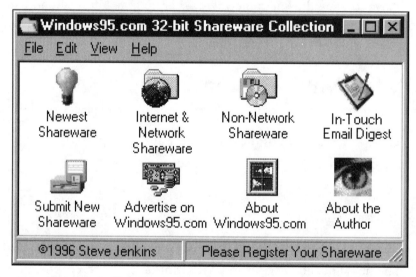

Figure 5.2   This is a brilliant metaphor for an image map at a site for Windows software. Users immediately understand how to navigate using this graphic.

Another example of a good metaphor is shown in Figure 5.3. Artistically, this image is very simple, but it relates well to the site, since it looks "audio" in an abstract way—like a speaker or disks in a jukebox.

Here are a few more general metaphors that could easily be turned into workable image maps:

   ◎ Objects on a table or desk

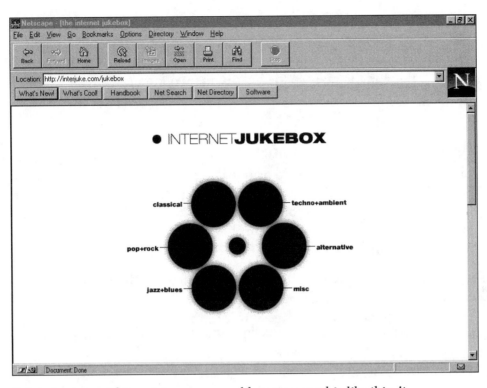

Figure 5.3   Anyone with a paint program could create a graphic like this. It doesn't necessarily take great artistic talent to design a good image map—simple symbols that are easy for users to understand can do just as well.

- Files in a filing cabinet
- Books on a shelf
- Postcards and stamps on letters
- Floppy disks
- Buttons in an elevator
- A menu
- Billboards and street signs

With a little brainstorming, you'll probably be able to think of dozens more. If you have a scanner, you can scan in the images you need from everyday objects, such as office supplies and envelopes. If you don't have a scanner, you can modify clip art, use abstract graphics that you make yourself in a paint program, or, if your budget allows, have a custom graphic designed for you.

Never change the original GIF or JPEG after you've created an image map from it. If you do, you might change the size or shape of elements in the graphic. Their coordinates won't match those in the map, so the links won't work properly.

AN IMAGE-MAPPING UTILITY

All Web wizards agree that a good map-making program is really indispensable for making image maps. While it is possible to map out an image by hand, it's difficult and tedious, because you need to get the exact pixel positions that make up each hot spot, and then write them all up in a way your server (or browser, for client-side maps) understands.

Fortunately, image-mapping utilities are easy to find on the Web, and most of them are free. The one most frequently mentioned by PC-based Web wizards is MapThis, a Windows program generously provided as freeware by Todd C. Wilson. MapThis is included on the CD-ROM and is used for the examples in this chapter. (The Mac equivalent, a program called WebMap, is available from the http://www.city.net/cnx/software/ Web site.)

HERE COMES THE CGI!

Once you've got a GIF or JPEG that you want to use and the image-mapping utility that will turn it into a map, you need to know what kind of server your site is on, if you want a server-side image map. The most common server standard is NCSA, followed by CERN. (Actually, there's another server called Apache which has recently become more popular than CERN for new installations, but it bases its server-side mapping on NCSA.)

Server-side image maps are device-dependent. Each server uses a different CGI script to process the user clicks, and each server expects the coordinates that make up the hot spots to appear in a particular way. Fortunately, MapThis, like most image-mapping utilities, takes care of all these tedious details, but you need to tell it which server's rules to use.

If you don't have either NCSA or CERN at your site (a fairly rare situation), you can still use image maps, but you'll have to either manually write out all the coordinates or stick with client-side image maps. Either of these options has drawbacks: writing the map file for images by hand is very slow going, while client-side maps can only be understood by Netscape and Internet Explorer.

Assuming that you have either CERN or NCSA, you also need to format the lines of HTML that refer to the image map in the proper way for your particular server. Basically, this means adding a few lines of HTML to call the right CGI script. For NCSA, the script is *imagemap* (or just *imap* in the Apache variation), and for CERN it's *htimage*. These scripts are stored in a special directory on the server called *cgi-bin*.

Suppose you had a graphic called hiking.gif that you wanted to be an image map at your site, http://www.outdoors.com/~hike-it, which is on an NCSA server. Processing it with MapThis would produce a text file called hiking.map that holds information about the hot spots, in addition to the original hiking.gif. Since you have an NCSA server, you'd use HTML like this to add the map to a Web page:

```
<A HREF="http://www.outdoors/cgi-bin/imagemap/~hike-it/hiking.map">
<IMG SRC="hiking.gif" ISMAP>
</A>
```

If you had a CERN server, the HTML would look almost identical, with *htimage* substituted for *imagemap* in the <A HREF> tag:

```
<A HREF="http://www.outdoors/cgi-bin/htimage/~hike-it/hiking.map">
<IMG SRC="hiking.gif" ISMAP>
</A>
```

The URLs in these <A HREF> lines probably look different from what you're used to. They actually combine two different directory paths: the place where the CGI script is and the place where your particular map is. In effect, the hiking example reads, "Use the map-processing script called imagemap (or htimage) found at http://www.outdoors.com/cgi-bin to process whatever is at /~hike-it/ hiking.map."

Fortunately, you don't have to worry about what exactly the imagemap or htimage CGI script does—you just have to know where it is and what it's called.

If you're comfortable with Unix directory conventions, you don't have to use complete URLs in the <A HREF>. For example, instead of writing <A HREF="http://www.outdoors/cgi-bin/htimage/~hike-it/hiking.map""> you could write <A HREF="..cgi-bin/htimage/~hike-it/hiking.map">. Some browsers can get confused by relative codes in the actual map files, however, so it's always a good idea to stick to complete URLs there. To keep from having to remember when relative URLs are okay and when they're not, I just use the complete URLs throughout my image-mapping code.

"Why Didn't I Think of That?":
Testing for Server Type

Not sure whether you have a CERN or NCSA server? A telephone call to your service provider is one way to clear things up, as long as it's during business hours and you can get through to the right person. If you can't wait for that, you can just test the server yourself by uploading both CERN and NCSA versions of the same map to your Web site. Whichever one responds correctly when you click the hot spots is the server you've got.

There is a collection of simple files already on the CD-ROM for the purpose of testing your server:

- Maptestc.htm
- Maptestn.htm
- Star.htm
- Ball.htm
- Square.htm
- Cernmap.map
- Ncsamap.map
- Maptest.gif

Before you use them, you'll need to modify the maptestc.htm, maptestn.htm, cernmap.map, and ncsamap.map files to reflect your own directory structure. All five of these files are just plain text, so you can open them in any word processing program to change the URLs. For example, the Webmaster at http://www.outdoors.com/ ~hike-it would change maptestn.htm from this:

```
<HTML>
<HEAD>
<TITLE>NCSA Map Test</TITLE>
</HEAD>
<BODY><H2>Click the map image to test for an NCSA server</H2>
<A HREF="http://www.your-isp.net/cgi-bin/imagemap/yoursite/
  ncsamap.map">
<IMG SRC="maptest.gif" WIDTH=314 HEIGHT=287 ISMAP></A>
</BODY>
</HTML>
```

to this:

```
<HTML>
<HEAD>
<TITLE>NCSA Map Test</TITLE>
</HEAD>
<BODY><H2>Click the map image to test for an NCSA server</H2>
<A HREF="http://www.outdoors.com/cgi-bin/imagemap/~hike-it/
  ncsamap.map">
<IMG SRC="maptest.gif" WIDTH=314 HEIGHT=287 ISMAP></A>
</BODY>
</HTML>
```

Similarly, ncsamap.map file would go from this:

```
#$MTIMFH
#$-:Image Map file created by Map THIS!
#$-:Map THIS! free image map editor by Todd C. Wilson
#$-:Please do not edit lines starting with "#$"
#$VERSION:1.20
#$TITLE:NCSA version of map test
#$AUTHOR:Marianne Krcma
#$DATE:Mon Mar 11 15:53:01 1996
#$PATH:C:\NETSCAPE\bkstuff\
#$GIF:maptest.gif
#$FORMAT:ncsa
#$EOH
default http://www.your-isp.net/yoursite/maptestn.htm
poly http://www.your-isp.net/yoursite/star.htm 16,78 71,78 88,45
```

```
99,74 145,76 105,110 117,165 73,132 33,160 52,116 10,77 13,78 16,78
circle http://www.your-isp.net/yoursite/ball.htm  205,52 243,90
rect http://www.your-isp.net/yoursite/square.htm 127,174 288,262
```

to this:

```
#$MTIMFH
#$-:Image Map file created by Map THIS!
#$-:Map THIS! free image map editor by Todd C. Wilson
#$-:Please do not edit lines starting with "#$"
#$VERSION:1.20
#$TITLE:NCSA version of map test
#$AUTHOR:Marianne Krcma
#$DATE:Mon Mar 11 15:53:01 1996
#$PATH:C:\NETSCAPE\bkstuff\
#$GIF:maptest.gif
#$FORMAT:ncsa
#$EOH
default http://www.outdoors.com/~hike-it/maptestn.htm
poly http://www.outdoors.com/~hike-it/star.htm 16,78 71,78 88,45
99,74 145,76 105,110 117,165 73,132 33,160 52,116 10,77 13,78 16,78
circle http://www.outdoors.com/~hike-it/ball.htm  205,52 243,90
rect http://www.outdoors.com/~hike-it/square.htm 127,174 288,262
```

When you've got the files loaded at your site and you call maptestn.htm, you should see something like Figure 5.4a. If you click on the star and see Figure 5.4b, you've got an NCSA server. If you get an error message, first make sure all your directory information is correct, then repeat the test. If it still doesn't work, try maptestc.htm. If neither one works, you're back to square one: either call your service provider to find out what's up, or just stick to client-side maps.

The Wizards Speak:
The Making of an Image Map

Moshe-Dovid Teitelbaum is the Web wizard who created the Bethesda Softworks Web site at http://www.bethsoft.com/. Since it is a computer games publisher, Bethesda Softworks decided on a site that could be "played" like an adventure game—and that means lots of clickable images, just like in a real computer game.

(a)

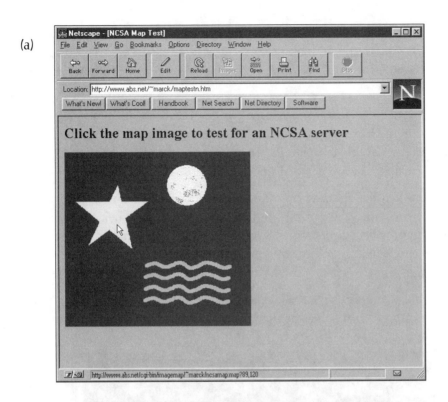

(b)

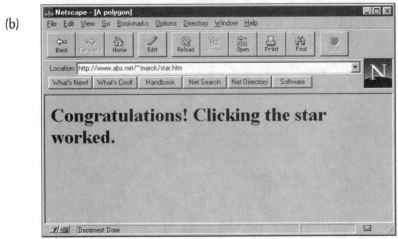

Figure 5.4   The map (a) tests for an NCSA server. It was successful at this Web site (b).

According to Teitelbaum, the opening image map, shown in Figure 5.5, was designed mainly for its graphic effect, as well as providing the way for users to navigate through the site. He explains how it came to be:

"Once the decision was made to go ahead with a game-like Web site, the basic page design was thought up. (Each page should have the same basic template/design so as not to confuse the user.) Then the images were decided upon, based on the page's contents.

"When the opening image map was designed, certain objects were thrown into the composition for the sole reason of being hot spots. Specifically, three books were added: one for text-based viewing, one for light graphics, and one for full graphics. Other objects were put into the image for later use as hot spots [such as the bottles].

"For commercial Web sites, it is important to grab the users' attention right from the start. Make them want to see what other cool

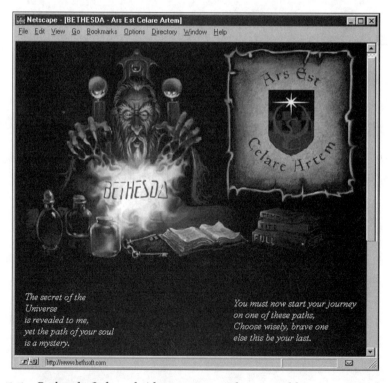

Figure 5.5 Bethesda Softworks' home page is dominated by an eye-catching image map. Hot spots include the keys and books.

stuff can be found if they delve deeper into the site. To that end, the image of the wizard peering into the crystal ball was used. It's just such a great image; you look at it and go 'Wow!'

"Another thing that commercial sites want is for people to keep them in mind, even after getting off the Net. Of course, you want them to keep you in mind because of the product, but don't rely on that in designing the Web site. Create some other reason for people to come back to your site. At the Bethesda site, we added the title 'ARS EST CELARE ARTEM' to the image map. If you don't know Latin, you leave the site wondering what that was—a great way to be kept in mind!"

Like other Web wizards, Teitelbaum advises using client-side image maps to lighten the load on your server. "However," he continues, "always assume that the client won't be able to handle client-side image maps. Prepare a server-side map just in case." Here is the relevant HTML for the server-side and client-side versions of the image map at Bethesda Softworks' home page:

```
<A HREF="http://www.bethsoft.com/cgi-bin/imagemap/Maps/wizard.map">
<IMG SRC="Graphics/wizard.gif" BORDER=0 ALT="Ars Est Celare Artem"
height=362 width=580 ISMAP USEMAP="#ARS EST CELARE ARTEM">
</A>
<MAP NAME="ARS EST CELARE ARTEM">
   <AREA SHAPE=POLY COORDS="410,284,410,274,462,285,462,295,410,284"
HREF=http://www.bethsoft.com/cgi-bin/gateway.cgi?Text>
   <AREA SHAPE=POLY COORDS="407,291,421,287,461,295,407,291"
HREF=http://www.bethsoft.com/cgi-bin/gateway.cgi?Lite>
   <AREA SHAPE=POLY COORDS="396,309,396,327,490,343,488,322,396,309"
HREF=http://www.bethsoft.com/cgi-bin/gateway.cgi?Full>
   <AREA SHAPE=POLY
COORDS="273,351,392,327,375,309,366,310,339,291,327,299,312,296,282,303,-
   265,306,254,303,236,315,272,351,273,351" HREF=http://
www.bethsoft.com/cgi-bin/register.cgi?Lite>
   <AREA SHAPE=POLY
COORDS="174,323,232,313,236,321,223,325,216,321,191,331,205,342,-
   252,344,253,346,251,352,237,351,198,353,193,354,183,344,177,335,174,323"
HREF=http://www.bethsoft.com/cgi-bin/alias.cgi>
   <AREA SHAPE=default HREF=http://www.bethsoft.com>
</MAP>
```

As you can see, all of the hot spots in the map call CGI scripts, except the <AREA SHAPE=default>, which just reloads the home page when a user clicks on the image map's background. The CGI calls are necessary because Bethesda Softworks requires users to register; otherwise, the hot spots would just point directly to pages at the site.

To minimize possible problems with your image maps, Teitelbaum advises, "Make sure your hot spots don't overlap. What happens when multiple hot spots overlap depends on the script you're using to handle image maps. NCSA's imagemap CGI script, for example, will return the URL of the last hot spot defined in the map file. CERN's htimage script, on the other hand, returns the first hot spot defined for the overlapping area.

"An image should have as many hot spots as are required, but you shouldn't cram the entire image full of hot spots. Try to make it perfectly obvious where each hot spot will take the user (unless your intention is to be confusing, that is). Similarly, the hot spots should be as large as needed. In general, you should try to keep a fair amount of free space between the hot spots, but it really depends on the image that you're using. Also, it's better to use full URLs instead of partial URLs when you're defining hot spots."

When you test an image map that you've made this way using an image-mapping utility like MapThis, there are really very few problems to look out for, according to Teitelbaum.

"Just make sure that the URL resolves correctly, and that the areas you wanted defined as hot spots are," he suggests. "I always use a number of browsers to make sure that the code works despite the differences between browsers, and to ensure that the layout works well on every browser." For the image maps at Bethesda Softworks, the browsers he tested on included Netscape Navigator, Internet Explorer, AOL browser (Windows version), and Mosaic (SPRY and NCSA versions).

A Home-Page Image Map

The great job you did on the Blue Ball tourist bureau's site (Chapter 4) has led to another design project: one of the tourist bureau's member businesses, the Lancaster County Quilters' Guild. This time, you decide on an image map as the central element of the home page. The Guild is certain that their site will run on an NCSA server, but they're not sure what browsers people will use to access it, so you'll need to prepare both client-side and server-side versions of the map.

Note that all of the URLs in the following step-by-step example are fake, so you won't actually be able to test the map. If you want to test it thoroughly, substitute the URLs of real pages at your site in the hot spots in the map files, as well as in the <A HREF> and <IMG SRC> tags.

 In creating the home-page image map, you decide to start with the client-side version, then do the server-side one. (This is arbitrary; you could just as easily have done it the other way around.) Here are the steps:

1. Find or create a GIF or JPEG that would make a good image map. This is actually the hardest part of the whole process. In this case, the image of a quilt is a fairly obvious choice. Using your favorite paint program to create one, you'll get something like Figure 5.6, which is available on the CD-ROM as quilt2.gif.

2. Install the MapThis program from the CD-ROM and start it. In the main screen of MapThis, select File|New. From the Make a New Image Map dialog box, click the Let's Go Find One button.

3. Navigate through your directory structure until you find quilt2.gif. Double-click it to load it into MapThis.

4. Select File|Preferences to bring up the General Preferences dialog box. It should be set up as shown in Figure 5.7, with CSIM as the default map type and all the check boxes turned on.

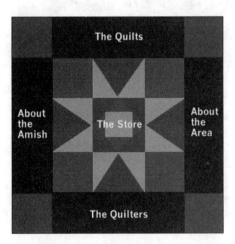

Figure 5.6 This is the graphic that will become the image map.

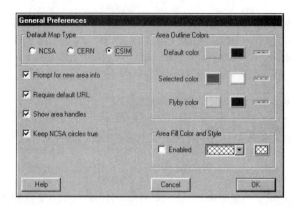

Figure 5.7 To make it as easy as possible to create the client-side map, set up the preferences as shown here.

5. Now you're ready to make your first hot spot. Use whatever system works best for you when mapping the hot spots. I prefer to start with the most important hot spot, and then work my way clockwise through the rest of the map. The most important hot spot in this case is "The Store," in the middle of the image. You want this spot to be fairly big and easy to click on, so choose the Define Rectangle Area tool as shown in Figure 5.8.

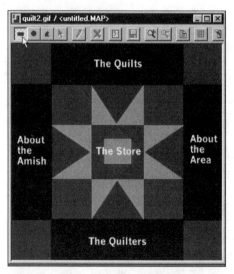

Figure 5.8 Choose the Define Rectangle Area tool to make the hot spot.

6. Click and drag this tool to make the hot spot. Remember, you want it fairly big, but you don't want it to overlap areas that will be used by other hot spots. As soon as you let go of the mouse button, a dialog box will pop up, asking for the URL for this spot. Type in the complete URL, http://www.blueball.com/quilters/thestore.htm, as shown in Figure 5.9. Don't worry about what's on that page for now, but do make a note of it so you give it the correct name when you create it.

7. Again using the Define Rectangle Area tool, create the hot spot for "The Quilts" square, being careful not to overlap onto other squares. If you do accidentally overlap, fix the problem by dragging by the black handles that appear at the corners and midpoints of the selection until the selected area is the right size. The URL for this area is http://www.blueball.com/quilters/stock.htm; again, make a note of it for future reference.

8. Repeat step 7 for the other hot spots in your image, using these URLs:

```
http://www.blueball.com/quilters/tourism.htm
http://www.blueball.com/quilters/theguild.htm
http://www.blueball.com/quilters/theamish.htm
```

When you're finished, you should have a series of coordinates like the ones in Figure 5.10.

9. Click Save to bring up the Info About This Mapfile dialog box shown in Figure 5.11. The only important things to be filled in here are the title and the default URL. The title is not required in server-side image maps, but it's needed in client-side maps like this one to serve as the name in the USEMAP call. The easiest thing is just to give it the same name as the image file itself, quilt2, minus the .gif extension.

The default URL is always needed, whether you're making a client-side or server-side map; it's the page that the browser will call up if the user clicks an area that isn't a hot spot. Usually, this URL will be the same as the one for the image map itself, so a click in the "wrong" area won't have any effect as far as the user can see. Since the image map is on the home page in this example, the default URL will be http://www.blueball.com/quilters/home.htm.

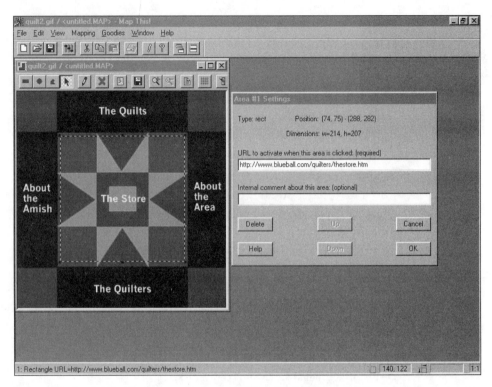

Figure 5.9 Note the size and shape of the first hot spot: big enough, but not too big.

10. In the Save As dialog box, save this client-side map with the name of the home page itself, home.htm, since it will be part of the home page you're going to make. Note that you'll actually have to type the .htm extension here.

11. If you were just making a client-side map, you could skip to step 13 and make the rest of the home page. For this example, though, you'll need to choose File|Save As from MapThis again, to create the server-side version.

12. In the Save As dialog box, click the NCSA radio button for File Format. In the File Name area, type quilt2.map (again, you have to actually type the *.map* extension) and save the server-side map. Close out of MapThis.

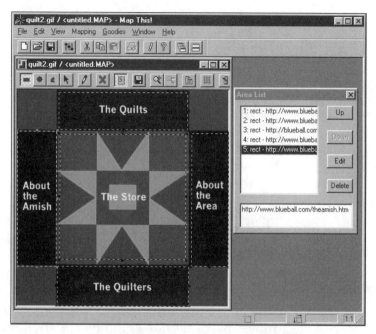

Figure 5.10   Here are the hot spots to put on the image map.

13.   Open the home.htm file in your HTML editor or word processor. It should look like this:

```
<BODY>
<MAP NAME="quilt2">
<!-- #$-:Image Map file created by Map THIS! -->
<!-- #$-:Map THIS! free image map editor by Todd C. Wilson -->
<!-- #$-:Please do not edit lines starting with "#$" -->
<!-- #$VERSION:1.20 -->
<!-- #$DATE:Tue Mar 12 12:52:34 1996 -->
<!-- #$PATH:C:\NETSCAPE\bkstuff\ -->
<!-- #$GIF:quilt2.gif -->
<AREA SHAPE=RECT COORDS="74,75,288,282" HREF=http://
   www.blueball.com/quilters/thestore.htm>
<AREA SHAPE=RECT COORDS="72,5,291,66" HREF=http://www.blueball.com/
   quilters/stock.htm>
<AREA SHAPE=RECT COORDS="299,73,360,293" HREF=http://blueball.com/
   quilters/tourism.htm>
<AREA SHAPE=RECT COORDS="70,295,293,360" HREF=http://
   www.blueball.com/theguild.htm>
<AREA SHAPE=RECT COORDS="1,70,67,294" HREF=http://www.blueball.com/
   theamish.htm>
<AREA SHAPE=default HREF=http://www.blueball.com/quilters/home.htm>
</MAP></BODY>
```

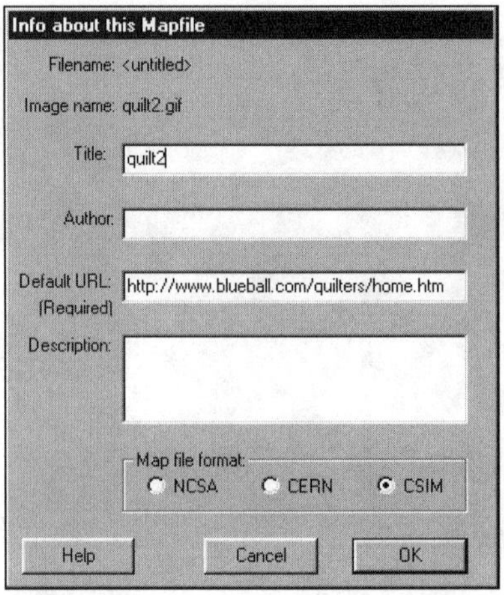

Figure 5.11   A title and default URL are required for client-side image maps.

14. Add the normal <HTML>..</HTML> and <TITLE>..</TITLE> tags. (The title is "Traditional Lancaster County Quilts.") Also, add the attribute BGCOLOR="#FFFFFF" to <BODY> to turn the background of the page white.

15. After the <BODY> tag, put in the <A HREF> and <IMG SRC> tags that will call the image maps:

```
<A HREF="http://www.blueball.com/cgi-bin/imagemap/quilters/
  quilt2.map">
  <IMG SRC="quilt2.GIF" WIDTH=360 HEIGHT=360 ISMAP
USEMAP="#quilt2">
</A>
```

If you were using only a client-side map, you could skip the <A HREF>..</A> tags and just use <IMG SRC="quilt2.gif" WIDTH=360 HEIGHT=360 USEMAP="#quilt2">. The hashmark before *quilt2* indicates that it's the name of another area on the same page.

16. To make the page at least usable, if not very attractive, to people using text browsers, provide text links that match those on the image map in a separate paragraph below the image, like this:

```
<P>
  <A HREF="stock.htm">|The Quilts|</A>
  <A HREF="thestore.htm">|The Store|</A>
  <A HREF="theguild.htm">|The Quilters|</A>
  <A HREF="tourism.htm">|About the Area|</A>
  <A HREF="theamish.htm">|About the Amish|</A>
</P>
```

17. As a final touch, add "Welcome to the Lancaster Quilters' Guild" as an H1 heading and center everything on the page.

Since you don't actually have a site called http://www.blueball.com/quilters/ and all the associated pages, you can't completely test all the links. Still, loading the home.htm file locally in your browser should produce the image map shown in Figure 5.12. When you run your mouse over the hot spots, you can check the status bar to find out whether they point to the right pages.

Here is the complete HTML for the home.htm page:

```
<HTML>
<TITLE>Traditional Lancaster County Quilts</TITLE>
<BODY BGCOLOR="#FFFFFF">
<CENTER>
<H1>Welcome to the Lancaster Quilters' Guild</H1>
<A HREF="http://www.blueball.com/cgi-bin/imagemap/quilters/
  quilt2.map">
  <IMG SRC="quilt2.GIF" WIDTH=360 HEIGHT=360 ISMAP USEMAP="#quilt2">
</A>
<P>
  <A HREF="stock.htm">|The Quilts|</A>
  <A HREF="thestore.htm">| The Store|</A>
  <A HREF="theguild.htm">|The Quilters|</A>
  <A HREF="tourism.htm">|About the Area|</A>
  <A HREF="theamish.htm">|About the Amish|</A>
</P>
</CENTER>

<!-- Here's where the client-side map, quilt2, starts -->
<MAP NAME="quilt2">
<!-- #$-:Image Map file created by Map THIS! -->
<!-- #$-:Map THIS! free image map editor by Todd C. Wilson -->
<!-- #$-:Please do not edit lines starting with "#$" -->
<!-- #$VERSION:1.20 -->
<!-- #$DATE:Tue Mar 12 12:52:34 1996 -->
<!-- #$PATH:C:\NETSCAPE\bkstuff\ -->
<!-- #$GIF:quilt2.gif -->
<AREA SHAPE=RECT COORDS="74,75,288,282" HREF=http://
  www.blueball.com/quilters/thestore.htm>
<AREA SHAPE=RECT COORDS="72,5,291,66" HREF=http://www.blueball.com/
  quilters/stock.htm>
<AREA SHAPE=RECT COORDS="299,73,360,293" HREF=http://blueball.com/
  quilters/tourism.htm>
<AREA SHAPE=RECT COORDS="70,295,293,360" HREF=http://
  www.blueball.com/theguild.htm>
<AREA SHAPE=RECT COORDS="1,70,67,294" HREF=http://www.blueball.com/
theamish.htm>
```

```
<AREA SHAPE=default HREF=http://www.blueball.com/quilters/home.htm>
</MAP>
</BODY>
</HTML>
```

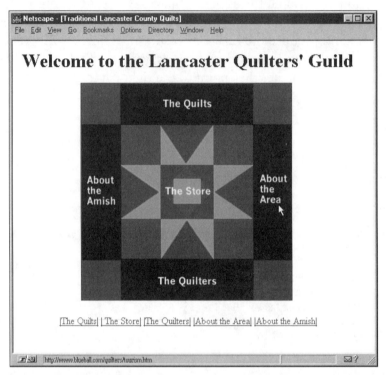

Figure 5.12   In this screen shot of the finished map, the mouse pointer is in the "About the Area" hot spot. As you can see in the lower-left corner, clicking here would take the user to http://www.blueball.com/quilters/tourism.htm, which is just what it's supposed to do.

Varying the Steps

Image maps can be used for all kinds of things besides large graphics. Probably the most common use of image maps is for button bars. Just create the whole bar as one graphic file, then use MapThis or a similar mapping program to break it up into separate areas (usually rectangles). The button bar in Figure 5.13 is a typical example of this kind of image map. It's from BusinessWire (http://www.hnt.com/bizwire/).

Figure 5.13   This "set" of navigational buttons is actually just one graphic, made into an image map.

A site map is another good use of image maps. It's helpful for visitors and easy for you to do, since you've probably already got a diagram of your site, anyway. Figure 5.14 shows the site map from the fairly large Macromedia site (http://www.macromedia.com/). It happens to be server-side only (but it could just as easily be a client-side version), with over 50 hot spots, all of them rectangles.

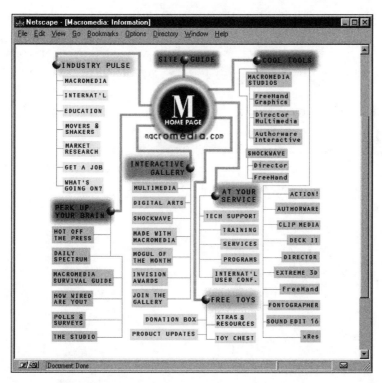

Figure 5.14   Turning your site schematic into an image map can be very helpful to users, particularly at larger sites like this one.

Web Wizard's Touchstones for Image Maps

Do use an image-mapping utility like MapThis (included on the CD-ROM) to create your map files.

Don't make users guess where a hot spot will take them. If the graphic itself isn't descriptive enough, add labels to it.

Do supply both client-side (USEMAP) and server-side (ISMAP) versions of your image maps if you're not sure what browsers your visitors use.

Don't let your hot spots overlap.

Do test both the client-side and the server-side versions of your image map thoroughly to make sure all the links work.

Don't edit a graphic after you've made an image map out of it.

Do provide text links that match the ones on your image map somewhere on your page, in case the link to the image map is broken or a visitor is using a text-based browser.

VI

CUSTOM FRAMING

T he boxes in a graphical interface that are know as "windows" everywhere else in the computing world are called "frames" on the Web. The Web page in Figure 6.1, for example, is made up of four frames, each containing its own file. Clicking in one frame can change the contents of another.

Unlike normal GUI windows, frames don't float on the screen (at least not now, in Netscape Navigator 2.0). They stay wherever you've placed them when you designed the Web page, and they can't overlap. They can, however, be resized by the users, unless you specifically decide not to allow that when you're coding the frames.

Some Web wizards have found unique uses for frames, such as the FURL site (http://www.dscnet.com/furl/) shown in Figure 6.2. Created by Brian Wilson, this site uses a combination of frame tags and Java to enable visitors to view as many as four sites at once.

Not all Web sites that use frames use them well, however. Frames are one of those Web tools that seem to be used either really well or really poorly, with not

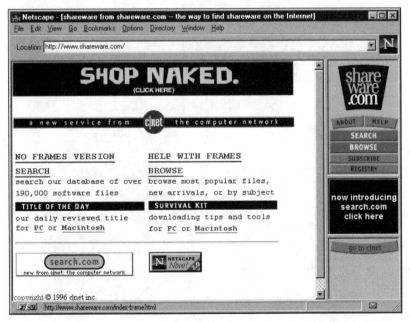

Figure 6.1   This page at http://www.shareware.com/ has four frames.

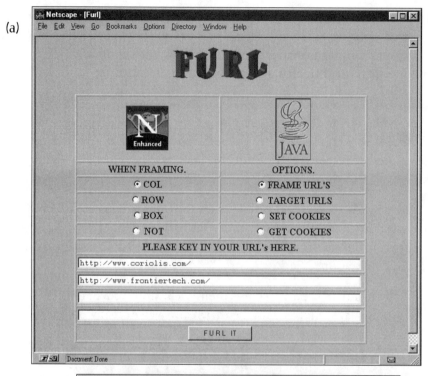

Figure 6.2 The FURL site (a) uses frames and Java to show several Web sites at once (b)—a concept in search of a buzzword, if ever there was one. "Preemptive multisurfing," anyone!

much in between. Figure 6.3 shows one of these unsuccessful implementations of frames. Ironically, it is supposed to demonstrate the advantages of frames. There are five frames on this page, including a tiny one that's just big enough for three one-word links.

"Why Didn't I Think of That?": Viewing Two Sites at Once

Using frame tags, you can do a little Web magic of your own to show two different sites in the same browser window. The effect, shown in Figure 6.4, is similar to the one at the FURL site, but with fewer options: you will be able to select the contents of two different frames from a bookmark list shown in a third frame. One particularly cool thing about this page is that you don't need to load it on your server to use it; it will work just as well loaded locally (with File|Open File in Browser, for Netscape users).

The interaction and layout of the frames on this page is sketched in Figure 6.5. To turn the sketch into a working Web page, start by creating a special HTML file, twosites.htm, to hold the <FRAMESET> and <FRAMES> tags that define the structure of the frames, like this:

```
<HTML>
<HEAD>
<TITLE>It's two, two, two sites in one!</TITLE>
</HEAD>
<FRAMESET ROWS="15%,*">
    <FRAME SRC="hotlist.htm" NAME="hotlist">
    <FRAMESET COLS="50%,*">
        <FRAME SRC="holder1.htm" NAME="site1">
        <FRAME SRC="holder2.htm" NAME="site2">
    </FRAMESET>
</FRAMESET>
<NOFRAMES>
Sorry, but you need a frames-enabled browser such as _
   Netscape Navigator 2.0 to use this page.
</NOFRAMES>
</HTML>
```

One of the first things you'll probably notice about this code is that the <BODY>..</BODY> tag pair is missing. That's because there are, in effect, two mutually exclusive pages defined in this file: one

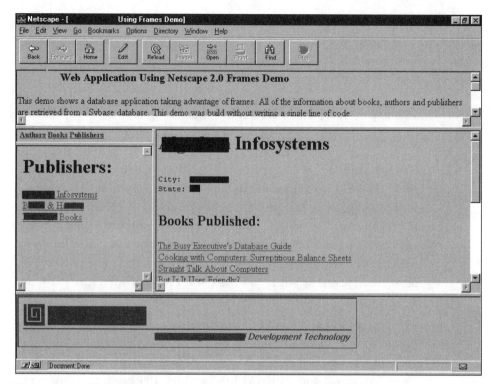

Figure 6.3 This is an example of how not to use frames. Names have been erased to protect the guilty.

for browsers with frames and the other for browsers without. The HTML for the frames' structure *must* come first and be surrounded by <FRAMESET>..</FRAMESET>. The HTML for frameless browsers follows, surrounded by <NOFRAMES>..</NO FRAMES>. Browsers that don't support frames will just ignore everything before <NOFRAMES>, while browsers that do support frames will ignore everything after it.

It's important to realize that the tags within <FRAMESET>..</FRAMESET> just define the overall structure of the page's frames, not the content. At this point, since hotlist.htm, holder1.htm, and holder2.htm don't exist yet, a frames-enabled browser would show the frame structure without anything actually in the frames. A frameless browser, on the other hand, would show "Sorry, but you need a frames-enabled browser such as Netscape Navigator 2.0 to use this page." Figure 6.6 illustrates this difference.

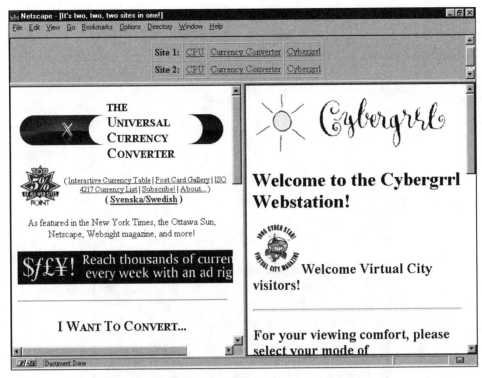

Figure 6.4   Using frames and basic HTML, you can create this "fake FURL."

Frame tags are very similar to table tags in the way that they divide up space on a Web page. Like tables, you define your frames in terms of rows and columns. You can assign specific percentages or pixel sizes to each row and column, or just use the * wildcard to indicate that the frame should be automatically sized by the browser.

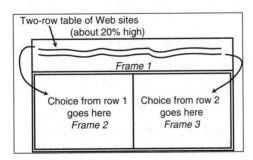

Figure 6.5   Frames are divided into rows and columns like tables, but each "cell" holds a separate file.

(a)

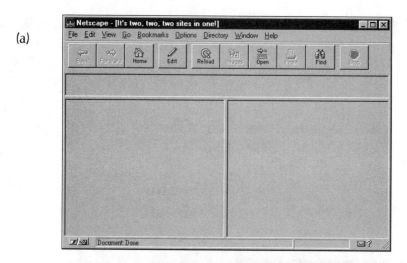

(b)

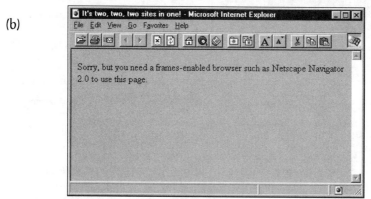

Figure 6.6 If the files referred to in the <FRAMES> tags don't exist, a frames-enabled browser would just show the frame structure (a). Whether or not the files exist, a browser without frames (b) would show whatever comes after <NOFRAMES>.

The line <FRAMESET ROWS="20%, *">, for example, divides the screen into two rows. The first row is 20 percent of the available screen height. The second row is automatically sized, in this case to 80 percent of the screen height.

Also like tables, framesets are often embedded to provide greater design flexibility, allowing different parts of the page to have different row and column layouts. For example, the line <FRAMESET COLS="50%, *"> creates an embedded frameset with two equal columns in the second row of the larger frameset.

However, frames are unlike tables in a very important way. In a table, all the contents of each cell is included within the <TABLE>..</TABLE> tags, but each frame in a frameset is a separate HTML file that can change independently of the others. The interaction among files in a frameset is handled using the NAME and TARGET attributes. If you give a frame a name when you define it, such as <FRAME SRC="holder1.htm" NAME="site1">, you can tell the browser to put a different file in that specific frame, using a line such as <A HREF="http://www.cybergrrl.com/" TARGET="site1">.

The page in this example is made up of four different files:

- Twosites.htm, as already mentioned, is the "main" file that defines the frame structure. It also includes a message for users without frames-capable browsers.

- Hotlist.htm is the file that holds a two-row table of site names for the user to choose from.

- Holder1.htm just puts some dummy text in the Site1 frame, which is replaced when the user selects a site from the first row of the table in Hotlist.htm.

- Holder2.htm puts some dummy text in the Site 2 frame until the user selects a site from the second row in Hotlist.htm.

Here's the HTML for hotlist.htm:

```
<HTML><HEAD><TITLE>My Hot List</TITLE></HEAD>
<BODY>
<CENTER>
<TABLE BORDER CELLSPACING=0 CELLPADDING=4>
<TR>
<TD VALIGN=middle><STRONG>Site 1:</STRONG></TD>
<TD><A HREF="http://www.comma.com/authors.htm" TARGET="site1">CPU</
A></TD>
<TD><A HREF="http://www.xe.net/currency/" TARGET="site1">Currency
Converter</A></TD>
<TD><A HREF="http://www.cybergrrl.com/" TARGET="site1">Cybergrrl</
A></TD>
</TR>
<TR>
<TD VALIGN=middle><STRONG>Site 2:</STRONG></TD>
<TD><A HREF="http://www.comma.com/authors.htm" TARGET="site2">CPU</
A></TD>
<TD><A HREF="http://www.xe.net/currency/" TARGET="site2">Currency
```

```
Converter</A></TD>
<TD><A HREF="http://www.cybergrrl.com/" TARGET="site2">Cybergrrl</
A></TD>
</TR>
</TABLE>
</CENTER></BODY></HTML>
```

Notice the use of the TARGET attribute in each <A HREF> line. It's what really drives the whole page, by putting the results of any link from the first row in the table into the Site1 frame (replacing holder1.htm), and the results of any link from the second row into the Site2 frame (replacing holder2.htm). For this example, just a few links are included in the hotlist.htm table, but you could have many more.

The HTML for holder1.htm and holder2.htm is very simple and basically identical, except for the site number:

```
<HTML>
<HEAD><TITLE>Site 1</TITLE></HEAD>
<BODY>
<H1>Site 1</H1>
When you pick a site from the first row in the list above, it _
  will be loaded here.
</BODY>
</HTML>
```

When you load twosites.htm in a browser that supports frames, all of the pieces will come together to produce a page like the one in Figure 6.7.

The NAME attribute can only be used with the <FRAME> tag. The TARGET attribute can be used with these tags:

⌖   <A HREF> for normal links.

⌖   <AREA> for client-side image maps, discussed in Chapter 5.

⌖   <BASE> to specify the default frame where you want most files to appear.

⌖   <FORM> for forms processing, discussed in Chapter 7.

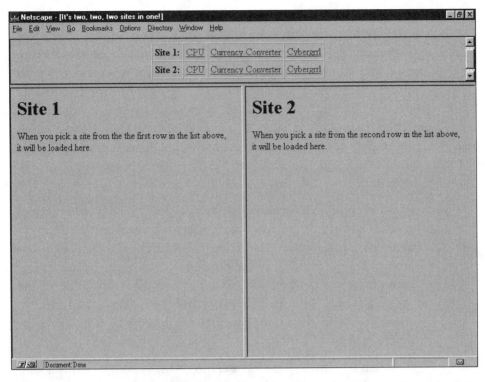

Figure 6.7   When you initially load twosites.htm, you should see a page like this.

The Wizards Speak:
Putting Frames in Their Proper Place

The most important thing to know about frames, according to many Web wizards, is when *not* to use them. "Whenever you're thinking about using a frame, ask yourself if you really need it or if it's a solution in search of a problem," advises Web designer Michael Herrick. "There's no point in a frame just to put a ledge at the top of a page. Frames *are* useful for things like shopping lists and bookmark lists. You can also use them for freezing headers and footers. Each frame requires its own URL, though, so now you've got a content page, minus the header and footer. For the <NOFRAMES> version [for people whose browsers don't support frames], you'll have to bring all these pieces back together again on a single page."

At this point, Netscape is the only major browser to support frames (although Microsoft has announced support in the unreleased Internet Explorer 3.0), so providing a <NOFRAMES> version of a framed page is a must for most Webmasters. Even if your site attracts mainly Netscape users, you should still consider providing a frameless version because frames can take much longer to load. And, says Web wizard Moshc-Dovid Teitelbaum, some people "find frames annoying and feel they take up too much space in the Web browser," especially on a 14- or 15-inch monitor.

Another thing that limits many Web wizards' current use of frames is the inability to control the borders between frames. Herrick explains, "Right now, you're basically stuck with a rectangular layout. If you could hide the borders, you could do much more interesting stuff. The frame structure would be invisible to the user." (In fact, Microsoft is proposing just such enhancements when they add frames to Internet Explorer 3.0. Can Netscape be far behind?)

By default, frame tags allow users to change the size and shape of frames. However, Herrick usually disables this for design considerations by adding the NORESIZE attribute to each <FRAME> tag he uses. That way, he can be fairly sure that the pages will look the way they're supposed to.

It's true that frames make site-management much more complicated, but they can do two things that are difficult or impossible to do any other way:

@ Keep a tool bar, list of links, advertisement, image map, or similar content onscreen all the time.

@ Enable a choice in one part of the screen to affect what happens in another part.

Because of these two important benefits, Web wizards agree that frames are worth exploring, despite their limitations.

Dealing with frame sizes means dealing with monitor sizes. If you just specify percentages in <FRAMESET ROWS=..> and <FRAMESET COLS=..>, you shouldn't have many problems, since the browser will handle sizing for you. However, if you must specify particular pixel sizes because of your page design, Web wizard Michael Herrick recommends keeping frames within seven inches wide (504 pixels, at 72 pixels per inch). Also, if you must specify the frames in pixels, use the * "wildcard" for at least one of them, to allow for the wide variations in monitors' pixel counts. For example, <FRAMESET COLS="200,200,320"> might look perfect on your monitor with 10 inches of horizontal viewing space and exactly 72 pixels per inch, but strange on a monitor that's 1,024 pixels across. Instead, use something like <FRAMESET COLS="200,200,*">.

A Frame to Hold Navigation Buttons

Frames provide an effective solution to the problem of where to put the button bars that users need to navigate through your site. Without frames, you'd probably put the button bar at the top or bottom of your screen, but then users have to keep scrolling to find it. Also, you have to repeat basically identical bars over and over again on all of your pages. By putting button bars in frames, you can keep them available to users all the time, with minimal scrolling for the users—and minimal repetition of HTML for you. Many professionally designed Web sites use this technique, including the Gamelan site at http://www.gamelan.com/, shown in Figure 6.8.

Suppose you want to create an online catalog for the (fictional) up-and-coming clothing store, K. Paulman. You design a set of buttons for the various departments and supporting pages, as shown in Figure 6.9. (They're all GIFs that I made freehand in Photoshop for this example, available on the CD-ROM.) These buttons would work best if they were in a frame that could serve as an always-available table of contents for the catalog. You could use either a vertical frame going down the left side of the screen or a horizontal frame along the top or bottom, but since many

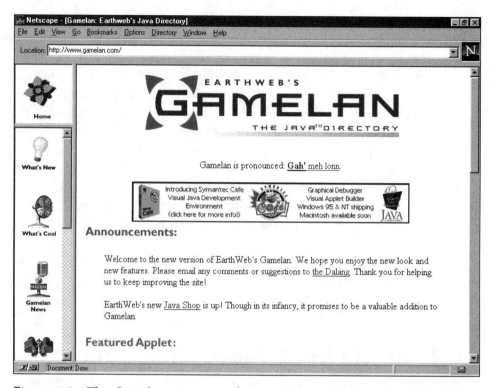

Figure 6.8 The Gamelan site is one of many Web sites that use frames to hold navigational buttons.

of the buttons in this particular example are long and narrow, a vertical frame is a logical choice.

At this point, you've got a page with two frames: one to hold the buttons and the other to hold all the rest of the information. For the sake of convenience and to allow for future interaction among the pages at the site, it's a good idea to label your frames, such as "bar" and "page," as shown in Figure 6.10.

You're almost ready to start coding, but you've still got one big decision to make: how much support to give to frameless browsers. Usually, the best choice is a compromise between the extremes of providing *only* "framed" versions of your pages and creating two completely separate, mostly redundant versions of your site, one with frames and the other without.

Figure 6.9   Putting these buttons in a separate frame will make it easier for users to move through the site.

For this example, you decide to re-create only the home page in a frameless version. For all the supporting pages, you're mainly concerned with users whose browsers support frames, so you don't have to repeat the button bar over and over. As a help to users of the frameless version, though, you decide to add a small link to the home page on every supporting page, even though it will seem redundant to users with frames.

The page you want to end up with is shown, both with frames and without, in Figure 6.11. Here are the steps to create it:

1. Create the basic structure of the framed pages in the main file, called kpframes.htm:

```
<HTML>
<HEAD><TITLE>A Framed Button Bar</TITLE></HEAD>
<FRAMESET COLS="20%,*">
    <FRAME NAME="bar" SRC="kpbtns.htm" NORESIZE>
    <FRAME NAME="page" SRC="kphome.htm">
</FRAMESET>
<NOFRAMES>
</NOFRAMES>
</HTML>
```

2. You'll go back and fill in the <NOFRAMES> area of kprames.htm later. For now, create the kpbtns.htm file, with each button in a separate paragraph on a beige background with khaki-green links and darker-beige visited links. One special requirement of this frame is to ensure that it stays onscreen all the time. To keep it from possibly getting overwritten when a user clicks one of its

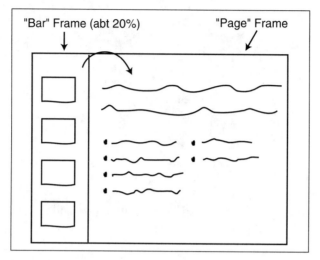

Figure 6.10 Here's a rough sketch of the interaction between the frames.

links, you add the <BASE TARGET="page">. Now, links will default to the "page" frame. Here is the HTML for kpbtns.htm:

```
<HTML>
<BASE TARGET="page">
<BODY BGCOLOR="#F7E4C4" LINK="#008000" VLINK="#FF8000">
<CENTER>
<P><A HREF="kphome.htm"><IMG WIDTH=72 HEIGHT=96 BORDER=0
SRC="kphome.gif"><BR>Home</A></P>
<P><A HREF="kporder.htm"><IMG WIDTH=86 HEIGHT=82 BORDER=0
SRC="hanger.gif"><BR>Ordering</A></P>
<P><A HREF="shirts.htm"><IMG WIDTH=85 HEIGHT=72 BORDER=0
SRC="shirt.gif"><BR>Shirts</A></P>
<P><A HREF="pants.htm"><IMG WIDTH=55 HEIGHT=126 BORDER=0
SRC="pants.gif"><BR>Trousers</A></P>
<P><A HREF="dresses.htm"><IMG WIDTH=72 HEIGHT=136 BORDER=0
SRC="dress.gif"><BR>Dresses</A></P>
<P><A HREF="access.htm"><IMG WIDTH=72 HEIGHT=34 BORDER=0
SRC="hat.gif"><BR>Accessories</A></P>
<P><A HREF="mailto:webmaster@kpaulman.com"><IMG WIDTH=50 HEIGHT=30
BORDER=0 SRC="kpmail.gif"><BR>Feedback</A></P>
</CENTER>
</BODY>
</HTML>
```

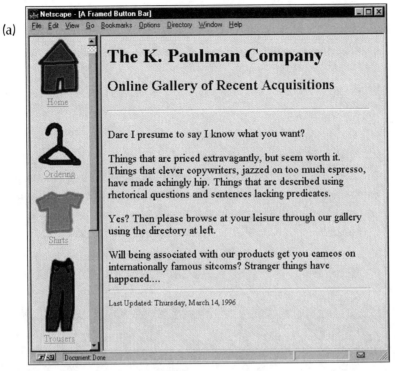

Figure 6.11   To viewers whose browsers support frames (a), the button bar will always be available as they move through the site. The frameless home page (b) almost duplicates the one that uses frames, but other pages in the frameless version won't show a button bar. (continued)

3. Create kphome.htm file, which will act as the home page for frames-enabled browsers. Remember to specify the same color scheme as in kpbtns.htm:

```
<HTML>
<HEAD><TITLE>The K. Paulman Company</TITLE></HEAD>
<BODY BGCOLOR="#F7E4C4" LINK="#008000" VLINK="#FF8000">
<BASEFONT SIZE=4>
<H1>The K. Paulman Company</H1>
<H2>Online Gallery of Recent Acquisitions</H2>
<HR>
<P>Dare I presume to say I know what you want?
<P>Things that are priced extravagantly, but seem worth it. Things _
   that clever copywriters, jazzed on too much espresso, have made achingly
   hip. Things that are described using rhetorical questions and sentences
```

```
      lacking predicates.
<P>Yes? Then please browse at your leisure through our gallery _
using the directory at left.
<P>Will being associated with our products get you cameos on in _
   ternationally famous sitcoms? Stranger things have happened....
<HR>
<FONT SIZE=-2>Last Updated: Thursday, March 14, 1996</FONT>
</BODY>
</HTML>
```

4. Using kpbtns.htm and kphome.htm as a model, you're ready to create the frameless version of the page. To make it look as much as possible like the version with frames, you can use table tags to put the buttons in a vertical column down the left side of the screen. (Chapter 4 explains in detail how to do this.)

You could put the HTML for the frameless page in yet another separate file, with just a link to it in <NOFRAMES>..</

(b)

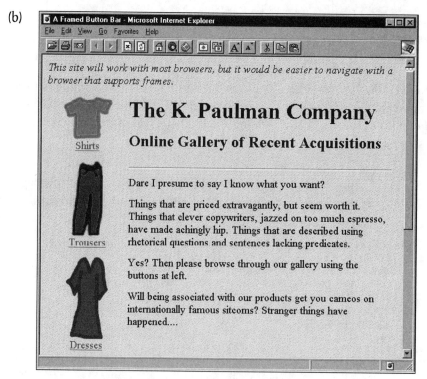

Figure 6.11 (continued)

NOFRAMES>, but you decide instead to include its HTML right in kpframes.htm, like this:

```
<HTML>
<HEAD><TITLE>A Framed Button Bar</TITLE></HEAD>
<FRAMESET COLS="20%,*">
    <FRAME NAME="bar" SRC="kpbtns.htm" NORESIZE>
    <FRAME NAME="page" SRC="kphome.htm">
</FRAMESET>
<NOFRAMES>
<BODY BGCOLOR="#F7E4C4" LINK="#008000" VLINK="#FF8000">
<BASEFONT SIZE=4>
<I>This site will work with most browsers, but it would be easier _
   to navigate with a browser that supports frames.</I>
<TABLE BORDER=0 CELLSPACING=15>
<TR VALIGN=TOP>
<TD ALIGN=CENTER WIDTH=200><P><A HREF="shirts.htm"><IMG WIDTH=85
HEIGHT=72 BORDER=0 SRC="shirt.gif"><BR>Shirts</A></P>
<P><A HREF="pants.htm"><IMG WIDTH=55 HEIGHT=126 BORDER=0
SRC="pants.gif"><BR>Trousers</A></P>
<P><A HREF="dresses.htm"><IMG WIDTH=72 HEIGHT=136 BORDER=0
SRC="dress.gif"><BR>Dresses</A></P>
<P><A HREF="access.htm"><IMG WIDTH=72 HEIGHT=34 BORDER=0
SRC="hat.gif"><BR>Accessories</A></P>
<P><A HREF="kporder.htm"><IMG WIDTH=86 HEIGHT=82 BORDER=0
SRC="hanger.gif"><BR>Ordering</A></P>
<P><A HREF="mailto:webmaster@kpaulman.com"><IMG WIDTH=50 HEIGHT=30
BORDER=0 SRC="kpmail.gif"><BR>Feedback</A></P></TD>
<TD><H1>The K. Paulman Company</H1>
<H2>Online Gallery of Recent Acquisitions</H2>
<HR>
<P>Dare I presume to say I know what you want?
<P>Things that are priced extravagantly, but seem worth it. _
   Things that clever copywriters, jazzed on too much espresso, have
   made achingly hip. Things that are described using rhetorical
   questions and sentences lacking predicates.
<P>Yes? Then please browse through our gallery using the buttons at
left.
<P>Will being associated with our products get you cameos on _
   internationally famous sitcoms? Stranger things have hap
   pened....</TD>
</TR>
</TABLE>
</CENTER>
<HR>
<FONT SIZE=-2>Last Updated: Thursday, March 14, 1996</FONT>
</BODY>
</NOFRAMES>
</HTML>
You need the <BODY> tag here to be able to specify the color _
   scheme for the frameless page, but it must come after the
   <NOFRAMES> tag.
```

5. As a finishing touch to kpframes.htm, add some space around the inside of the "bar" frame so the buttons don't come too close to the edges of the frame. You can do this by setting the MARGINWIDTH and MARGINHEIGHT attributes of the bar's <FRAME> tag to specific pixel values:

```
<FRAME NAME="bar" SRC="kpbtns.htm" NORESIZE MARGINWIDTH=1
MARGINHEIGHT=20>
```

6. With all the basic elements in place for the main page, you're ready to create the pages for each department. They'll all have the same format, including a small home-page link for the benefit of users who don't have frames. To make the small home page, just use the regular kphome.gif scaled to a smaller size with HEIGHT=50.

Here's a dummy page for the shirts department, to test the basic HTML:

```
<HTML>
<HEAD><TITLE>Shirts</TITLE></HEAD>
<BASE TARGET="page">
<BODY BGCOLOR="#F7E4C4" LINK="#008000" VLINK="#FF8000">
<P><A HREF="kpframes.htm" TARGET="_top"><IMG HEIGHT=50 BORDER=0
SRC="kphome.gif" ALIGN=right></A></P>
<H1>Shirts</H1>
This page will hold information about our shirts and blouses.
<UL>
<LI><A HREF="shirt1.htm">Shirt 1: Picture and Info</A>
<LI><A HREF="shirt2.htm">Shirt 2: Picture and Info</A>
</UL>
</BODY>
</HTML>
```

Note the TARGET="_top" attribute of <A HREF>. It's one of several special variations of TARGET that help keep frames from nesting too deep; the others are "_blank" and "_full" (which are functionally identical); "_self"; and "_parent" (which would have done the same thing as "_top" in this example). If TARGET="_top" weren't there and a user with frames clicked the home button on the shirt page (which was added for the benefit of frameless browsers), kpframes.htm would load in the space where shirts.htm was. The user with frames would then see a strangely nested set of frames, like Figure 6.12.

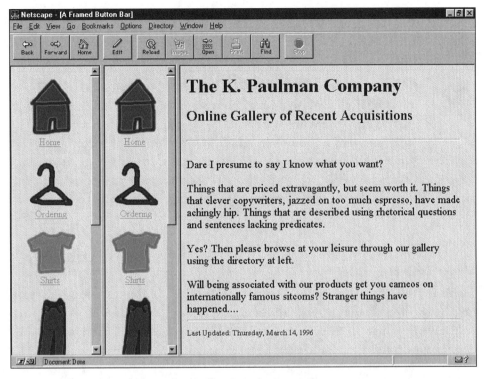

Figure 6.12   Including the TARGET="_top" attribute would avoid this kind of problem when a lower-level frame calls a higher-level one.

7. Create at least one of the lowest-level pages, for the individual items, so you can test the interaction of pages at all the levels. Here's the dummy HTML for one of the shirts:

```
<HTML><HEAD><TITLE>Shirt 1</TITLE></HEAD>
<BODY BGCOLOR="#F7E4C4" LINK="#008000" VLINK="#FF8000">
<P><A HREF="kpframes.htm" TARGET="_top"><IMG HEIGHT=50 BORDER=0
SRC="kphome.gif" ALIGN=right></A></P>
<H1>The First Shirt</H1>
<IMG WIDTH=150 HEIGHT=200 SRC="shirt1.gif"><I>Replace with _
  real picture</I><BR>
Colors: Wax Paper, Wet Cement, Beef<BR>
Fabric: Linen/Cotton Blend, Dry-Clean<BR>
Sizes: Small through Extra-Large, Unisex<BR>
Price: $74.95
</BODY>
</HTML>
```

8. Test the pages thoroughly, both with and without frames, to make sure all the links and frames work properly.

The special attributes of TARGET, such as "_parent" and "_top," must begin with the underscore character. Also, they must be all lowercase. Avoid "_full" and "_blank," since they open up new browser windows in addition to the one that the original page is in. For more details, read what Netscape has to say about the TARGET attribute at http://home.netscape.com/eng/mozilla/2.0/relnotes/demo/target.html.

VARYING THE STEPS

There are lots of ways you could further customize the frames setup for a catalog. Note, though, that as your frames become more complicated, you'll probably have to put the frameless version in a file by itself, with just a link to it on the home page. Here are a few simple modifications:

@ If you put the order form in a small frame below the main frame, users could keep track of their orders as they browsed through the site, easily adding and deleting items. It wouldn't be very hard to implement, since a form automatically continues to hold its information until it is explicitly cleared by the user.

@ A banner frame could be added across the top or bottom of the screen that displays information on sales.

@ When a user picks a particular item, the main frame could be divided into two smaller frames, one holding an animation such as an animated GIF (see Chapter 2) that loops through various views of the item, the other holding catalog copy and ordering information about the item. Note, though, that this would about double the number of files you have to keep track of, since every item would require four files instead of two: an HTML file for the frame structure, an HTML file for the frame that holds the animation, a GIF for the animation itself, and an HTML file for the item's text.

To implement this for the second shirt, for example, you'd need a file called shirt2.htm that would look something like this:

```
<HTML>
<HEAD><TITLE>Shirt 2</TITLE></HEAD>
<FRAMESET COLS="50%,*">
    <FRAME NAME="views" SRC="s2pic.htm">
    <FRAME NAME="info" SRC="s2info.htm">
</FRAMESET>
<NOFRAMES>
Put the shirt's picture and info for frameless browsers here, with _
   a link to the order form.
</NOFRAMES>
</HTML>
The s2pic.htm file is only necessary to align the animated GIF and
have _
   its color scheme match the other frames. It's a very short HTML
file:
<HTML>
<HEAD><TITLE>Shirt 2 Animation</TITLE></HEAD>
<BODY BGCOLOR="#F7E4C4" LINK="#008000" VLINK="#FF8000">
<CENTER><IMG SRC="shirt2.gif" WIDTH=188 HEIGHT=250></CENTER>
</BODY>
</HTML>
The s2info.htm is also a fairly short, simple file:
<HTML>
<HEAD><TITLE>Shirt 2 Info</TITLE></HEAD>
<BODY BGCOLOR="#F7E4C4" LINK="#008000" VLINK="#FF8000">
<H1>The Second Shirt</H1>
<P>Lots of catalog copy goes here.</P>
Colors: Whitewash, Filing-Cabinet Gray<BR>
Fabric: 100% Cotton, Hand Wash<BR>
Sizes: Extra-Small through Extra-Large, Women's<BR>
Price: $69.95
</BODY>
</HTML>
```

When a user selects Shirt2, all of these file will come together to produce something like Figure 6.13.

You can add some Java or CGI programming (discussed in later chapters) to provide even greater control of the frames. When they're added to the mix, the possibilities for making the catalog really interact with the user are endless.

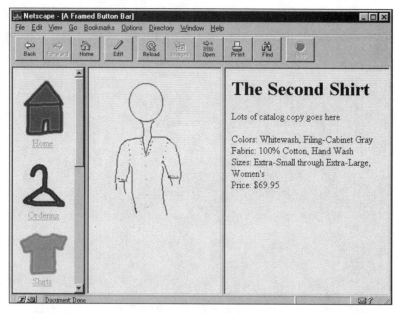

Figure 6.13   When a user selects a particular item from the catalog, he or she gets frame running an animation of the item (with a better picture than the "dummy" GIF here) and another frame with information about the item.

Even users who have been surfing the Web for quite a while might not be used to navigating through a frames-based site. If you use frames at your site, consider providing some way for visitors to get a brief explanation of what frames are, how to use them, and what to do if things don't work right. Include tips like clicking the right mouse button to get a frame's menu and using their browser's Home button if they feel like they're going around in circles (although that really shouldn't happen if you design your frames carefully—putting in a <BASE TARGET="_top"> line provides a good escape mechanism).

You might want to link this information to a Help button in your button-bar frame or put it in a small, separate frame by itself.

The Wizards Speak:
Using Frames for Interactive Pages

Frames should generally be used sparingly on typical Web pages, but they're great for pages that involve step-by-step instructions, queries, and similar types of user interaction. The choices a user makes in one frame can affect another one, so you can give instructions or select a question in, say, the left third of the screen, and have the results appear in the remaining two-thirds.

Arnold Kling puts this idea to good use on his Relocation Salary Calculator page, part of the ASK Real Estate Information Services at http://www.homefair.com. This site was one of the first thousand to be put on the Web, coming online in the Spring of 1994. (Of course, it didn't use frames then.) Kling created and maintains it from a PC running Unix and NCSA's server.

As you can see in Figure 6.14, the Relocation Salary Calculator page is divided into three frames. Frames are an especially good choice

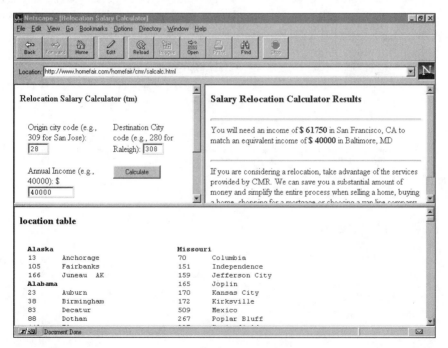

Figure 6.14 Frames are a natural choice for interactive pages such as the Relocation Salary Calculator at http://www.homefair.com/homefair/cmr/salcalc.html.

on this page because, Kling explains, "The main design issue is that there are 450 city names in a list that has to be accessed twice for each query. Lots of people who use my site don't have much bandwidth, so I wanted to make sure that a user would just have to download the list once, and be able to keep it onscreen. Everything else [in the page design] flows from that."

The upper-left frame is a form that the user fills out with the help of the reference material in the city-list frame. The data from the form is processed by a CGI script to produce the results in the upper-right frame. Thanks to the frame-based design, users can repeat the salary recalculation process for as many different cities as they want without ever having to leave or reload this page.

Although frames make the Relocation Salary Calculator easier and faster to use, Kling needed to supply a version without frames as well, since most of his traffic comes from the consumer-oriented commercial services like AOL and Prodigy instead of Netscape. Fortunately, frames allow this kind of backwards compatibility with the <NOFRAMES> tag. Kling uses it to add HTML to the bottom of the main file, salcalc.html, that produces a page like the one shown in Figure 6.15 on browsers that don't support frames.

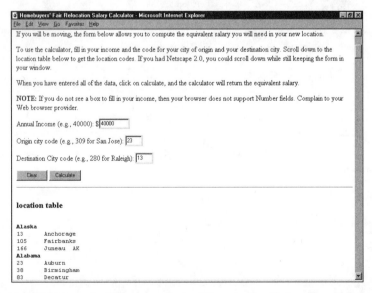

Figure 6.15 This is part of the page that visitors to the Relocation Salary Calculator see if their browsers don't support frames.

Like all frames-based pages, the Relocation Salary Calculator is actually a set of several HTML files. The main one, salcalc.html, provides the basic frame structure, as well as the code for the frameless version. Here's a portion of the salcalc.html file, with some of the text and most of the cities in the <NOFRAMES> section omitted:

```
<HTML>
<HEAD><TITLE>Relocation Salary Calculator</TITLE></HEAD>

<FRAMESET ROWS="50%,*">
  <FRAMESET COLS="45%,55%">
    <FRAME SRC="salform.html">
    <FRAME SRC="results.html" NAME="output">
  </FRAMESET>
  <FRAME SRC="citylist.html" >
</FRAMESET>
<NOFRAMES>
<Title>Homebuyers' Fair Relocation Salary Calculator</Title>
<BODY bgcolor="#FFFFFF" text="#000000">

<PRE><A HREF="/homepage.html"><IMG ALT="welcome screen" SRC="/
homefair/welcome.gif"></A>
<A HREF="/homefair/map.html"><IMG ALT="map of the fair" SRC="/ _
  homefair/compass.gif"></A>
</PRE>

<H1>Relocation Salary Calculator (tm)</H1>

To use the calculator, fill in your income and the code for _
  your city of origin and your destination city. Scroll down to the
  location table below to get the location codes.  If you had
  Netscape 2.0, you could scroll down while still keeping the form
  in your window.
<P>
When you have entered all of the data, click on calculate, and _
  the calculator will return the equivalent salary.
<P>
<FORM METHOD="GET" ACTION="/cgi-bin/salarycalc3">
<B>NOTE:</B> If you do not see a box to fill in your income, _
  then your browser does not support Number fields.  Complain to
  your Web browser provider.
<P>
Annual Income (e.g., 40000): $<INPUT TYPE="NUMBER" NAME="income"
MAXLENGTH="10" SIZE="10">
<P>
Origin city code (e.g., 309 for San Jose):
<INPUT TYPE="TEXT" NAME"from" MAXLENGTH="4" SIZE="4">
<P>
Destination City code (e.g., 280 for Raleigh): <INPUT TYPE="TEXT"
NAME="to" MAXLENGTH="4" SIZE="4">
<P>
```

```
<INPUT TYPE="reset" VALUE="Clear">
<INPUT TYPE="submit" VALUE="Calculate">
</FORM>
<HR>
<h3>location table</h3>
<PRE>
<B>Alaska</B>
13      Anchorage
105     Fairbanks
166     Juneau  AK
<B>Alabama</B>
23      Auburn
38      Birmingham
83      Decatur
</PRE>
</BODY>
</HTML>
```

The Relocation Salary Calculator page requires all of these HTML files:

- ☺ Salcalc.html—the main page
- ☺ Salform.html—the frame in the upper-left of the screen
- ☺ Results.html—the frame in the upper-right of the screen when a user first enters the site
- ☺ Citylist.html—the frame in the bottom half of the screen
- ☺ Salcalc3.html—the frame in the upper-right of the screen after a user has submitted a query

The relationships among these files is sketched in Figure 6.16.

Note that the upper-right frame is named with <FRAME NAME="output"> in salcalc.html because its content changes. Kling

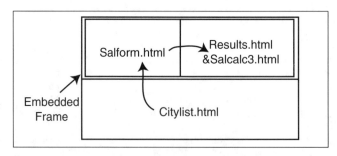

Figure 6.16 Visitors use the information in citylist.html to fill in the form in salcalc.html, which is processed to produce salcal3.html.

uses the TARGET attribute in salform.html to change the contents of the "output" frame from results.html to salarycalc3.html when the user submits the filled-out form.

```
<HTML><HEAD><Title>Homebuyer' Fair Relocation Salary Calculator</
Title></HEAD>

<body bgcolor="#FFFFFF" text="#000000">
<FORM METHOD="GET" ACTION="/cgi-bin/salarycalc3" Target = "output">
<B>The Salary Calculator (tm)</B><BR>
<TABLE BORDER=0 cellpadding=13><TR><TD WIDTH=50% VALIGN=TOP>
Origin city code (e.g., 309 for San Jose):
<INPUT TYPE="TEXT" NAME="from" MAXLENGTH="4" SIZE="4"><P>
Annual Income (e.g., 40000): $<INPUT TYPE="NUMBER" NAME="income"
MAXLENGTH="10" SIZE="10">
<P>
</TD><TD VALIGN = TOP>
Destination City code (e.g., 280 for Raleigh): <INPUT TYPE = "TEXT"
NAME = "to" MAXLENGTH = "4" SIZE = "4">
<P>

<INPUT TYPE="submit" VALUE="Calculate"></TD></table>
If you haven't already been to the <A HREF = "cmr.html" TARGET =
"HFW">Center for
Mobility Resources</A> home page to see the other information we _
    have to offer, please stop by when you are finished.  We have a _
    <A HREF =
"faq.html" TARGET = "HFW">Frequently Asked Questions</A> page for _
    the salary calculator.<P>
</FORM></body></HTML>
```

The TARGET attribute in this case is placed in the <FORM> tag because a CGI script on Kling's Web server looks up cost-of-living data and calculates the resulting salary when a user submits a form.

Kling is pleased with the way frames streamline his Relocation Salary Calculator, and plans to expand his use of them. In particular, he intends to add a frame to the bottom of the screen that will include advertising and other information relevant to the user's destination city.

Frames work best when the structure of the pages to be put in the frames is fairly flat, with only two or three levels. The deeper the frames hierarchy is, the more complicated it is to manage, and the harder it is to create a reasonably similar frameless version.

Web Wizard's Touchstones for Frames

Do   provide some information after the <NOFRAMES> tag for visitors to your site whose browsers don't support frames, even if it's just a message that your pages require a frames enabled browser.

Don't   use frames just because they look cool. Make sure they add value to the page.

Do   test your frames-based pages thoroughly for possible circular references and incorrect nesting.

Don't   include a link in a frame that loads another frames-based page unless you use the TARGET="_parent" or TARGET="_top" attribute, either in the link itself or in the <BASE> tag.

Do   label your frames using the NAME attribute of the <FRAME>tag if you want to control them independently.

Don't   use TARGET="_full" or TARGET="_blank." Either one will open a completely new browser window on top of the existing one, confusing the user and making the Back button unavailable in the new window.

Do   put the frameless version of your main page in a file by itself, instead of within <NOFRAMES>..</NOFRAMES>, if the frame structure is complicated.

Don't   put the <BODY> tag anywhere before </FRAMESET>, or your frames will be ignored even by frames-enabled browsers.

VII

A FORM FOR EVERY FUNCTION

Forms are everywhere on the Web. They provide the front ends for everything from enormous search engines like Yahoo to simple one- or two-question surveys. If you want to get information from users, and especially if you want to have your Web pages respond to that information in real-time, forms such as the one in Figure 7.1 are a must.

In the wild world of Web wizardry, though, just because a technique is important doesn't mean it's easy to use. Nowhere is this more true than with forms. It's not really the forms themselves that are hard to work with; they're just collections of HTML tags. It's the processing of forms that can require really heavy-duty Web wizardry, mostly involving the intricacies of CGI scripts. Fortunately, many Web wizards are hard at work coming up with ways to make forms easier to create and manage. You'll read about some of their successes in this chapter.

Figure 7.1 This "front door" from The Coriolis Group's Web site is typical of the kinds of forms built by Web wizards to support their sites and their users.

Oh, No—More CGI!

At least for the near future, most forms require some kind of processing by the server itself. This involves CGI (*Common Gateway Interface*) scripts. CGI scripts are programs written in languages like C or the Unix-based Perl. They can do lots of things, but what they're most often used for on the Web is to read the information that users submit in forms and respond accordingly. For example, a simple CGI script might take a filled-out survey, format the data in it by removing weird characters so it is human-readable, send it to a particular file or account, and load a page of HTML that thanks the user for taking the time to complete the survey. If you are already a programmer, you probably won't have much trouble picking up the syntax needed for CGI scripts. If you aren't a programmer, you can set yourself the goal of mastering C or Perl—a worthy, although fairly time-consuming, task—or you can "cheat" and use shareware and public-domain scripts.

Suppose you are lucky enough to find a ready-made, public-domain CGI script that exactly fits the form you want to process. You just load that script wherever all your other Web site files are, and you're ready to go, right? Probably not. Unless whoever manages your server specifically permits you to put your scripts wherever you want, which is pretty unlikely, you've got to put that script in the directory where the server expects such scripts to be. Usually, this is the special directory called *cgi-bin*, not the directory that holds your HTML files and GIFs.

The first thing to do before you get too deep into forms and CGI, then, is to contact your server administrator to find out how much access you have to your server's cgi-bin. Access levels fall into these general categories:

- *No access at all*—If you are totally blocked from the cgi-bin, don't despair! You can still use forms on your Web pages to get all kinds of information from users, as you'll see in this chapter. You just won't be able to give automatic feedback from the forms.

- *"Read" rights only*—This is very common, especially if you're working from a non-commercial Internet account. With "read" rights to the cgi-bin, you can't add or customize any CGI scripts, but you can use certain scripts that are already on the server. If server-side image maps work on your Web pages (discussed in Chapter 5), you have this level of access for at least some scripts.

@ *Limited "write" rights*—Many commercial sites have this level of access, where you can add, edit, and delete only the scripts you've put on the server, not any that might already be there. In some cases, you have to upload your scripts to a server administrator who actually installs them on the server; in other cases, you have your own virtual cgi-bin that you can play with to your heart's content. Be careful, though, to find out whether any custom CGI scripts you put on the server are still considered your legal property, or whether you're "contributing" to the server's CGI collection. This could have serious implications if you change service providers.

@ *Full "write" rights*—You have complete freedom to add, remove, or change CGI scripts in whatever way works best for you, wherever they reside, probably because you're the server administrator or have made a special agreement with him or her.

No matter what level of access you have, you can use forms. The more rights you have, though, the more options you have for processing those forms.

Form Formatting

To put a form on your page, you use the <FORM>..</FORM> tag pair. The <FORM> tag has two attributes: METHOD=.., which is almost always set to METHOD=post, and ACTION=.., which holds the URL of the CGI script you want to use or the e-mail address where you want the results sent. All the elements of the form need to be within the <FORM>..</FORM> tag pair.

The <FORM> tags in this chapter use the attribute METHOD=post. There is also another version of this attribute, METHOD=get, that you might see if you view other people's HTML source files. In fact, if you leave METHOD out altogether, it defaults to GET. It's generally best to avoid GET, though. It turns all the results from a form into, basically, a giant URL instead of a text string. Some servers limit the maximum size of a URL, so form data sent with GET can get cut off, totally messing up its processing.

There are eight major elements that you can put on your form, listed in Table 7.1. If you don't format the form elements any other way, they will just appear one right after another onscreen until they fill a line, then wrap down to the next line—just like text. Usually, though, you'll want your form elements to align in a very specific way, possibly to duplicate a paper-based form that you already have. To get the form elements to line up properly, use regular alignment tags like <BR> and <CENTER>, or use table tags. (If you're not familiar with table tags, you might want to review Chapter 4.)

Some of the form tags can have other attributes than those shown in Table 7.1. Specifically, you could put default text into the <INPUT TYPE="text"> or <TEXTAREA> boxes by adding the VALUE=.. attribute, like this:

```
<INPUT TYPE="text" NAME="status" VALUE="full-time student">
```

That way, if most of your users are full-time students, that information will be automatically entered for them. Similarly, to have a radio button or checkbox turned on by default, add the CHECKED attribute. To set an absolute limit for the number of characters allowed in a text box, use the MAXLENGTH=.. attribute, like this:

```
<INPUT TYPE="password" NAME="pswd" MAXLENGTH=10>
```

With this line of HTML, the browser will only accept the first ten characters that the user enters for a password.

To Do This:	Use This Form Tag:	Like This on the Page:	With These Results:
Have users enter one short piece of data.	<INPUT TYPE="text">	<P>First name: <INPUT TYPE="text" NAME="fname" SIZE=15>	A text box that is 15 characters big appears; what's typed there is stored in the "fname" field.
Have users enter a password.	<INPUT TYPE="password">	<P>Password: <INPUT TYPE="password" NAME="pword" SIZE=10>	A text box appears, but typing is masked by asterisks onscreen. The value of "pword" is sent to the server as a normal text string, so this is not terribly secure.
Have some data sent without the	<INPUT TYPE="hidden">	<INPUT NAME="status" TYPE="hidden" VALUE="neworder">	Nothing appears onscreen, but the "status" field is set to "neworder," perhaps for processing in an orders database.

Table 7.1 The major elements of a form given here are illustrated in Figure 7.2.

To Do This:	Use This Form Tag:	Like This on the Page:	With These Results:
Have users type in multiple lines of text.	\<TEXTAREA\>.. \</TEXTAREA\>	\<P\>Comments:\<BR\> \<TEXTAREA NAME="comments" ROWS=6 COLS=60\>\</TEXTAREA\>	An area for typing appears, 6 lines long and 60 characters wide; what's typed there is stored in the "comments" field.
Have users choose from mutually exclusive items (using radio buttons).	\<INPUT TYPE="radio"\>	\<P\>How do you want to view this site? \<INPUT TYPE="radio" NAME="sitepath" VALUE="hi"\> Full graphics \<INPUT TYPE="radio" NAME="sitepath" VALUE="low"\> Light graphics	Users can click the circle (radio button) for only one choice. The "sitepath" field holds that choice: either "hi" or "low."
Have users select multiple items (using checkboxes).	\<INPUT TYPE="checkbox"\>	\<P\>Interests/hobbies:\<BR\> \<INPUT TYPE="checkbox" NAME="interest" VALUE="hike"\>Hiking\<BR\> \<INPUT TYPE="checkbox" NAME="interest" VALUE="bike"\>Biking\<BR\> \<INPUT TYPE="checkbox" NAME="interest" VALUE="raft"\>Rafting	Users can click in any or all of the three boxes that appear. The "interest" field holds the values selected, if any.
Have users make a choice from a drop-down list box.	\<SELECT\>.. \</SELECT\>	\<P\>Preferred shipping method: \<SELECT NAME="ship"\> \<OPTION\>UPS \<OPTION\>U.S. Mail \<OPTION\>Fedex 2nd-Day \<OPTION\>Fedex Overnight \<OPTION\>Fedex Same-Day \</SELECT\>	Users can choose one item from the list box, stored in the "ship" field. To allow the user to choose multiple items from a scrollbox, add the MULTIPLE attribute to the \<SELECT\> tag.
Have a push-button to send or clear the form.	\<INPUT TYPE="submit"\> \<INPUT TYPE="reset"\>	\<P\>\<INPUT TYPE="submit" VALUE="Send it!"\> \<INPUT TYPE="reset" VALUE="Let me start over"\>	Buttons appear with the values on them as text. Clicking the TYPE= "submit" button sends the form, clicking the TYPE= "reset" button sets all values in the form back to defaults.

Table 7.1   Continued

Two new attributes related to forms were added in the Netscape extensions for version 2.0: WRAP for <TEXTAREA> and ENCTYPE="multipart/form-data" for <FORM>.

The WRAP attribute for the <TEXTAREA> tag handles word wrapping in multiple-line text blocks. The default is <TEXTAREA WRAP="off">, for no wrapping. The other possible values are <TEXTAREA WRAP="virtual"> to show word wrapping to the user but not in the forms processing, and <TEXTAREA WRAP="physical">, to include word wrapping both onscreen and in the data sent from the form.

The ENCTYPE="multipart/form-data" attribute for the <FORM> tag lets you accept files from the user in your form. To go along with it, the TYPE attribute of the INPUT tag has a new value, "file." You might use this option, for example, to get entries for a "Greatest GIF" contest:

```
<FORM ENCTYPE="multipart/form-data" METHOD=POST ACTION="http://
www.gifbase.com/cgi-bin/contest">

My greatest GIF: <INPUT TYPE="file" NAME="entry">
<INPUT TYPE="submit" VALUE="Enter Contest">
</FORM>
```

Simple CGI-less Forms

If you just need to get information from users without immediately passing anything back, you don't necessarily need any CGI scripts at all. You can use MAILTO in the ACTION part of the <FORM> tag to have the form response sent to you as email. This is especially helpful when automatic, programmed responses aren't appropriate.

For example, lots of people have "guestbook" pages at their sites that automatically append whatever a visitor writes on a form to the guestbook page, as soon as he or she clicks the "submit" button. But you might not want to let anyone post whatever they want at your site, without taking a look at it yourself first. There are all kinds of liability issues here, not to mention the fact that some people use guestbooks as a low-risk outlet for their spamming urges. You could program a CGI script to reject guestbook entries under certain conditions, but unless you're getting lots of entries all the time, that could easily evolve into a bigger project than just looking the entries over yourself and adding them to the page with a little copying and pasting.

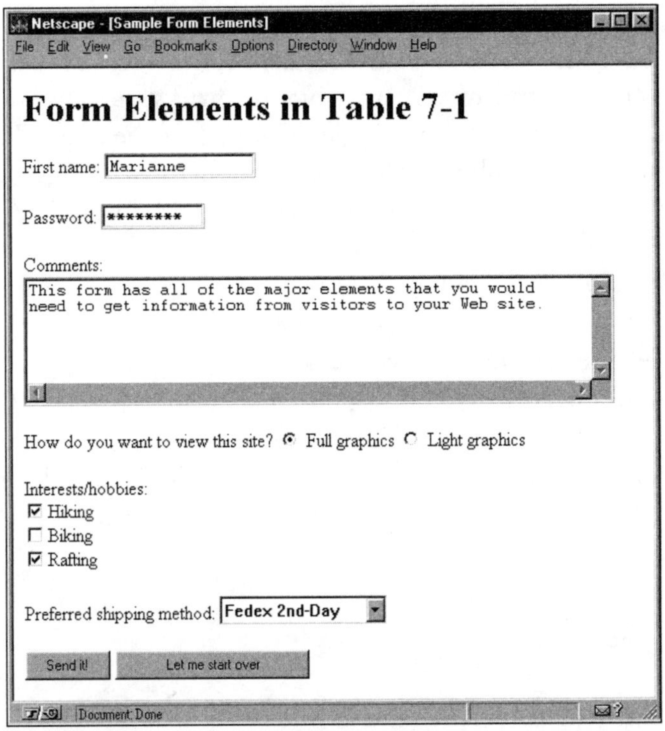

Figure 7.2 The code samples in Table 7.1 would look like this on a Web page. Note that nothing shows on screen for the <INPUT TYPE="hiden"> field.

By far the most important benefit of using MAILTO is that you don't have to tangle with CGI scripts. If you don't have CGI access on your server, MAILTO is the only way to get forms to work without some kind of third-party software. An additional benefit is that you can test a MAILTO form online right from the hard drive on your computer, without the usual cycle of loading a file on the server, debugging, then reloading.

There are, of course, several drawbacks to using MAILTO instead of a CGI. The most important one is that you won't be able to give a real-time response. You can't, for example, have a page of HTML that pops up when the user submits the form to thank him or her. Another drawback is that MAILTO in the <FORM> tag is not supported by all browsers—but then, neither are form tags themselves. Unlike tables, frames, image maps, and other high-end Web page elements, there's no acceptable substitute for forms. If a user's browser doesn't support forms or your use of MAILTO, about the best you can do is provide a link to a downloadable version of the form to be filled out offline and faxed or emailed back to you.

The final major drawback to using MAILTO is that the email you'll receive will be *URL encoded*, which basically means it will have lots of garbage characters instead of spaces, quotation marks, new lines, commas, and so on. If your form is just a single field, such as the one in Figure 7.3, that's not much of a problem. Most forms, though, are things like surveys and order forms, which have multiple fields. The results of such forms will need to be formatted (*parse*) to make them easier to read. That's not as difficult to do offline as you might think.

A SINGLE-FIELD FORM SANS CGI

Suppose you want to create the simple, one-field form in Figure 7.3. A visitor to your page can use it to vote on whether or not you should include frames at your Web site. You'll need just two form elements: <INPUT TYPE="radio"> and <INPUT TYPE="submit">. Here's the HTML for the page:

```
<HTML>
<HEAD>
<TITLE>Frame Vote</TITLE>
</HEAD>
<BODY>
<H1>Should this site be framed?</H1>
<P>Cast your vote here to help determine whether the final version of _
   this site should use Netscape's frames to create "windows" onscreen.
<P>If you're not sure, check out the <A HREF="frsamp.htm">framed</A> _
   and <A HREF="nfsamp.htm">frameless</A> samples.
<FORM METHOD=POST ACTION="MAILTO:me@my.isp.net">
<P><INPUT NAME="frames" TYPE="radio" VALUE="yes"> I love frames; give me more!
<P><INPUT NAME="frames" TYPE="radio" VALUE="no"> Get those frames th' heck
outta here!
<P><INPUT TYPE="submit" VALUE="Cast my ballot">
</FORM>
<BR><HR>
<FONT SIZE="-1"><ADDRESS>Last Updated: Friday, March 29, 1996 by <A
HREF="mailto:me@my.isp.net">Marianne Krcma</A></ADDRESS></FONT>
</BODY>
</HTML>
```

When someone casts a vote, you'll get an email message with an attachment. The attachment will contain one of these two strings:

```
frames=yes
frames=no
```

Figure 7.3 This simple form would be easy to process, even without any special programs or scripts.

Not much processing necessary there! It's just a matter of tallying the votes and announcing the outcome.

> On a single-field form that uses <INPUT TYPE="text">, you don't even need a "submit" button. When the user presses the Enter key, the form data will automatically be submitted.

PROCESSING A **MAILTO** MULTIPLE-FIELD FORM

Suppose that your business sends out free samples of your products to qualified leads. At your Web site, you want to put up a form that enables people to request samples, but you need to have someone examine these forms to see who is actually qualified to receive the samples, and possibly follow up for more information. A Web page with such a form is shown in Figure 7.4.

If this were a real form, you'd probably want each element of the address in a different field to make it easier to export to your database of names and addresses. For this example, though, the address is all in a single text block so you can see what the <TEXTAREA> form element looks like in use.

Here's the HTML that creates this page, with the tags that actually create the form:

```
<HTML>
<HEAD>
<TITLE>Widget Sample Request Form</TITLE>
</HEAD>
<BODY>
<BODY BGCOLOR="white">
<H1>Request Your Free Samples from Widget, Inc.</H1>
<P>Thank you for taking a few moments to fill this out. Your request _
   will be processed within 48 hours of its receipt. Please be sure to
   include an e-mail address to which we can send verification informa
   tion.</P>
<HR>
<FORM METHOD=POST ACTION="MAILTO:sampler@widget.com">
<TABLE>
<TR>
<TD>Your name:</TD>
<TD><INPUT TYPE="TEXT" NAME="name" SIZE="30"></TD>
</TR>
<TR>
<TD>Your title:</TD>
<TD><INPUT TYPE="TEXT" NAME="title"></TD>
</TR>
<TR>
<TD>Your company:</TD>
<TD><INPUT TYPE="TEXT" NAME="company" SIZE="40"></TD>
</TR>
<TR>
<TD>Your email address:</TD>
<TD><INPUT TYPE="TEXT" NAME="e-mail" SIZE="40"></TD>
</TR>
</TABLE>
<BR>
Your complete street address for delivery:<BR><TEXTAREA NAME="address"
ROWS=6 COLS=60></TEXTAREA>
<BR><BR>
Which of these products does your company currently use?
<TABLE>
<TR>
<TD><INPUT TYPE="CHECKBOX" NAME="use" VALUE="sprockets">Sprockets</TD>
<TD><INPUT TYPE="CHECKBOX" NAME="use" VALUE="supersprockets">Super _
   Sprockets</TD>
</TR>
<TR>
```

```
<TD><INPUT TYPE="CHECKBOX" NAME="use" VALUE="widgets">Widgets</TD>
<TD><INPUT TYPE="CHECKBOX" NAME="use" VALUE="wonderwidgets">Wonder _
  Widgets</TD>
</TR>
<TR>
<TD><INPUT TYPE="CHECKBOX" NAME="use" VALUE="doodads">Doodads</TD>
<TD><INPUT TYPE="CHECKBOX" NAME="use" VALUE="deluxedoodads">Deluxe _
  Doodads</TD>
</TR>
</TABLE>
<P>Which sample would you like? (Sorry, only one per request.) _
  <SELECT NAME="sample">
<OPTION>Doodad
<OPTION>Deluxe Doodad
<OPTION>Sprocket
<OPTION>Super Sprocket
<OPTION>Widget
<OPTION>Wonder Widget
</SELECT>
<P>Do you have purchasing authority for widgets and related items?
<INPUT TYPE="RADIO" NAME="canbuy" VALUE="yes"> Yes
<INPUT TYPE="RADIO" NAME="canbuy" VALUE="no"> No
<BR><BR>
<INPUT TYPE="SUBMIT" VALUE="SEND FORM"> <INPUT TYPE="RESET" VALUE="CLEAR
FORM">
</FORM>
<HR>
<P><STRONG>Please note that this form will not provide immediate feedback._
After submitting your request, <A HREF="postform.htm">go on to the next
page.</A></STRONG></P>
Comments or questions? <A HREF="mailto:sampler@widget.com">Send e-mail.</a>
</BODY>
</HTML>
```

The table tags in this HTML file just help align the various elements of the form. The paragraph letting users know not to expect immediate feedback and providing a link off the page is important when you use a MAILTO form. Without it, users might be confused about what to do after they click the "submit" button. If they don't know that they should just move on after submitting the form, users will typically keep clicking the "submit" button for a while, waiting to see something happen, then eventually give up and use their browser's Back button to leave the page. Not only does this frustrate your users, but it skews whatever data you're trying to select, since each click of the "submit" button posts another copy of the filled-out form to you.

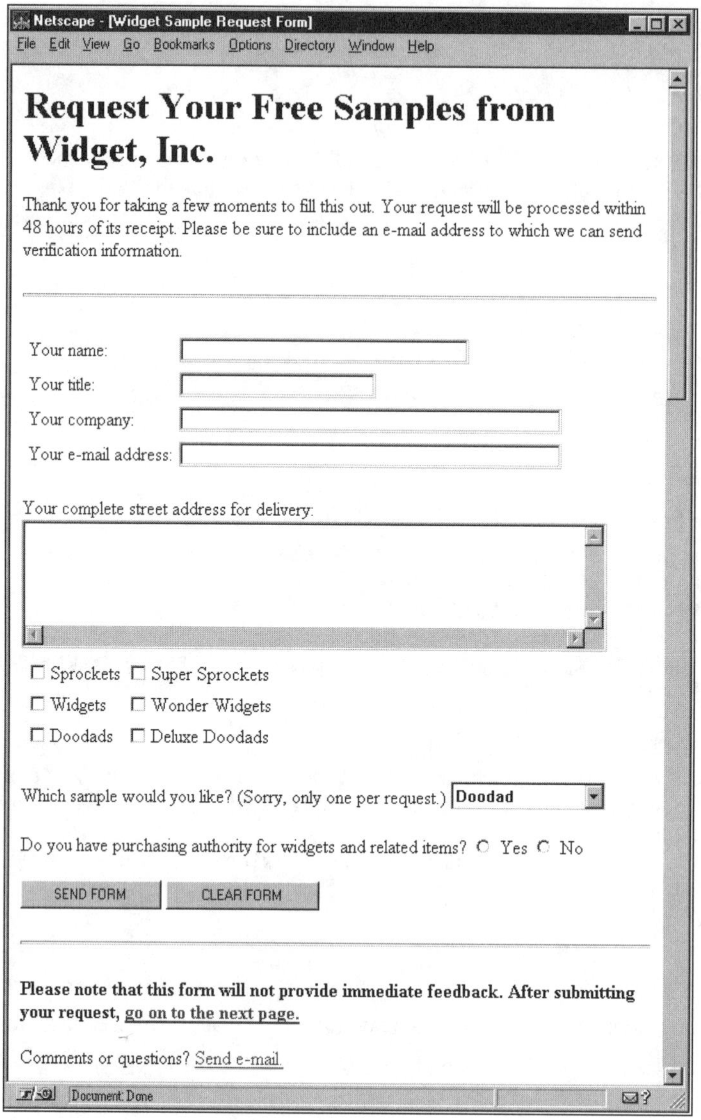

Figure 7.4 You don't necessarily need a CGI script to process even a fairly complex form like this.

When a user fills out and submits the form as shown in Figure 7.5a, an email with the message in Figure 7.5b appears in sampler@widget.com's mailbox. Clicking on *attachment* produces this string:

```
name=Jane+Smith&title=VP%2C+Purchasing&company=Thingies+R+Us&e-
mail=jsmith@tru.com&address=1+Main+Street%0D%0ABuilding+2%0D%0
AAnywhere%2C+ST++12345&use=supersprockets&sample=Wonder+Widget&canbuy=yes
```

(a)

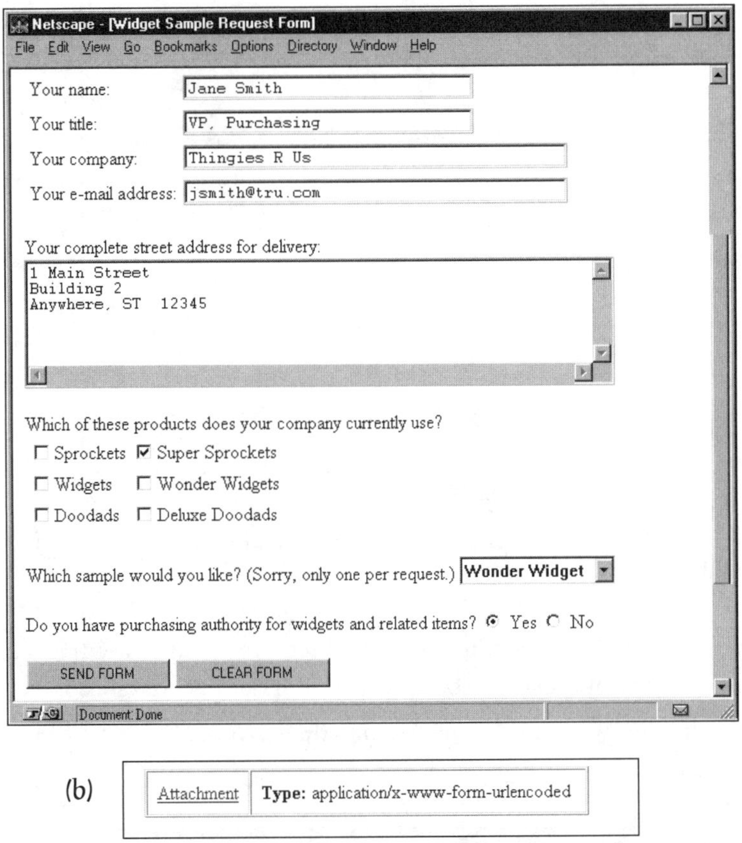

(b)

Figure 7.5   When a user fills out the form (a) and submits it, the file is sent to the appropriate mailbox (b).

This string might look like gibberish at first, but if you look carefully you can see that it's the data from Figure 7.5a, with strange character combinations instead of spaces, commas, and other symbols. One of the main things CGI scripts do for forms is reformat these kind of results so they're readable. Not to worry, though. There are freeware and shareware programs that do the same thing, just offline. One of these, a freeware program called Mailto Formatter, is included on the CD-ROM. Install the program, then follow these steps to convert the sample-request string with it:

1. Copy the string from the attachment file using Ctrl-C.

2. In the opening screen of the Mailto Formatter, shown in Figure 7.6, click in the Original String box and paste the string with Ctrl-V.

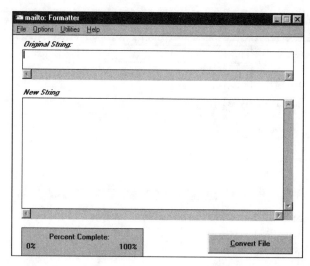

Figure 7.6   Use the Mailto Formatter to make the data from the MAILTO form easily readable.

3. Click the Convert File button to produce the results shown in Figure 7.7. This data is now ready to be read by a person or a database.

4. Save the file with File|Save As, or add it to an existing file with File| Append To.

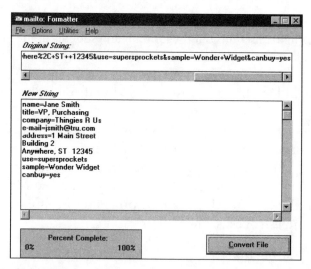

Figure 7.7   Each field of the new string is separated by a line break, but you could also choose comma-delimited or pipe-delimited fields if you're putting the results into a database that requires them.

If the volume of responses to your form is relatively light, it's not a very big deal to go through these four steps. If the volume is heavy, you can either consider using a CGI script instead of MAILTO or, if that's not possible, using a shareware program to automatically put the results into a database. In fact, the same company that makes Mailto Formatter also makes a program called Mailto Manager that does just that. A demo version is available from http://homepage.interaccess.com/~rpfries/mtf.html.

"Why Didn't I Think of That?": A Real, Old-Fashioned Button Bar

As mentioned in Chapter 2, you can use a one-field form with <INPUT TYPE="submit"> to create a beveled button that links pages together just like a normal <A HREF> navigational link would. The problem, though, is that you can't normally put more than one "submit" button on a line, so you can't create a button bar with them—at least, not without a little Web wizardry.

By combining table tags with form tags, you can create pages with professional-looking button bars like the one in Figure 7.8 with a minimum of effort and no artistic ability. The key to this trick is

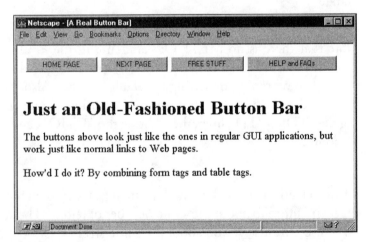

Figure 7.8 A simple, one-button form is relatively easy to make, but how do you make this whole bar?

that each cell in a table is treated like a miniature page, so you can have several cells side-by-side, each with its own form. Here's the HTML:

```
<HTML>
<HEAD>
<TITLE>A Real Button Bar</TITLE>
</HEAD>
<BODY BGCOLOR="white">
<TABLE>
<TR>
<TD><FORM ACTION="home.htm"><INPUT TYPE="submit" VALUE= _
  "HOME PAGE"></FORM></TD>
<TD><FORM ACTION="bartest.htm"><INPUT TYPE="submit" VALUE="NEXT
PAGE"></FORM></TD>
<TD><FORM ACTION="files.htm"><INPUT TYPE="submit" VALUE="FREE
STUFF"></FORM></TD>
<TD><FORM ACTION="help.htm"><INPUT TYPE="submit" VALUE="HELP and
FAQs"></FORM></TD>
</TR>
</TABLE>
<H1>Just an Old-Fashioned Button Bar</H1>
<FONT SIZE=4>
<P>The buttons above look just like the ones in regular GUI _
  applications, but work just like normal links to Web pages.</P>
<P>How'd I do it? By combining form tags and table tags.</P>
</BODY>
</HTML>
```

Note that there is no METHOD attribute in the <FORM> tag. The method really doesn't matter for this, so you might as well spare yourself some typing by letting it default to GET. Also, note that you could easily add more buttons to the bar by copying and pasting the <TD>..</TD> lines, then editing the ACTION and VALUE attributes.

When creating button bars with form tags, try to keep the text on each button to about the same number of letters. That way, all of the buttons will be about the same size. Also, note that visitors won't see the URL for the button's link in the status bar, like they would with normal <A HREF> links.

Counting Down the Hits

A hits counter is one of those little "odometers" that lets visitors see how incredibly popular your page is with other denizens of the Web. A typical hits counter is shown in Figure 7.9. Okay, it isn't really a form, but I wanted to give you information on hits counters somewhere in this book, since they're such popular elements of Web pages. This chapter, with all its discussions of CGI, seemed the logical choice.

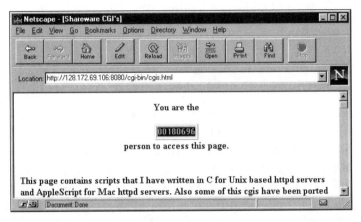

Figure 7.9   The little "odometer" on this page is called a hits counter. Even if you don't have cgi-bin access at your server, you can still put one on your page.

Hits counters are, in the words of Web wizard Muhammad A. Muquit (who co-wrote the very popular WWWCount program), "no way accurate" because any access to your page, such as loading a graphic, clicking the Reload button, or being the target of a keyword search, will increment the counter. Even though they're not accurate indications of the traffic at your site, you still might want to put one on your page. They're fun and, perhaps most important, Web surfers seem to like seeing them.

If you want to get a better idea of how people are actually interacting with your site and you have administrator-level rights to the server, you can look at the access logs. For a list of programs that will analyze the logs for you, check out http://

www.yahoo.com/Computers/World_Wide_Web/HTTP/ Servers/Log_Analysis_Tools. If you really want to know all about the people who are hitting your site, you might want to look into a commercial service like I/Pro (http:// www.ipro.com/index.html). These are apparently the same folks who do the Nielsen ratings.

There are several ways to add a hits counter to one or more of your Web pages:

- The ridiculously easy way, no matter what hardware and software you have.
- The easy way if your server is set up with a particular set of permissions.
- The "I can do this myself, dammit" way.

The ridiculously easy way is to use someone else's server to keep track of your hits. Typically, all you have to do is fill out a form online and you'll get a line of HTML to add where you want a counter to appear. There are several pub-lic-spirited types on the Web who provide this service. My current favorite is John Anthony Ruchak's Homepage Access Counter at http:// www.microserve.net/~john/counter-def.html (Figure 7.10a, 7.10b, and 7.10c), although you can find others by doing a keyword search on "hits counter" in a directory service like Yahoo.

Ruchak's form is very clear and easy to use, with plenty of neat-o options for customizing the look of your counter. All you have to do is copy the line of HTML that his form gives you into your Web page, and you're ready to roll. For example, when I filled out the form, it returned this line of HTML:

```
<img src="http://www.microserve.net/cgi-bin/public/Count20.cgi?md=5|
dd=odometer|st=100|df=krcma1">
```

I copied and pasted it onto a page of HTML, loaded it onto my Web site, and got the results shown in Figure 7.11.

The only problem with using the ridiculously easy approach is that, if the server where you've got your counter is down, visitors will see a broken link on your page. Also, as a courtesy to the nice people providing space on their servers for these counters, don't overuse this technique. In fact, some of these sites will start

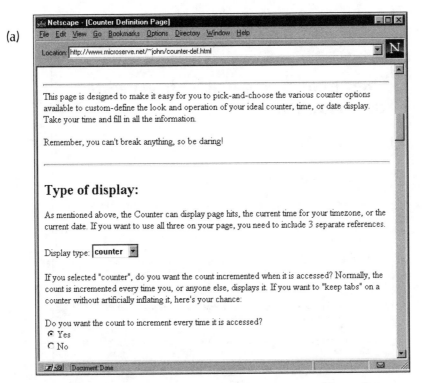

Figure 7.10   At the Homepage Access Counter site, just fill out the easy-to-use form (a) and you'll get a line of HTML to copy onto your page for an instant counter (b).

billing at a nominal rate if you get more than a certain number of hits in a given time, although the allowed number of "free" hits is very reasonable, typically several thousand per month.

The slightly less easy way to add a hits counter is to use a *server-side include (SSI)*. SSIs are ways to put dynamic information on a Web page based on data that the server already has or can easily get, such as the current date, or the name of the host computer from which a visitor is accessing your page. This method of creating a hits counter is less easy because it requires several things from your server:

◎ A server that can support SSIs.

◎ A server administrator who has set permissions so your page can access the SSIs.

(b

> Netscape - [Counter preview...]
> File   Edit   View   Go   Bookmarks   Options   Directory   Window   Help
>
> Location: http://www.microserve.net/~john/cgi-bin/count22query.pl.cgi
>
> # Your input has been used to generate the following...
>
> `<img src="http://www.microserve.net/cgi-bin/public/Count20.cgi?md=5| dd=script|st=100|df=myctr1">`
>
> and will look like this: `00101` on your web page.
>
> If the above image has the look you desire, copy the `<img src>` line shown above into your HTML document. Please note that the entire `<img src>` tag needs to be on *ONE* continuous line (no spaces) in your page. It is broken into multiple lines here for readability and to make it easier for you to copy & paste the tag into your Web page.
>
> If it doesn't have the look you want, you can use your browser's "Back" feature to go back to the form and change your settings, or you can simply start over with a clean new form.
>
> Please be sure to let me know if you see an error message where the counter should be. Of course, if you have any comments or suggestions, those are welcome too!
>
> If you're something of a "propeller-head", you might enjoy seeing all the gory details for possible syntax. ☺
>
> Document Done

Figure 7.10b   At the Homepage Access Counter site, just fill out the easy-to-use form (a) and you'll get a line of HTML to copy onto your page for an instant counter (b).

> @ A CGI script on the server to perform the count, usually called *counter* or *counter-ord*.

If these three things check out, you can add a counter wherever you want it on your Web page using a line of HTML like this:

```
Counting down the current hits: <!--#exec cgi="http://www.your-isp. _
  net/cgi-bin/counter"-->
```

Note that you'll probably have fewer options for controlling the look of the counter than you would with the first way of adding a counter.

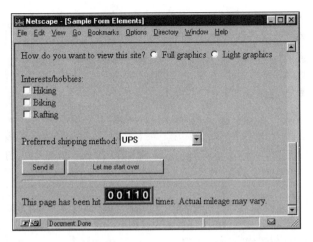

Figure 7.11 Every time this page is accessed, the counter will increase by one. You can choose lots of "looks" for your hits counter other than the one shown here.

Server-side includes can do lots of things other than run a counter CGI. If you've ever seen pages that automatically show the current date and time, size of a file, or similar information, chances are they're using server-side includes. SSIs are extremely easy to use if your Web server is set up to support them, especially if you use an HTML editor like Ken Nesbitt's WebEdit, which will add them to your page for you. For example, these lines of HTML (with SSIs bolded for easier reference) will produce Figure 7.12.

```
<P>It's <STRONG><!--#echo var="DATE_GMT"--></STRONG>. Having a great
time. Wish you were here.
<P>This file was last modified <STRONG><!--#echo
var="LAST_MODIFIED"--></STRONG>.
At that time, it was <STRONG><!--#fsize virtual=""--></STRONG> big.
```

Many new server-side includes are in the process of being implemented as this is being written. You can find out about the latest developments with SSIs straight from the source at http://hoohoo.ncsa.uiuc.edu/docs/tutorials/includes.html.

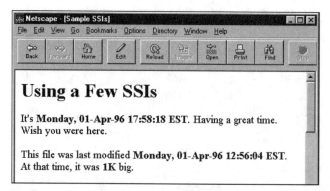

Figure 7.12 The partial Web page shown here uses three SSIs: the first gives the current date and time in Greenwich Mean Time, the second gives the complete timestamp from the last time the file was modified, and the third gives the size of this file.

The third way to add a hits counter is to find or write a CGI script that makes one, load it to an appropriate directory on your server (probably the cgi-bin), configure it to work properly with your server, and call it from a page of HTML. The most popular CGI scripts for this purpose are in a program called WWWCount, currently in version 2.2. In fact, this program is the basis for John Anthony Rushak's Homepage Access Counter form. You can download WWWCount 2.2 from ftp://ftp.probe.net/pub/wwwcount2.2/, among other places. Detailed instructions for installing, using, and modifying the scripts are provided at http://yoda.semcor.com/~muquit/.

There's actually another way to add a hits counter: use a shareware Java applet like LiveCounter from http://www.chamisplace.com/prog/lc/. For more on Java applets, see Chapter 10.

The Wizards Speak: CGI Secrets

Sooner or later, you'll have to deal with CGI scripts if you want to claim true Web mastery. Fortunately, you don't have to start completely from scratch. There are many good sources for shareware and freeware CGI scripts on the Web, including these sites:

- Selena Sol's Public Domain CGI Script Archive and Resource Library at http://www2.eff.org/~erict/Scripts/
- Matt Kruse's Perl Scripts at http://cs.sau.edu/~mkruse/www/scripts/
- Dave's List of CGIs at http://www.cyserv.com/pttong/cgi.html
- The CGI Collection at http://www.wolfenet.com/~rniles/cgi.html
- Matt's Script Archive at http://www.worldwidemart.com/scripts/
- NCSA's HTTPD Web site (http://hoohoo.ncsa.uiuc.edu/cgi/)

Many Web wizards use the concepts in these scripts as the basis for their own CGIs. Joe Maissel of Soundwire, for example, recommends, "Try to get canned CGIs to work on your pages" rather than coding them from scratch. It's rare, however, to find a "canned" script that exactly suits your needs right off the virtual shelf, so you'll need to know a few CGI scripting secrets to be able to get the script working for your particular situation. The rest of this chapter is devoted to giving you those secrets.

Web wizard Moshe-Dovid Teitelbaum has this advice about writing CGI scripts: "Never assume. For example, you might assume that all browsers submit form info in the same order. However, some browsers send the info back in the order you wrote it on the web page (Name1=Val1&Name2=Val2&...& NameX=ValX) and others send it back in reverse order (NameX=ValX&... &Name2= Val2&Name1=Val1)." In other words, if you have a form that requests a first name, last name, and e-mail address, you can't write a script that just finds the last field and adds it to an address book. In some cases, you'd be adding the person's first name, not the e-mail address.

To avoid these problems, you need to parse the form values. Basically, parsing strips all the garbage characters and matches field names with values in an *array* (a programming word for a table). Teitelbaum wrote a special C script for this purpose, but unless you happen to be a programmer, you'll probably want to use one of the several freeware and shareware parsers available. One of the best, cgi-lib.pl, is included on the CD-ROM. You can install it in the /cgi-bin directory of your server and then let it handle the parsing for your other scripts.

If you have lots of CGI scripts at your site, you probably don't want to have them all depending on a parser like cgi-lib.pl, warns Web wizard Dave Friedel. Otherwise, an error in one script could tie up the parser and bring down the whole site. Instead, Friedel handles the parsing within each CGI script, using a fairly standard routine that can be adapted for each CGI he writes. You can check out this routine in the section "The Wizards Speak: Real-Life CGI."

Processing a Form with a Simple CGI Script

Suppose you want the sample-request form shown in Figure 7.13 to be automated. As a first step, you need to make the form itself using the form tags discussed earlier in this chapter, like this:

```
<HTML>
<HEAD>
<TITLE>Widget Sample Form</TITLE>
</HEAD>
<BODY>
<BODY BGCOLOR="white">
<H1>Request a Free Sample from Widget, Inc.</H1>
<P>Please use the following form to request a sample. Your order will _
   be processed within 2 business days of its receipt.</P>
<HR>
<FORM METHOD=POST ACTION="http://www.coriolis.com/cgi-bin/ordsub.pl">
<TABLE>
<TR>
<TD>Your customer number: </TD>
<TD><INPUT TYPE="TEXT" NAME="cust" SIZE=15></TD>
</TR>
<TR>
<TD>Your full name:</TD>
<TD><INPUT TYPE="TEXT" NAME="name" SIZE=30></TD>
</TR>
<TR>
<TD>Your title:</TD>
<TD><INPUT TYPE="TEXT" NAME="title" SIZE=30></TD>
</TR>
<TR>
<TD>Your company:</TD>
<TD><INPUT TYPE="TEXT" NAME="company" SIZE=40></TD>
```

```
</TR>
<TR>
<TD>Your e-mail address:</TD>
<TD><INPUT TYPE="TEXT" name="email" size="40"></TD>
</TR>
</TABLE>
<BR>
Your complete street address for delivery:<BR><TEXTAREA NAME= _
  "address" ROWS=6 COLS=60></TEXTAREA>
<P>Which of these products would you like? (One sample per order,
please.)
<TABLE>
<TR>
<TD><INPUT TYPE="radio" NAME="item" VALUE="sprockets">Sprockets</TD>
<TD><INPUT TYPE="radio" name="item" VALUE="supersprockets">Super _
  Sprockets</TD>
</TR>
<TR>
<TD><INPUT TYPE="radio" name="item" VALUE="widgets">Widgets</TD>
<TD><INPUT TYPE="radio" name="item" VALUE="wonderwidgets">Wonder Wid-
gets</TD>
</TR>
<TR>
<TD><INPUT TYPE="radio" name="item" VALUE="doodads">Doodads</TD>
<TD><INPUT TYPE="radio" name="item" VALUE="deluxedoodads">Deluxe
Doodads</TD>
</TR>
</TABLE>
<P>Preferred shipping method: <SELECT NAME="ship">
<OPTION>UPS
<OPTION>U.S. Mail
<OPTION>Fedex 2nd-Day
<OPTION>Fedex Overnight
<OPTION>Fedex Same-Day
</SELECT>
<BR><BR>
<INPUT TYPE="SUBMIT" value="SEND FORM"> <INPUT TYPE"RESET" value= _
  "CLEAR FORM">
</FORM>
<HR>
<P><A HREF="mailto:sampler@widget.com">Widget, Inc. Webmaster</a>
</BODY>
</HTML>
```

Several assumptions are necessary to keep this sample CGI script relatively simple:

© You'll put the finished script in the cgi-bin of a server that has Perl, as most of them do.

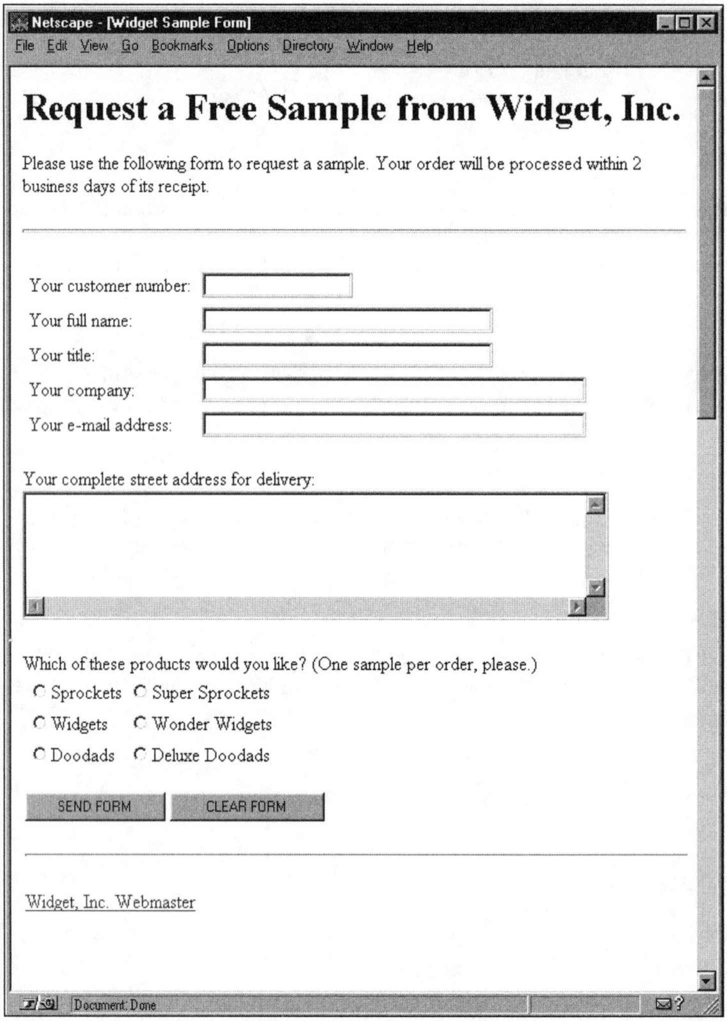

Figure 7.13   This form is very similar to the one in Figure 7.4, but the results are processed by a CGI script instead of by ACTION=MAILTO.

- You're using the freeware parsing script cgi-lib.pl, which has been installed in your server's cgi-bin.

- You aren't doing any validity checking for things like the customer number. By including the customer number in the form data, though, you're planning ahead to a time when you might want to use it as a password.

- The customer can only request one item at a time.

- The address is all in one field, to minimize the number of variables.

- The "thank-you" page is a very simple one, basically just echoing back to the customer some of the information he or she submitted in the form.

- You're adding the form results to the bottom of a simple text file that holds the orders, not a database. In real life, sending the information straight to a database would be better, but a text file is easier to handle for this example.

- You're also sending the information as an email message to whoever processes these requests.

Before you get to the CGI itself, you need to figure out what the Web page that it produces should look like. Then, you can use those lines of HTML in the script. The page shown in Figure 7.14 was produced with this HTML:

```
<HTML><HEAD>
<TITLE>Order Acknowledgment</TITLE>
</HEAD><BODY><FONT SIZE=4>
<P>Thank you very much, <EM>name</EM>.<BR>
Your order has been processed. The <EM>item</EM> will be sent to:
<BR><BR> <EM>address</EM><BR><BR>
If you have any questions, please call our customer-service department at
1-800-123- _
  444-5555.
</FONT></BODY></HTML>
```

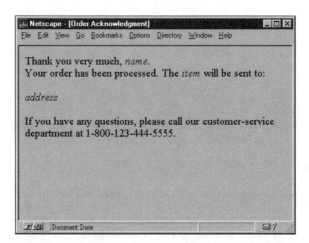

Figure 7.14   Sketch out the page of HTML that you want the script to produce, using form names where the data will go.

Now that everything is ready, you can work on the script. The easiest way to produce a CGI script (or, more accurately, the somewhat less difficult way) is to look at some freeware ones that are similar to what you want, and then "swipe" bits and pieces for your own needs. In this case, Brian Exelbierd's joke-sub.pl script (from http://www.catt.ncsu.edu/~bex) and Selena Sol's eff_form.pl script (from http://www.eff.org/~erict/Scripts/) provided inspiration. Both are included on the CD-ROM.

You'll usually need to modify any scripts you swipe to remove references to local directories and form-specific values. You can use any text editor that saves files as straight text to modify the scripts, or you can get a programmer's tool called a *line editor*. Web wizard Dave Friedel recommends PFE (Programmer's File Editor), included on the CD-ROM. The main benefits of a line editor like PFE are that it counts the lines for you. That way, you'll know when you get a message saying "ERROR LINE 29" where line 29 is. Also, it automatically creates a backup copy of the old version of your script when you save a new version.

In the case of the ordsub.pl script, the main modifications were to make it as general and simple as possible, so it will work on whatever server you have. In Perl, comments start with one or more hashmarks (#) and variables start with a dollar sign. I've commented the ordsub.pl script so you can see what each line does:

```
#!/usr/bin/perl
# ordsub.pl
#
# The first line above says this is a Perl script and says where Perl
# is on the server. You might need to change it slightly for your server.
# The second, optional, line gives the name of the script.
#
# This script accepts a single-item sample request and
# returns a page of HTML verifying the request and thanking the customer.
# It then appends the request to a log file and sends it via e-mail to _
  the Webmaster.


##### The following statement tells the server to "print working directory"
##### and store it in the variable $mydir. Always start a Perl script
##### this way, so it figures out the path the cgi-bin for you.
##### Then, even if your administrator moves it to a different
##### server with a different directory tree, the script will still work.
##### The backwards apostrophes around pwd are required. This character
##### is usually on the same key as the tilde (~) on your keyboard.
$mydir='pwd';
```

```
##### Remove the extra linefeed that the pwd command adds:
chop $mydir;

##### Use the cgi-lib.pl script in the cgi-bin The space-period-space
##### links $mydir and /cgi-bin/cgi-lib.pl into one directory string.
require $mydir . '/cgi-bin/cgi-lib.pl';

##### Create two variables, one to hold the order log
##### and the other to hold your e-mail address:
$orders = $mydir . "/temp/order.log";
$email="me@my.isp.net";

##### Add the standard command to parse the form data with cgi-lib.pl:
&ReadParse(*in);


##### All of the following print statements make the HTML page that
##### thanks the customer, by printing normal HTML codes onscreen.
##### Whenever you use Perl to write a Web page, the first line should be
##### Content-type, formatted exactly as shown. The \n symbols are
##### linefeeds. Since this script uses cgi-lib.pl, the form data needs
##### indicated as $in{'name-of-form-field'}.
##### Make sure you use curvy brackets around form fields, not parentheses.

print "Content-type: text/html\n\n";
print "<HTML><HEAD>\n";
print "<TITLE>Order Acknowledgment</TITLE>\n";
print "</HEAD><BODY>\n";
print "<FONT SIZE=4>\n";
print "<P>Thank you very much, " . $in{'name'} . ".\n";
print "<BR>Your request has been processed.";
print "The " . $in{'item'} . " will be sent to: \n";
print "<BR><BR>" . $in{'address'} . "<BR><BR>\n";
print "If you have any questions, please call ";
print "our customer-service department at 1-800-123-444-5555.\n";
print '</FONT></BODY></HTML>\n";


##### All of the following print statements add the order information
##### to the order.log file held in the $orders variable.
##### The first line says to append everything called ORDER to the
##### $orders variable. If the order.log file doesn't exist yet,
##### it will be created.
##### The two "greater-than" signs are important. If you
##### used just one, you would be creating the file, not appending to it,
##### which would overwrite the file every time the script was called.

open (ORDER,">>$orders");
print ORDER "Customer: ",$in{'cust'},"\n";
print ORDER "Name: ",$in{'name'},"\n";
print ORDER "Title: ",$in{'title'},"\n";
print ORDER "Company: ",$in{'company'},"\n";
```

```
print ORDER "E-mail: ",$in{'email'},"\n";
print ORDER "Address: ",$in{'address'},"\n";
print ORDER "Ordered: ",$in{'item'},"\n";
print ORDER "----------------------------\n";
close (ORDER);

##### All of the following lines send the order information to the
##### e-mail account held in the $email variable. The first line
##### creates a new variable to store the words that will make up
##### the subject line of the e-mail. You need to use a variable
##### because Perl could get confused by a text string in the open _
    statement.
##### The open statement says to pipe (|) anything in MAIL to e-mail
##### with a subject (-s) of $subject and a destination account $email.

$subject = "New Order";
open (MAIL, "| mail -s \"$subject\" $email");
print MAIL "Customer: ",$in{'cust'},"\n";
print MAIL "Name: ",$in{'name'},"\n";
print MAIL "Title: ",$in{'title'},"\n";
print MAIL "Company: ",$in{'company'},"\n";
print MAIL "E-mail: ",$in{'email'},"\n";
print MAIL "Address: ",$in{'address'},"\n";
print MAIL "Ordered: ",$in{'item'},"\n";
close (MAIL);
```

Part of the results from ordsub.pl, the email to order-processing, is shown in Figure 7.15. There are other ways to code CGI scripts that produce the same results as ordsub.pl. In particular, you might not want to have a separate print statement for each line that you want to add to a file or an email message. It's faster to use some code like this instead:

```
print "Content-Type: text/html\n\n";
print <<EOF;
<HTML><HEAD>
<TITLE>Order Acknowledgment</TITLE>
</HEAD><BODY>
<FONT SIZE=4>
<P>Thank you very much, $in{'name'}.
<BR>Your request has been processed.
EOF
```

The first line of this code starts the HTML file out in standard format. Then, everything else between <<EOF; and EOF is echoed into the HTML file. The main problem with this approach is that it can make debugging more difficult. You'll either get everything printed out or nothing. By using separate print statements for each line instead, you can more easily see where a problem happened because any lines after it won't print, while those before it will. Also, according

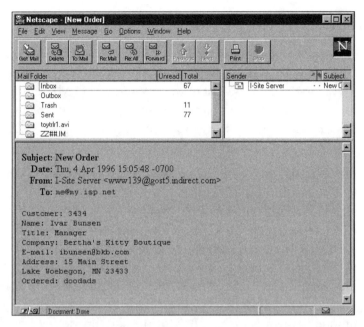

Figure 7.15   This email was sent by the ordsub.pl script. The same information was appended to the order.log file.

to Dave Friedel, the EOF won't register if you have more than 1,000 lines of code, causing a "Missing End of File" error. However you choose to develop a CGI script, the important thing is to have one that works for you, even if the programming is a little "messy."

There is no automatic debugger for Perl, so if you make a mistake, you'll have to search for it manually, line by line. To speed up the process, here are some typical problems to look for:

@ Lines that are missing the required semicolon at the end.

@ Parentheses instead of curly brackets around variables.

@ Any extra characters on an EOF line (especially spaces, since they're easy to overlook).

@ Accidentally uploading a Perl script as binary instead of ASCII, usually signaled by a "malformed header" error.

@ Referring to a value using an invalid name; for example, using NAME="items" in a form but $item in the script.

@ Misspelled or incorrectly capitalized words.

The Wizards Speak: Real-Life CGI

As the network engineer of The Coriolis Group, Dave Friedel manages a Web site with nearly a thousand pages (http://www.coriolis.com/). Most of the day-to-day HTML on these pages isn't hand-coded by him; it's generated by a collection of CGI scripts he's written. Friedel also uses CGI scripts to manage the online book ordering and to control access to restricted sites.

Friedel's method for password-based access to restricted areas of the Coriolis Group site is relatively easy to implement and reasonably secure. It's based on email. He explains, "When someone passes an email address and name [via a form], the password is emailed back. That way, the email address must be valid" in order for the person to gain access. The user is basically doing validity-checking for you; if the user doesn't send the correct email address, he or she won't get the password. Rather than keep track of an ever-growing list of unique passwords for this part of the site, Friedel reuses a limited number of passwords over and over, which can be coded right into the CGI script and checked with simple IF statements.

Friedel does use unique passwords, though, in the ordering process. "I use the time feature with random letters appended, so it [the order number] is unique for everybody who comes in, even if two people are placing an order at the same time. The unique number is then appended to the order database." Speaking of databases, Friedel recommends them over ordinary files in CGI scripts as being at least 20 to 30 times faster to work with, although he concedes that they take a little longer to initially set up. He warns, "If someone tries to append to a file while it's open [by someone else], you'll get an error and only bits and pieces of the orders because file locking doesn't work in Perl. A file stays open until it's closed [by a CLOSE statement in the CGI script], while a database updates and then closes instantly."

Friedel has contributed the Example.cgi script to the enclosed CD-ROM. It contains several useful, multi-purpose routines that he adapted from those he uses at the Coriolis group site:

- A general-purpose parsing routine.
- A routine that opens or creates a database, and then appends data to it or erases data from it.

@ A routine that sends mail to a user-supplied email address.

@ A routine that checks to see if a password typed by the user is valid for entry into a restricted Web page.

If you want to test the script without loading it on your server, it's available at the Coriolis Group site. Point your browser to the Coriolis Group, using this line:

```
http://www.coriolis.com/cgi-bin/Example.cgi?page=main
```

When you send that line, you should see the form in Figure 7.16. This form is actually created by the script itself.

Of course, you wouldn't want your users to have to enter a cryptic URL like that. You'll need a Web page to server as a kind of "front door" into the script. Here's some very simple HTML that serves the purpose for this example, as shown in Figure 7.17:

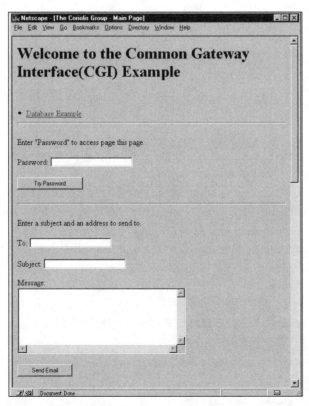

Figure 7.16 The Example.cgi script produces this form, among other things.

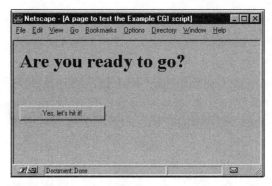

Figure 7.17 In real life, you'd probably want a more elaborate way to get the user to the Example.cgi script, but this serves the purpose for this example.

```
<HTML>
<HEAD>
<TITLE>A page to test the Example CGI script</TITLE>
</HEAD>

<BODY>
<H1>Are you ready to go?</H1>
<FORM ACTION="http://www.coriolis.com/cgi-bin/Example.cgi"
METHOD="Post">
<BR><BR>
<INPUT NAME="page" TYPE="hidden" VALUE="main">
<INPUT TYPE="SUBMIT" value="Yes, let's hit it!'>
</FORM>
</BODY>
</HTML>
```

Here is the complete code for Example.cgi. As you examine it, remember that you don't necessarily have to figure out why each particular character is where it is. Instead, the goal is to recognize what items could be changed to adapt the script to your purpose. Note that I expanded the comments (which start with one or more #) from Friedel's original script to make it a little easier to follow:

```
#!/usr/bin/perl
#
#
###############################################
# Written by David H. Friedel Jr.
# Network Engineer, The Coriolis Group
# I am not responsible for any damage that may
# occur as a result of using this script for
# purposes other than learning
###############################################
#
```

```
#Prepare all information for Web browser: _
  print "Content-Type: text/html\n\n";


# Retrieve current directory:
$mydir='pwd';

# Chop off return character appended when information is retrieved:
  chop $mydir;

###### Parse the info from the server using the following code,
###### which is basically getting the data from the form with either
###### the GET or POST method, checking to make sure it's not _
###### a spam (over 32,768 characters), and splitting
###### each form item into a name ($reqType) and value ($reqValue),
###### and stripping off all the characters that got added
###### when it was sent from a Web page:

$method = $ENV{'REQUEST_METHOD'};
if ($method eq "GET")  {
        $request = $ENV{'QUERY_STRING'};
} elsif($method eq "POST") {
        $length = $ENV{'CONTENT_LENGTH'};
        if ($length > "32768") {
                die "too big";
        }
        while ($length--) {
        $request .= getc(STDIN);
        }
}
foreach (split(/&/, $request)) {
        ($reqType, $reqValue) = split(/=/, $_);
        $reqType =~ s/\+/ /g;
        $reqType =~ s/%([0-9|A-F]{2})/pack(C,hex($1))/eg;
        $reqValue =~ s/\+/ /g;
        $reqValue =~ s/%([0-9|A-F]{2})/pack(C,hex($1))/eg;
        $reqData{$reqType} = $reqValue;
        }


##### Done parsing.

############## Let's begin the main program by checking
############## what page the person wants, using an IF statement.
############## Each choice sends the program to a different _
  subroutine.

############## Main page
if ($reqData{'page'} eq "main") {

   &main; # Main Page calls subroutine
```

```
############# Mail page
} elsif ($reqData{'page'} eq "mail") {

   &mail; # Mail Page calls subroutine

############# Database page
} elsif ($reqData{'page'} eq "dbase") {

   &dbase; # Database Page calls subroutine

############# Password page
} elsif ($reqData{'page'} eq "password") {

   &password; # Password Page calls subroutine

# If nothing is passed, this page is displayed
} else {
print qq|Default Text|;

}

##### End of main program



########### Subroutines

########### Main Form
sub main {

### Append lines of HTML to the end of a file, in this case the
empty text/html file
print <<EOF;
<HTML>
<HEAD>
<TITLE>The Coriolis Group - Main Page</TITLE>
</HEAD>
<body>
<H1>Welcome to the Common Gateway Interface(CGI) Example</H1>
<br>
<li><a href='/cgi-bin/Example.cgi?page=dbase">Database Example</a>
<hr>
<form method=post action="/cgi-bin/Example.cgi">
<input type=hidden name=page value="password">
Enter "Password" to access this page.<br><br>
Password: <input type=password name=password><br><br>
<input type=submit value="Try Password">
</form>
<hr>
<form method=post action="/cgi-bin/Example.cgi">
<input type=hidden name=page value="mail">
Enter a subject and an address to send to.<br><br>
```

```
To: <input type=text name=to><br><br>
Subject: <input type=text name=subject><br><br>
Message:<br> <textarea name=message cols=40 rows=8></
textarea><br><br>
<input type=submit value="Send Email">
</form>
<hr>
</BODY>
</HTML>
EOF
##### Exit the script
exit;
}
###########

########### Database Form
sub dbase {

##### When the user comes to this page from the main page, the
hidden variable "section"
##### will be empty (eq ""). In that case, print the introduction _
##### and either create or open the database.
if ($reqData{section} eq "") {

print <<EOF;
<HTML>
<HEAD>
<TITLE>The Coriolis Group - Database Page</TITLE>
</HEAD>
<body>
Here is an example of a database.  If this is the first time it is
being read, it will display nothing.  To add or delete information,
fill in the appropriate fields below.
<hr>
<h4>Example:</h4>
<dl><dt><h4>Key</h4><dd><h4>Data</h4></dl>
<h4>***Data Starts Below***</h4>
EOF

##### Open or create the database for Example
dbmopen(%DBASEFILE,"$mydir/Example", 0644);
while (($key, $value) = each %DBASEFILE) {
    print qq|<dl><dt>$key<dd>$value</dl>|;
}
dbmclose(%DBASEFILE);

##### Print HTML lines that tell the user what to
print <<EOF;
<hr>
<form method=post action="/cgi-bin/Example.cgi">
<input type=hidden name=page value="dbase">
<input type=hidden name=section value="add">
```

```
Enter information to add.<br>
Key: <input type=text name=key><br>
Data: <input type=text name=data><br>
<input type=submit value="Add">
</form>
<form method=post action="/cgi-bin/Example.cgi">
<input type=hidden name=page value="dbase">
<input type=hidden name=section value="erase">
Enter information to erase.<br>
Key: <input type=text name=key><br>
<input type=submit value="Erase">
</form>
</BODY>
</HTML>
EOF
exit;
#####
#### Check if the hidden variable, "section," equals add

} elsif ($reqData{section} eq "add") {

##### If so, open the database and add "key" and "data" variables
dbmopen(%DBASEFILE,"$mydir/Example", 0644);
$DBASEFILE{$reqData{key}} = $reqData{data};
dbmclose(%DBASEFILE);


##### Print HTML lines responding to the add
print <<EOF;
<HTML>
<HEAD>
<TITLE>The Coriolis Group - Password Page</TITLE>
</HEAD>
<body>
Thank you for the deposit!
</BODY>
</HTML>
EOF
exit;
#####
#### Check if the "section" variable being passed equals erase

} elsif ($reqData{section} eq "erase") {

##### If so, open the database and erase the "key" variable, _
##### which gets rid of the data automatically
dbmopen(%DBASEFILE,"$mydir/Example", 0644);
delete $DBASEFILE{$reqData{key}};
dbmclose(%DBASEFILE);

##### Print HTML lines responding to the erase
print <<EOF;
```

```
<HTML>
<HEAD>
<TITLE>The Coriolis Group - Password Page</TITLE>
</HEAD>
<body>
Thank you for the withdrawal!
</BODY>
</HTML>
EOF
exit;
}


}
###########

########### Password Form
sub password {

#### Check the "password" variable being passed to the script.
#### If the password does not check out, the script drops down
#### to the } else { line.
if ($reqData{password} eq "Password") {

#### If the password checks out, print a welcome page
print <<EOF;
<HTML>
<HEAD>
<TITLE>The Coriolis Group - Password Page</TITLE>
</HEAD>
<body>
Welcome to a secret Web Page
</BODY>
</HTML>
EOF
exit;

} else {


##### If the password doesn't check out, print this page
print <<EOF;
<HTML>
<HEAD>
<TITLE>The Coriolis Group - Password Page</TITLE>
</HEAD>
<body>
You have entered an invalid password!
</BODY>
</HTML>
EOF
exit;
```

```
}
}
##########

########## Mail Form
sub mail {

#### Check for the "to" variable; if not equal to zero,
then
#### perform the mail message.
if ($reqData{to}) {
   open (MAIL, "| mail -s \"$reqData{subject}\" $reqData{to}");

#### You could send a password here, instead of whatever is in
#### the message variable.
      print MAIL "************Message***************\n";
      if ($reqData{'message'} ne ""){ print MAIL "They replied:\n
$reqData{'message'}\n";}
      print MAIL "*********************************\n";

   close(MAIL);
}
print <<EOF;
   <HTML>
   <HEAD>
   <TITLE> Coriolis Group - Mailer </TITLE>
   </HEAD>
   <BODY>
   <H2>Your mail has been sent...</H2>
   <P>
   You replied to:<br> $reqData{'message'}...
   <br><hr><br>
   Sent To: $reqData{to}<br>
   </BODY>
   </HTML>
EOF
exit;
}
##########
```

It doesn't matter whether you give a Perl CGI script a .PL
extension or a .CGI extension. In fact, you could leave off the
extension altogether if you wanted to, although most people
use .PL or .CGI.

A particularly useful and easy adaptation of this script would be to create and
validate passwords using the email method that Friedel mentioned. You'd keep

the parsing routine and main program basically intact, but delete all of the stuff that doesn't have to do with sending an email message or validating a password. You'd also delete the "message" text area on the main form as shown in Figure 7.17, since the message would be the password itself. With a few additional changes based on the comments in Example.cgi, you'd have a script like this (called passchk.cgi on the CD-ROM):

```perl
#!/usr/bin/perl
# passchk.cgi
#
#################################################
# Adapted from the Example.cgi script by David H. Friedel Jr.
# Network Engineer, The Coriolis Group,
# who is not responsible for any damage that may
# occur as a result of using this script for
# purposes other than learning
#################################################
#
# Prepare all information for Web browser:
print "Content-Type: text/html\n\n";

# Retrieve current directory:

$mydir='pwd';

# Chop off return character appended when information is retrieved:

chop $mydir;

###### Parse the info from the server using this standard code:

$method = $ENV{'REQUEST_METHOD'};
if ($method eq "GET")   {
        $request = $ENV{'QUERY_STRING'};
} elsif($method eq "POST") {
        $length = $ENV{'CONTENT_LENGTH'};
        if ($length > "32768") {
                die 'too big";
        }
        while ($length--) {
        $request .= getc(STDIN);
        }
}
foreach (split(/&/, $request)) {
        ($reqType, $reqValue) = split(/=/, $_);
        $reqType =~ s/\+/ /g;
        $reqType =~ s/%([0-9|A-F]{2})/pack(C,hex($1))/eg;
```

```
        $reqValue =~ s/\+/ /g;
        $reqValue =~ s/%([0-9|A-F]{2})/pack(C,hex($1))/eg;
        $reqData{$reqType} = $reqValue;
        }

##### Done parsing.

############## Let's begin by checking what the person wants to do:

############## Main page
if ($reqData{'page'} eq "main") {

    &main; # Main Page calls subroutine

############## Mail page
} elsif ($reqData{'page'} eq "mail") {

    &mail; # Mail Page calls subroutine

############## Password page
} elsif ($reqData{'page'} eq "password") {

    &password; # Password Page calls subroutine

# If nothing is passed, this page is displayed
} else {

print qq|Default Text|;

}
######

###### End of Program


########### Subroutines

########### Main Form
sub main {

#### Append lines of HTML to the end of a file,
#### in this case the empty text/html file
print <<EOF;
<HTML>
<HEAD>
<TITLE>The Coriolis Group - Main Page</TITLE>
</HEAD>
<body>
<H1>Welcome to the Password-Checking Example</H1>
```

```
<br>
<hr>
<form method=post action='/cgi-bin/passchk.cgi">
<input type=hidden name=page value="password">
Please type your password to access this site.<br><br>
Password: <input type=password name=password><br><br>
<input type=submit value="Try password">
</form>
<hr>
<form method=post action="/cgi-bin/passchk.cgi">
<input type=hidden name=page value="mail">
If you do not have a password, apply for one here via e-mail.<br>
Fill out your e-mail address and a subject, and a password will be sent _
  to your e-mail acount immediately.<br><br>
Your e-mail address: <input type=text name=to size=30><br><br>
Subject: <input type=text name=subject size=30><br><br>
<input type=submit value="Send Email">
</form>
</BODY>
</HTML>
EOF
#### Exit the script
exit;
}
###########

########## Password Form
sub password {

#### Check the "password" variable being passed to the script.
#### If the password does not check out, the script drops down to the }
#### else { line.

if ($reqData{password} eq "apr10bk") {

#### If the password checks out, print a welcome page
print <<EOF;
<HTML>
<HEAD>
<TITLE>The Coriolis Group - Password-Restricted</TITLE>
</HEAD>
<body>
Welcome to a secret Web page!
</BODY>
</HTML>
EOF
exit;

} else {
```

```
##### If the password doesn't check out, print this page
print <<EOF;
<HTML>
<HEAD>
<TITLE>The Coriolis Group - Password-Restricted</TITLE>
</HEAD>
<body>
Sorry, your password does not check out.<BR>
Would you like to <A HREF="/cgi-bin/passchk.cgi?page=main">try again?</A>
</BODY>
</HTML>
EOF
exit;
}
}
###########

########### Mail Form
sub mail {

##### Check for the "to" variable; if not zero, perform the mail message.
if ($reqData{to}) {
   open (MAIL, "| mail -s \"$reqData{subject}\" $reqData{to}");

      print MAIL "************Message*********\n";
      print MAIL "Your password is apr10bk\n";
      print MAIL "****************************\n";

   close(MAIL);
}

print <<EOF;
   <HTML>
   <HEAD>
   <TITLE> Coriolis Group - Mailer </TITLE>
   </HEAD>
   <BODY>
   <H2>Your password has been sent to your e-mail address.</H2>
   </BODY>
   </HTML>
EOF
exit;
}
###########
```

Had enough of forms and CGI scripting for the time being? It's definitely one of the more cryptic areas of Web wizardry to master, but also one of the most useful. And once you get that first CGI script to work, it's mostly a matter of practice and experimentation before you, too, are writing scripts that will amaze your friends and confound your enemies!

If you want more information on CGI, check out the resources that Yahoo has gathered at http://www.yahoo.com/Computers_and_Internet/Internet/ World_Wide_Web/CGI___Common_Gateway_Interface/. For more information on Perl programming, the book *Programming Perl* by Larry Wall (published by O'Reilly) is the definitive reference.

Web Wizard's Touchstones for Forms

Do rely as much as possible on "canned" CGI scripts that are available as shareware and freeware on the Web.

Don't leave users stranded on a form page where you've used ACTION=MAILTO. Tell them not to expect an immediate response, and include a link to leave the page.

Do use table tags to get the elements of your form to align properly.

Don't make your form longer than one or two screens unless you give the user a very strong incentive for filling out and submitting it.

Do use ACTION=MAILTO if you need to get information from users and you don't have any CGI rights.

Don't upload a CGI script as binary. If you do, extra blank lines will be added that will cause a "malformed header" error. Upload in ASCII instead, by typing ascii at the ftp prompt.

Do remember that Perl is case-sensitive.

Don't use a special character like $, ", or & in your CGI code unless you *escape* it first by adding a slash character before it, like this:

```
if ($reqData{price} > "/$49.95")
```

Do make sure permissions for any text files or databases that your CGI scripts use are set properly, usually with chmod 0644.

Don't overuse hits counters, especially if you're borrowing someone else's server to run them on.

VIII
THE SOUND OF MUSIC... OR VOICES... OR BARKING

F or most of its short life, the Web has been a remarkably quiet place. The reason for this was simple: the technology just hadn't been there—in software, hardware, or bandwidth—to support sound on the Web to anywhere near the extent that graphics have been supported. This is changing quickly, though. New HTML tags, add-ins, and audio formats are making it easier to deliver better and longer-playing sound clips in reasonable amounts of time. Sites like the Houston Chronicle Interactive, a page of which is shown in Figure 8.1, provide audio effects every bit as compelling as the visual effects, and your site can, too.

The Wizards Speak: The Highs and Lows of Audio Formats

In the "grand" microcomputing tradition of competing standards, there are many audio formats to choose from when adding sound to your Web pages. According to Web wizard Joe Maissel, owner of the Web-based music store Soundwire (Figure 8.2) at http://www.soundwire.com/, here are several of the current popular formats:

- AIFF is used mostly on Macintosh computers.

- AU, often called m-law ("mu-law") or Sun format, is very common in Net-based archives of sound clips.

- IWAVE provides real-time audio for Windows-based PCs.

- MPEG stands for Motion Picture Experts Group and is pronounced "em-peg." Although better known as a video standard, Maissel says it "provides the finest compression algorithm available, 10-to-1 compression with CD-quality sound." Currently, it's mostly for traditional downloads, but a few companies such as Xing (http://204.62.160.251/) have announced streaming technology using proprietary servers.

- RealAudio provides fast, real-time audio for most computer platforms. It comes in version 1.0 (also called 14.4) and version 2.0 (also called 28.8).

- TrueSpeech, like IWAVE and RealAudio, provides real-time audio over the Web, but it is designed primarily for speech, not music.

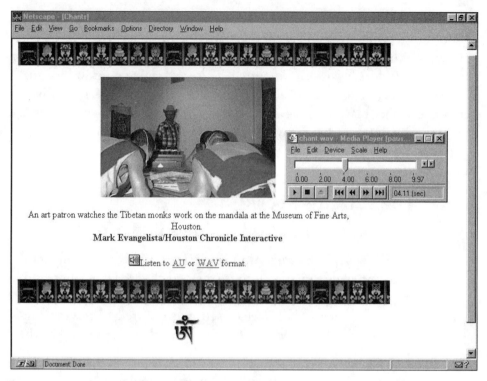

Figure 8.1 This special online exhibit of Tibetan art at the Museum of Fine Art Houston was complete with graphics, sound, and video.

WAV is used as the default audio format on most on Windows-based PCs.

Deciding which one(s) you want to use at your Web site depends on several factors:

- The operating systems your target audience uses.
- The sound quality you need.
- The amount of money you have to spend.
- Whether the clips are to be downloaded first and then played later, or automatically played while they are being downloaded (sometimes referred to as *streaming audio*).
- For streaming audio, how much access you have to your Web server.

At Soundwire, the sound quality needs to be as high as possible, since people are making buying decisions about the albums based

Figure 8.2 From Soundwire's home-page image map, you enter an online catalog that includes audio clips in MPEG and IWAVE formats.

in part on the clips they hear. At the same time, Soundwire is a small company in an industry with low profit margins, so the cost of putting the clips on Soundwire's Web page needs to be kept to a minimum.

Based on these factors, Maissel experiments with all of the major audio formats, but concentrates on two: MPEG for relatively long sound clips designed to be downloaded and played offline, and IWAVE for streaming audio on short clips where lower sound quality is acceptable. Most album samples at Soundwire are provided in one of these two formats, although a few have both.

Creating MPEG sound files involves the additional cost of special software and DSP (digital signal processing) hardware. Still, Maissel chooses MPEG over more common formats such as WAV and AIFF because of its superior sound quality and file compression. Also, it's a cross-platform format that is supported by Mac, Windows, and Unix players, and it can be used for video as well as audio.

For streaming audio, Maissel praises RealAudio for "its ubiquity, business sense, and marketing. Its development tools are the best of the bunch." On the other hand, he explains, "RealAudio uses its own proprietary server technology, which costs several thousand dollars [for the commercial version]. For relatively small companies, that price point is pretty high. Also, the sound quality is only good in the RealAudio 2.0 format, but you can't use that if you have a 14.4 modem." In addition to the commercial version, RealAudio also sells a personal server for about $100 (for noncommercial use only). As of this writing, however, it must be installed on a Windows 95 or Windows NT server instead of the more common Unix server. Also, it must be installed by someone who has administrator-level rights to the server; you can't just upload it to the type of directory where you put all your HTML files.

One unique solution to the problems of running a dedicated RealAudio server is to rent space on someone else's server. Soundwire, for example, segments its server so users can rent space for two or three RealAudio streams on a monthly basis. All the user has to do is record the clip, encode it with the (free) RealAudio encoder, and upload it to Soundwire's RealAudio server.

If you want to use RealAudio but don't have access to its server, you can put the encoded RA files on your Web pages to be downloaded whole and played like a WAV, AU, or AIFF. Make sure visitors understand that these clips can only be downloaded, not streamed. Although you don't get the major benefit of real-time audio, you do benefit from good compression rates; for example, a 600 KB AU file would become about a 75 KB RA file.

Another solution is to look at alternatives to RealAudio, such asIWAVE. Maissel says, "The definitive audio format isn't here yet, but IWAVE is a step in the right direction. It's almost as fast as RealAudio, and it's free."

Of course, in order to hear the sounds on your Web page, visitors will need a player that can handle the format(s) you supply. Maissel says that Soundwire's users don't mind having to download several different audio players to hear the various clips. To make it as easy as possible for his visitors, however, Maissel includes links to sites where they can get the players (Figure 8.3).

Your Audio Toolkit

The basic hardware and software you need to add audio to your Web pages include the following:

A SOUND CARD

Most computers sold in the last few years come with some kind of sound card. If you can hear the sound effects and music from today's computer games, you have one. If you don't, you can buy an acceptable sound card for recording effects and speech for less than $100. Sound cards that support more advanced features for studio-quality recording, however, can cost much more.

If you plan to create MPEG files, make sure your sound card has a DSP chip to handle the special audio compression needed by this format. Cards with this chip are sometimes called *digital audio adapters.* They range from a few hundred

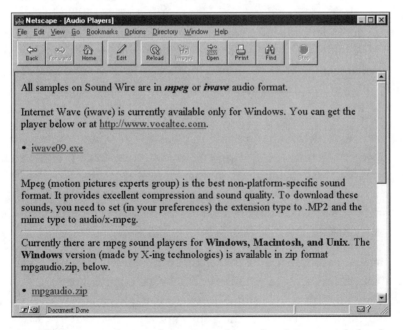

Figure 8.3 This page explains where to get the audio players needed to hear Soundwire's audio files.

dollars to several thousand dollars for top-of-the-line hardware such as the adapters from Antex (http://www.antex.com/).

A MICROPHONE

A cheap microphone is fine for short, basic sound effects, although not so great for music and extended speech clips. If a microphone didn't come with your system, you can pick one up for $10 or so from your local electronics store, plug it into the MIC port on your sound card, and you're ready to go. If you need to record high-quality clips, invest in a professional-quality, unidirectional microphone for upwards of $50.

> For better sound quality, put the microphone on a stable base instead of holding it. Also, don't speak down into it; position it so it's about level with your nose when you're looking straight ahead.

SOFTWARE FOR RECORDING, EDITING, AND ENCODING

Software for adding audio to your Web site is much less common than software for graphics, but it is out there. Microsoft Windows comes with a very basic sound recorder called, logically enough, Sound Recorder. However, since it only supports WAV files and doesn't provide much in the way of sound editing, it's really not adequate for Web-publishing purposes. Many sound cards come with more robust sound programs that handle several different audio formats and let you mix sounds.

Of course, there's always the Internet itself as a source of freeware, shareware, and demoware for audio recording and editing. For example, the shareware programs GoldWave (included on the CD-ROM) and CoolEdit (download-loadable from http://www.syntrillium.com/) can convert among all the major sound formats; cut, copy, mix, invert, and reverse sounds; and add all kinds of special effects.

If you have large sound or music files that you want to supply in a streaming format such as RealAudio, IWAVE, or TrueSpeech, you'll need additional software. Exactly how much additional software you'll need and where it will have to be installed varies for each of these formats.

All of the streaming-audio technologies require a special encoder to compress your audio file into their particular proprietary formats. The encoders are free from the Web sites of their vendors:

- IWAVE, http://www.vocaltec.com/iwave.htm
- RealAudio, http://www.realaudio.com/
- TrueSpeech, http://www.dspg.com/

You'll also need to create a special text file of "directions" for each audio file you make. RealAudio calls them *metafiles*. Finally, you'll need to have the server administrator modify your Web server's MIME types to tell it to recognize whatever file type your streaming program uses. Plus, in the case of RealAudio, you'll need to install separate, proprietary server software.

SOUND AND MUSIC FILES

There are lots of sources for audio clips on the Web. Unfortunately, most of them fall into a gray—or sometimes downright black—area of the current copyright law. That might not be too bad if you just want to download a sound to play when Windows starts up on your PC, but it's a major issue when you're putting the sound on a Web page that might be visited by hundreds of thousands of people—including copyright lawyers.

A few sites do provide at least some sound and music files that are royalty-free and explicitly allowed to be used on Web pages, including these:

- The World Wide Web Virtual Library: Audio at http://www.comlab.ox.ac.uk/archive/audio.html
- The sound area of SunSite at http://sunsite.unc.edu/pub/multimedia/sun-sounds/
- The sound effects archive at ftp://ftp.southern.com/pub/4th_Eye/
- The home page of Musicians Against the Copyrighting of Sound Clips at http://www.io.org/~macos/
- The SoundRoom at http://snhungar.kings.edu/SndrmNB.html
- Multi-Media Music at http://www.wavenet.com/~axgrindr/quimby.html

You can also buy collections of sounds like you buy clip art, but collections of audio clips are not nearly as easy to find as graphical clips. Look for CD-ROMs such as Kaboom! (whose sound effects were used in the Myst computer game, among others) or Janus Professional Sound Library (http://www.janusinteractive.com/). Also ask at larger music stores for audio CD collections of royalty-free sounds and music that you can copy directly from the CD player in your computer.

Note, though, that when you buy stock audio clips (or any stock clips, for that matter), you're really buying the rights to them, not the items themselves. There are various levels of rights you can buy, depending on how you want to use the clips. It usually costs more to buy clips with fewer usage restrictions. Broadcast rights, which is the level of usage you need to post the clips at your Web site, can be expensive. The Janus library, for example, costs around $600, although it does have several thousand sounds.

When you click a link to a sound clip, you don't usually get an option to save it after it's played. To download the sound clip instead of playing it (in Netscape), right-click on the link, choose Save Link As from the menu that appears, change directories if necessary, and click Save.

The Wizards Speak: Some Sound Copyright Advice

You'd like to have your home page play the opening bars from the Beatles' "Hard Day's Night." As a budding guitarist, you've recorded yourself playing it. Should you put it on your page? Definitely not, say the Web wizards, especially if yours is a commercial site.

As Joe Maissel explains, "*All* songs have copyright holders. These copyright holders are represented by very large, very powerful agencies that are aggressively pursuing their rights. Don't put any audio on a page that you didn't create [not just perform] unless you've cleared it with the copyright holder," which he does with the clips at his site.

What about all those sound files that you find in archives all over the Web of Homer Simpson saying "Doh!" or Worf asking permission to blow up some alien ship? Maissel says you should stay away from them as a source of sound for your page, too.

"Up until recently, most [copyright holders] didn't worry about people using their stuff too much—they considered it good publicity for their television programs or whatever. But as people integrate these clips into the content of their sites, and they become part of the draw and are used for advertising the site, repercussions start. Actually, they've already begun, especially for commercial sites."

Remember, too, that "royalty-free" does not mean "copyright free." Read the copyright and usage information that comes with collections of sound files, if possible before you buy. For example, the publisher of the Best of Media Clips CD-ROM does not allow its sound files to be resold in other clip collections—a very typical, understandable limitation. It also prohibits reproducing more than 20% of its files—still okay for most Web wizards.

Here's where it gets tricky, though: the publisher explicitly permits its clips to be used in print and digital media, but prohibits their use in broadcast media. The Web is a digital medium, but according to the most recent copyright laws, it is *also* a broadcast medium when people download things from it. Most likely, the copyright information for this CD-ROM was written before the new laws were enacted.

So what's a Web wizard to do? You can try contacting the owner of whatever audio clips you want to use for permission or clarification. That's feasible in some cases, but not in others—especially if you're on a tight deadline. The alternative is to make your own audio clips or have them made for you, with your own content. Having music or sound created for you involves hiring a freelancer, just like you can hire a graphic freelancer. Creating basic sound effects yourself, though, is really not that hard to do—in fact, it can be a lot of fun.

Sampling Simple Sounds

The way you record (*sample*) sounds and music has a dramatic effect on both the quality of the sound and the size of the finished file, as you can see from Table 8.1.

Sampling Rate	File Size	Filename on CD-ROM
44.1 kHz, 16-bit stereo	452 KB	wel4416s.wav
44.1 kHz, 8-bit stereo	226 KB	wel4408s.wav
44.1 kHz, 16-bit mono	226 KB	wel4416m.wav
44.1 kHz, 8-bit mono	114 KB	wel4408m.wav
32 kHz, 16-bit stereo	326 KB	wel3216s.wav
32 kHz, 8-bit stereo	163 KB	wel3208s.wav
32 kHz, 16-bit mono	163 KB	wel3216m.wav
32 kHz, 8-bit mono	82 KB	wel3208m.wav
22 kHz, 16-bit stereo	230 KB	wel2216s.wav
22 kHz, 8-bit stereo	115 KB	wel2208s.wav
22 kHz, 16-bit mono	115 KB	wel2216m.wav
22 kHz, 8-bit mono	58 KB	wel2208m.wav
16 kHz, 16-bit stereo	166 KB	wel1616s.wav
16 kHz, 8-bit stereo	83 KB	wel1608s.wav
16 kHz, 16-bit mono	83 KB	wel1616m.wav
16 kHz, 8-bit mono	42 KB	wel1608m.wav
11 kHz, 16-bit stereo	115 KB	wel1116s.wav
11 kHz, 8-bit stereo	58 KB	wel1108s.wav
11 kHz, 16-bit mono	58 KB	wel1116m.wav
11 kHz, 8-bit mono	29 KB	wel1108m.wav
8 kHz, 16-bit stereo	83 KB	wel0816s.wav
8 kHz, 8-bit stereo	42 KB	wel0808s.wav
8 kHz, 16-bit mono	42 KB	wel0816m.wav
8 kHz, 8-bit mono	21 KB	wel0808m.wav

Table 8.1 A spoken greeting, about 2.6 seconds long, can take up vastly different amounts of space depending on how it's sampled. WAV files are used here, but file sizes would be very similar for AU and AIFF formats.

When you consider that a 14.4 baud modem downloads about one kilobyte per second, you can see that most of the sampling rates in Table 8.1 are not feasible for simple WAV, AU, and AIFF sound clips. Who wants to wait two minutes just to hear, "Welcome to my Web site. Please let me know what you think of it"?

"Homemade" sound and music files are usually sampled at 22 kHz 16-bit mono or less. This is just fine for most purposes, especially since most people don't have the software or hardware on their computers to really do justice to high-end audio, anyway. As you can hear if you test the files in Table 8.1 from the CD-ROM, it doesn't make sense to record voice or sounds in stereo unless you have professional recording equipment because the left channel will just play static.

Whatever format you use, it's a good idea to let visitors know a little about what to expect. For each audio link, include text or a graphic indicating that the link is an audio file, and giving the format of the file and its size in bytes. If the file is fairly large, consider adding the details of its sampling rate or sound quality, as well. Many Web wizards provide the same audio file in different formats to accommodate visitors with different sound players.

Suppose you want to include a link to the pronunciation of a word on your Web page. Here's how to do it:

1. Start up the sound recorder of your choice to sample the sound. Window's own Sound Recorder would work for short, simple WAVs, but to supply the file in several different formats, use a more full-featured editor like GoldWave (included on the CD-ROM). Also, make sure the microphone is turned on in whatever software program controls your sound inputs and outputs (usually part of your sound card's utilities).

2. Select the format for your new sound. In GoldWave, click the New button or select File|New to bring up the New Sample dialog box. Set the options as shown in Figure 8.4 for a one-second, 8-bit mono sound at a sampling rate of 11025 Hz (11 kHz). Since you're just recording a single word, these settings should be adequate.

3. When you're ready, click the red record button in GoldWave's Device Controls dialog box and speak your word into the microphone.

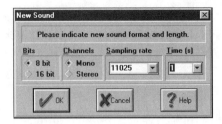

Figure 8.4 These settings will result in a fairly small file.

4. (Optional) Repeat steps 2 and 3 so you have several different "takes." Choose the best and close the others without saving them.

5. Trim the audio file to remove any silence at the beginning or end. *Trimming* an audio file is similar to cropping a graphic file; it keeps file sizes down and removes unnecessary parts. To trim, left-click at the place where you want your finished sound to start and right-click where you want it to end. The areas that will be trimmed are in black onscreen, and the selected sound is in blue. Figure 8.5 shows a recording of my last name ready for trimming. Click the Trim button to remove the areas in black.

6. There are lots of useful and fun effects you could add at this point, such as a flange, reverb, noise reduction, or change in pitch. Experiment with them, and when you've got the clip sounding the way you want it, bring up the Save As dialog box.

7. The format(s) you choose for saving your file depend on personal preference, both yours and what you think your audience's will be. For this example, use the three most popular formats. For the first one, choose WAV in the Save File as Type area, and 8-bit, mono, unsigned in File Attributes, as shown in Figure 8.6. Name the file and finish the save. You'll probably get a message that the file has been converted. Click OK to remove the dialog box. Keep the file opened because you're not finished yet.

8. Bring up the Save As dialog box again, but this time choose Sun (AU) as the file type and m-law, mono for the file attributes. Finish the save.

9. Bring up the Save As dialog box yet again, choosing Apple (AFC, AIFF), 8-bit, mono, signed. Note that you'll have to actually type in the filename extension, AIF, for this one. Finish the save and close GoldWave.

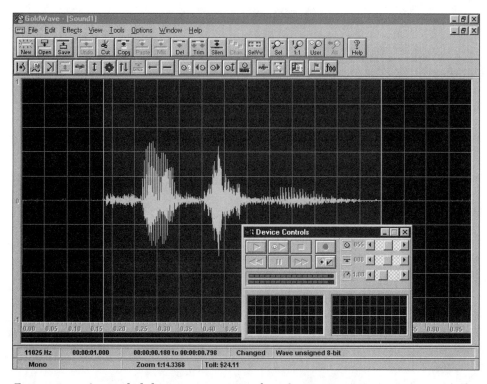

Figure 8.5   I recorded the pronunciation of my last name; now I want to trim the "dead air" at the beginning and end.

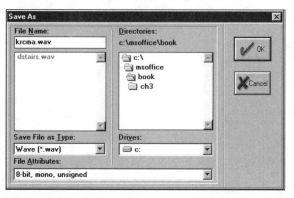

Figure 8.6   This file, being saved as an 8-bit mono WAV, will also be saved in AU and AIFF formats.

10. Now you're ready to put links to the audio files on a page of HTML. You can just use the standard <A HREF> tag for the links, but make sure to let people know that the links are to audio files, as shown in Figure 8.7. Here's the code:

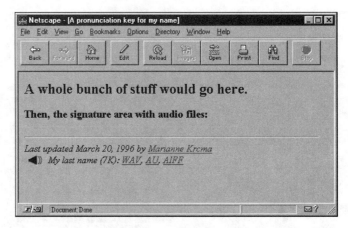

Figure 8.7 A small icon makes it immediately clear to visitors that the links are sounds. Visitors can also see that the sound's file size is 7 KB. If the files are large (more than about 60 KB), sampling details should also be included.

```
<HTML>
<HEAD><TITLE>A pronunciation key for my name</TITLE></HEAD>
<BODY>
<H2>A whole bunch of stuff would go here.</H2>
<H3>Then, the signature area with audio files:</H3>
<HR>
<ADDRESS>
Last updated March 20, 1996 by <A HREF="mailto:me@my-isp.net">Marianne _
  Krcma</A><BR>
<IMG SRC="/sounds/sndicon.gif" ALT="Sound Icon" WIDTH=36 HEIGHT=22
ALIGN=top> My last name (7K):
<A HREF="/sounds/krcma.wav">WAV</A>,
<A HREF="/sounds/krcma.au">AU</A>,
<A HREF="/sounds/krcma.aif">AIFF</A>
</ADDRESS>
</BODY>
</HTML>
```

 As a rule of thumb, record at 44.1 kHz 16-bit stereo on good-quality sound equipment for CD-quality music, 16 to 22 kHz 8-bit mono to 16-bit stereo for decent-quality music (similar to what you hear on AM radio), 11 kHz 8-bit mono for short speech clips, and 8 kHz 8-bit mono for sound effects.

"Why Didn't I Think of That?": Automatically Playing a Sound Clip

If you plan to support mainly Microsoft Internet Explorer users at your site, you can add a sound that will load automatically using Internet Explorer's special BGSOUND attribute of the <BODY> tag. It's pretty cool to have a welcome message or something similar automatically play when someone hits your page. However, no other browser supports BGSOUND, which means Netscape Navigator users, among others, will be left in silence.

But wait! There is a way to produce a similar effect without the BGSOUND attribute. First, you need a sound. For Figure 8.8, it would be interesting to have the sound of someone opening a door and walking downstairs "magically" play.

The sound itself is a combination of a public-domain clip of a door opening that I downloaded from http://sunsite-uncedu/pub/multimedia/sun-sounds/sound-effects (door-2.au) and the sound of someone walking downstairs (walk.wav), which I recorded

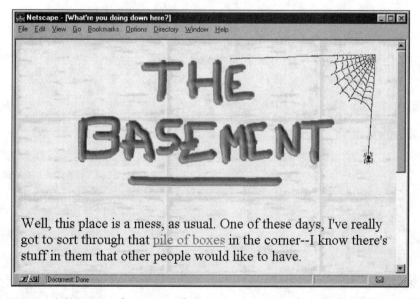

Figure 8.8   Visitors to this page whose computers can handle AU files will hear a door open and someone walk downstairs, even though there are no visible links to a sound file.

myself by simply "walking" a pair of shoes around on my desk. Both of these files are included on the CD-ROM. Here's how to put them together:

1. Start up the sound editor of your choice. GoldWave is used in this example.

2. Open the files you want to combine (door-2.au and walk.wav), as shown in Figure 8.9.

3. Edit the files, one at a time, starting with door-2.au, since it will be played first in the finished effect. Play the file several times, looking for a logical starting and ending point that you can trim to. A good place to trim door-2.au is between the 0.05-second mark and the 0.95-second mark. Left-click at 0.05 to trim everything before it and right-click at 0.95 to trim everything after it, as shown in Figure 8.10. Click the Trim button.

4. Minimize door-2.au and bring up stairs.wav for editing. The sixth step doesn't sound quite right. You only need seven steps anyway,

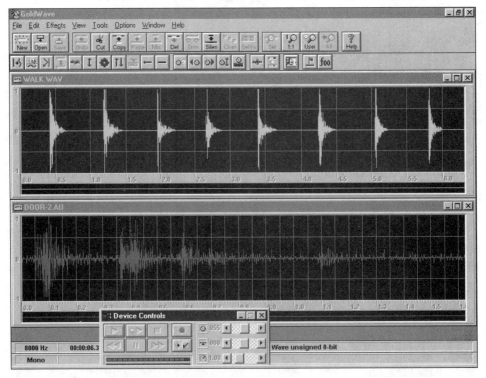

Figure 8.9   Here are the two files that you want to use for the sound effect.

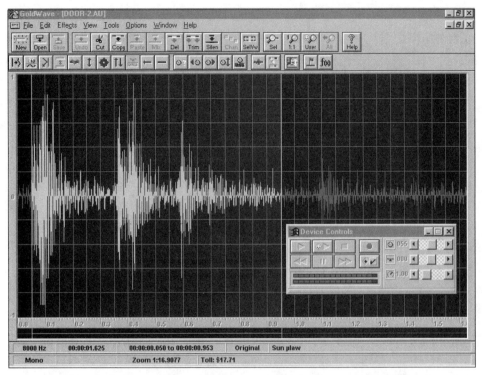

Figure 8.10 Only the area between 0.05 seconds and 0.95 seconds is selected.

not eight, so left-click at the 4.0-second mark, right-click at the 5.0-second mark, and click the Delete button to remove the step, as shown in Figure 8.11. (Note that pressing the Delete key on your keyboard won't work here.)

5. Click the Copy button or Edit|Copy to put the whole stairs.wav file in the clipboard. Bring up door-2.au, and select Edit| Paste at|Finish Marker to put the two files together.

6. To get the impression that you're standing in the basement and hearing someone else come downstairs, the sound should get progressively louder. With the entire file selected (blue), click the Fades In button or Effects|Volume|Fade In to bring up the Fade In dialog box. Set 25% as the initial volume, as shown in Figure 8.12.

7. Most of the background noise in the file was removed by the last step. Noise shows up onscreen as tiny squiggles in the areas that should be just flat lines. You can fix any remaining noise by click-

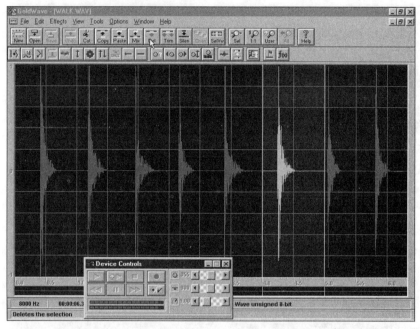

Figure 8.11   As soon as you click the Delete button, the selected area will be removed from the clip.

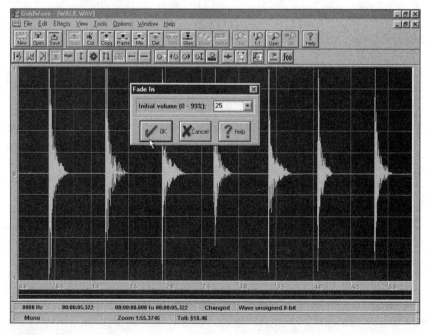

Figure 8.12   With this setting, the sound will start at 25% of full volume and gradually fade in.

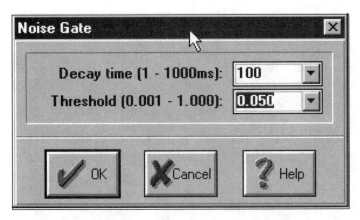

Figure 8.13   The Noise Gate settings to use depend on the particular sound you're editing, but these settings are a good starting point.

ing the Noise button to bring up the Noise Gate dialog box. Experiment with various settings; the ones in Figure 8.13 are a good place to start. Realistically, though, the audio quality you'll be able to deliver over the Net is not great for most formats, so you don't have to worry too much about eliminating every little pop and hiss (sometimes called *artifacts*).

8. Trim the silent area at the end of the file, from about the 6.0-second mark. Because sound files are so large, it's important to trim every unneeded bit.

9. Save the file in Sun (AU) format, m-law, mono, as dstairs.au. The finished file is shown in Figure 8.14.

Why AU format? Well, if you expect your site to be visited mostly by PC users, you could choose WAV instead. Similarly, if you expect mostly Mac users, you could use AIFF. The file sizes will be about the same, in any case. The AU format is used for this example because it's very common on the Net, and specifically because the Netscape Player that's included with Netscape comes preconfigured to handle this format on all major computer platforms.

Once you have your sound, use HTML 3.0's <META> tag to have it automatically play on a page. For example, consider this HTML excerpt from the home page shown in Figure 8.8:

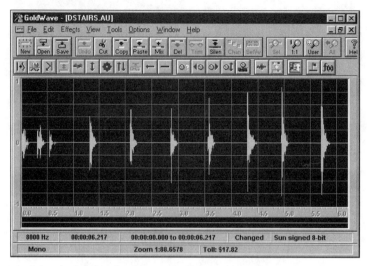

Figure 8.14 Here's the finished sound effect in AU format.

```
<HTML>
<HEAD>
<TITLE>What're you doing down here?</TITLE>
<META HTTP-EQUIV="refresh" CONTENT="5; URL=dstairs.au">
</HEAD>
<BODY BGCOLOR="#EFEFEF" LINK="808000" VLINK="#797979" ALINK="#COCOCO"
background="grwall1.gif">
<CENTER><IMG  SRC="baselogo.gif" width=600 height=250></CENTER>
<BASEFONT SIZE=5>
<P>Well, this place is a mess, as usual.</P>
</CENTER>
</BODY>
</HTML>
```

Five seconds after this page is loaded, the <META> tag will cause the browser to request the dstairs.au file from the server. The dstairs.au file will automatically be loaded and, assuming the browser has a helper application configured to handle AU files, the visitor will hear a door open and someone walk down a flight of stairs. This sort of technique, where the browser (the client) tells the server to send some sound, animation, or similar item, is called *client pull.*

Look carefully at the format of the <META> tag in the sample code, because it must be set up just like you see it here, with the quotation marks and semicolon in the right places. Also, it must be placed before the </HEAD> tag. (Actually, both Netscape and Internet Explorer would still interpret this particular use of the <META> tag correctly if it were in the body of the HTML file, but that's not proper use and could cause problems in other instances of <META>.) The <META> tag, like most HTML tags, is not case-sensitive, so the line of HTML could have been in lowercase instead of uppercase.

It's important with this trick to not use too large a number for the delay time in the "CONTENT=" attribute. Otherwise, the visitor will have gone on to other things before the sound file plays—and the sound file *will* play after the required delay, even if some other page is onscreen at the time.

In fact, if this were a page at a real Web site, it would probably be a good idea to add some more text to keep visitors with faster connections busy while the <META> tag was counting down the seconds until the sound loads. Figuring out how much time to allow in the CONTENT attribute is mostly a matter of trial and error, but since the sound won't play in Netscape 2.0 until after all the inline elements of the page are loaded, a fairly short delay is best.

VARYING THE STEPS

It would be nice to have a different home page for visitors who don't want to hear the sounds or don't have the software or hardware to handle them. The <META> tag can help here, too, by enabling you to create a "front door" to your site, as shown in Figure 8.15. Here's the HTML for it:

```
<HTML>
<HEAD>
<TITLE>Check out the basement</TITLE>
<META HTTP-EQUIV="refresh" CONTENT="15; URL=basement.htm">
</HEAD>
<BODY BGCOLOR="#EFEFEF" LINK="808000" VLINK="#797979" ALINK="#COCOCO"
background="grwall1.gif">
<H2>
A page with AU (Sun) sounds will appear in a few seconds. If you don't _
   have an AU player or don't want to hear the sounds, you should go to <A
HREF="nsbasemt.htm">the quiet basement</A> now.
</H2>
</BODY>
</HTML>
```

You can use a similar trick with the <META> tag to do a "live feed." Hook up a tape recorder, video camera and video capture card, or digital camera such as QuickCam so that it's constantly feeding data into your Web server. Actually, that's the hardest part of this trick, but there are just too many hardware and software variables to address in detail here. If you're using

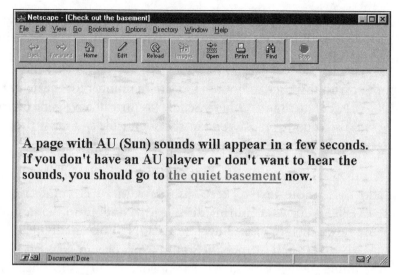

Figure 8.15 Use this kind of "front door" to present alternative paths through your site, in this case for visitors to either get a page with sound clips or one without.

QuickCam, use the instructions that come with it. If you're using an audio or video recorder, plug a feed from its LINE OUT jack to your sound card's LINE IN jack, get yourself some supporting software if it didn't come with your digitizing card, and test it out.

The feed should be sending output to a particular file. Put a link to that file on a page of HTML, using a line like this:

```
<IMG SRC="../video/highway.mp2">
```

or this:

```
<A HREF="../audio/baby.wav">Hear what she's doing now.</A>
```

Then, at the top of the page, add a tag like this:

```
<META HTTP-EQUIV="refresh" CONTENT="60">
```

Every minute, the page will be reloaded with whatever is in the audio or video file at the time.

Preparing an Audio Clip for Streaming Audio

Suppose that you want to put some bird calls on your Web page. The first one is of a kookaburra, kookaburra.au on the CD-ROM (from the Australian National Botanic Gardens Web site, http://155.187.10.12/anbg/). It was sampled at 8 kHz, mono and is about a minute long, with a file size of 478 KB. It could take a visitor to your site who has a 14.4 modem up to eight minutes to download this clip! To fix this problem, you decide to use a streaming format—RealAudio, in this case.

The first thing to do is install the RealAudio server or find someone who'll let you use theirs. Although it is possible to install the personal edition of the server on a computer that has only a dial-up connection to the Web, realistically, you'll need to have the RealAudio server running on a dedicated Internet computer (one that's always online). Otherwise, visitors will only be able to hear your clips when you happen to be online. Detailed instructions for installation are included with the server software and at http://www.realaudio.com/. There are different instructions for different Web servers, so rather than repeat them all here, I will assume for this example that you have access, one way or another, to a RealAudio server.

Once the server issue is resolved, preparing a clip for any streaming format involves these basic steps:

1. If this is a new clip, sample it at "radio quality," which is generally considered to be 22 kHz, 16-bit mono. The kookaburra.au clip is far below this quality, but since it's just sound rather than music or speech, it will still be okay.

2. Edit the sound to get the best quality, using your recording hardware, sound-editing software, or both. Progressive Networks, the maker of RealAudio, recommends boosting midrange frequencies, minimizing noise (*noise gating*) and normalizing the volume to 95 percent of maximum.

3. Save the sound in WAV or AU format.

4. Compress the file into the streaming format using a proprietary encoder. RealAudio's encoder, shown in Figure 8.16, produces a sound file with an .RA extension. This file is only 60 KB, as opposed to the original's 478 KB.

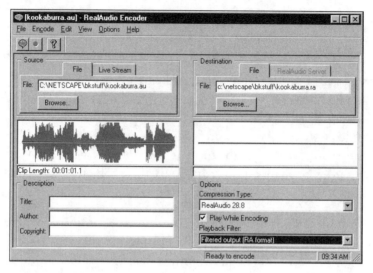

Figure 8.16   RealAudio's Encoder is set up to encode the file kookaburra.au in 14.4 format, playing the results as it goes.

5. Create the text file (metafile) that will serve as the "style sheet" for the sound, using the instructions for the particular streaming audio format you have. Each audio file you compress will need one. If you wanted to use the RealAudio file kookaburra.ra at your site at http://www.my.isp.com/~me, you would type in a line like this in your favorite word processor:

```
pnm://www.my.isp.com/~ me/kookaburra.ra.
```

6. Save the metafile with the appropriate extension for the sound format. In the case of the RealAudio file, you could use kookaburra.ram.

7. Add a link to the metafile on your HTML page, like this:

```
<A HREF="http://www.my.isp.com/~me/kookaburra.ram">A RealAudio
clip from down under</A>
```

8. Upload the HTML page and metafile as ASCII files to your server.

9. Upload the sound file as a binary file.

10. Test the results.

Varying the Steps

One of the really cool features of RealAudio 2.0 is its ability to synchronize Web pages with sound, creating a "filmstrip" or "slideshow" effect where you are automatically walked through a site in time to the audio. The Interactive History of the Wienermobile site at http://www.oscar-mayer.com/wienermobile/history.html uses this feature.

To synchronize a sound file with Web pages, you build what Progressive Networks calls an *event file*. It's basically a text file of timing cues and the URLs to go with them, which is compiled by RealAudio's special *cevents* utility. The resulting file is uploaded along with the RealAudio file. You can get complete, up-to-date instructions for this bit of Web wizardry from http://www.realaudio.com.

Web Wizard's Touchstones for Sounds

Do include links to the players your visitors will need to hear your audio files.

Don't limit yourself to one audio format only. Each format has its own strengths and weaknesses; use whatever is most appropriate for the particular sound file.

Do get to know what the MPEG standard is all about, advises Joe Maissel, especially if you want to put music on your site. Good places to start are with the list of MPEG links at http://www.yahoo.com/Computers_and_Internet/Multimedia/Video/MPEG/Technical_Information/ and the MPEG FAQ at http://www.crs4.it/HTML/LUIGI/MPEG/mpegfaq.html.

Don't save audio files at a higher sound quality than absolutely necessary, even when you initially record them at a high quality. Most Web surfers would rather have your message or sound effect play fast than crystal-clear.

Do consider providing the same audio clip in two or three different formats, such as RealAudio for immediate play and MPEG for high sound quality offline.

Don't hesitate to experiment with recording your own audio effects. Simple, everyday sounds like doors closing, water dripping, and dogs barking can make great effects, and there's no question that you own the rights.

Do trim your sound files as tightly as possible. Every fraction of a second counts toward reducing the final file size.

Don't ignore copyright and usage restrictions when you use sound and music files with content in them that you didn't create.

Do let visitors to your site know, through icons or text, which links are sound files, as well as the format, file size, and possibly the sampling rate of each sound.

IX

ELECTRIFYING SHOCKWAVE

Shockwave lets Web wizards add high-quality animation and interactivity to their Web sites without a lot of server overhead or exotic programming. Unlike all the other elements of Web wizardry discussed in this book, Shockwave is proprietary technology, owned by the Macromedia software company. It's a way to distribute, over the Web, animations produced with Macromedia's very successful Director authoring software, shown in Figure 9.1. You must have Director to create a Shockwave movie; no other program will do. And the Director package isn't cheap; the current street price is about $850.

So what's the big deal about Shockwave? For several years, Director has been the product of choice for professional multimedia developers working on corporate presentations, computer games like Myst and Iron Helix, and special effects for the movies and television. There's a large installed base of developers, therefore, who are already very comfortable with Director and have large libraries of Director material. These people can use Shockwave to put animation and

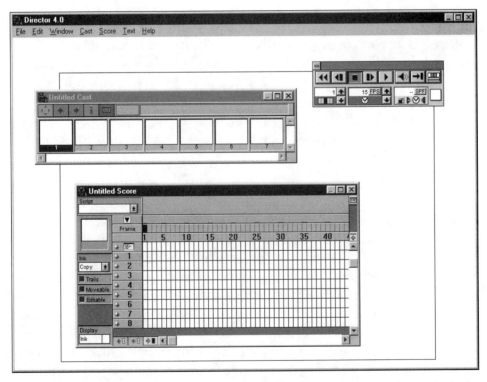

Figure 9.1 This is the opening screen of Macromedia Director 4.0. It might look strange at first, but it soon becomes familiar.

interactivity on the Web with a minimum of time and effort. And for newcomers, Director's flexibility and relatively gentle learning curve can offset its fairly steep price.

Usually, Director *movies*, as the finished multimedia files are called, are combined with a special runtime version of Director to produce a *projector* that runs the files on the user's machine regardless of whether he or she has Director installed. This process is completely transparent to the user. A Shockwave movie starts out as a Director movie, but it is then compiled by a special, free Macromedia program called *AfterBurner* to produce a compressed file that can run over the Web. To keep file sizes as small as possible, there's no runtime version of the Director software in a Shockwave file. A user, therefore, has to have the free Shockwave plug-in downloaded (from http://www.macromedia.com/) and installed in order to play a Shockwave movie. Right now, that plug-in is only available for Netscape.

The Wizards Speak: Shockwave and/or Java?

When writing about or discussing the relative merits of Shockwave, the unstated assumption is *...compared to Java programming*, as in "Shockwave animations are easy to make" compared to Java programming, or "Shockwave's entrance price for home users is pretty high" compared to Java programming. But does this comparison really make any sense, or is it the proverbial comparison of apples to oranges?

Any Web wizards you're likely to talk to on this subject, whether they are Shockwave developers or Java programmers, will tell you that Shockwave and Java are two different technologies, each with its own strengths and weaknesses. The obvious difference is that Java is a full-fledged language, while Shockwave's Director is an application that includes some language elements. As Mark Holt of Sun Microsystems (the creators of Java) puts it, "You could *write* Shockwave in Java." On the other hand, Web wizard and computer designer Larry Rosenthal, who used Director to make the Shockwave animations at his ThunkWorld site (http://www.thunk.com/, shown in Figure 9.2), says, "Lingo [the scripting language in Director] is more for animation and creative stuff. There's a huge group of people who already understand Director and don't have the time or interest in learning something else."

Figure 9.2   The animations at this site were created in Director and converted to Shockwave.

Despite the apparent differences, there does seem to be some convergence of the two technologies. You can, for example, do some C++ programming in the latest version of Director. At the same time, freeware Java applets let nonprogrammers put simple animations on their Web pages that would be indistinguishable from small Shockwave movies to an end-user. (For more on these applets, see Chapter 10.)

In real life, the Shockwave versus Java debate comes down to a matter of preference and suitability, just like any other computer product. For example, if you know you'll need Java to support the underlying math at an engineering site, it makes sense to use Java to make the models move, too. On the other hand, if you want to put the next Donkey Kong on the Web without a lot of programming, Shockwave is a better way to go. It might remind you of the great Mac versus PC debates that have raged for years on a much larger scale. (Macromedia started out on the Mac, and its origins are pretty evident, even in the Windows version.) In the end, people with creative and artistic backgrounds will probably tend to side with Shockwave/Director, while people with business and analytical backgrounds will probably prefer Java in its various varieties—and both sides will be convinced that the other would switch if only they *really* understood the situation.

The Wizards Speak: Shocking Secrets Revealed

The Pop Rockets site at http://www.poprockets.com/shockwave/ (Figure 9.3) supports the company's Total Distortion game, which is a commercial CD-ROM. Since Total Distortion was itself created with Macromedia Director, it was relatively easy for the folks at Pop Rockets to translate elements of it into interactive Shockwave movies for the Web. Kevin Krejci of Pop Rockets says, "To do the whole Web site, it took one person less than a year, working on it part-

Figure 9.3 The welcome page at Pop Rockets includes JavaScript and animated GIFs, as well as Shockwave.

time," to create all of the elements in-house, including the graphics and sound effects.

"Some of the Shockwave games took less than a week to complete," Krejci continues, "And now we have 'engines' for things like the slider puzzle, so we can use other artwork" to quickly create new Shockwave games for the site.

The arcade-style Shockwave games at Pop Rockets, such as Fat! ShooterMan!, shown in Figure 9.4a, and Lock (my personal favorite, shown in Figure 9.4b) are every bit as fun to play as their CD-ROM equivalents. More important—especially for arcade-type games—they're just as fast to play, since the whole game is downloaded and run on the user's computer. Keeping that downloading as short as possible is a major concern of Web wizards who work with Shockwave because Director file sizes can get very big very quickly. AfterBurner does a good job of reducing the file sizes of finished Shockwave movies, but files upwards of 300 KB are still not at all unusual. Krejci says the maximum file limit for a download at the Pop Rockets site is 2 MB, but they try hard to stay under 1 MB—that's still pretty big for today's bandwidths.

To keep animation fast and file sizes down, Krejci suggests these tricks:

- "Use the In-Between commands [Score|In-Between Linear and Score|In-Between Special] for things like someone walking across the screen. That way, you just put an object in one frame and another version of it at the end, and the command traces the path for it to go."

- "Make any animation that's going to repeat into a separate cast member. You might have a face where only the eyes move. Make one cast member for the face, and another for the eyes." That way, the entire face isn't being redrawn in every frame of the animation.

- "To keep graphics [files] small, use 1-bit or 2-bit graphics and assign specific colors from the 256-color palette." You can do this by using Cast|Transform Bitmap and then changing the foreground and background colors in the Tools window. For example, transforming a logo that's red and blue into a 1-bit

(a)

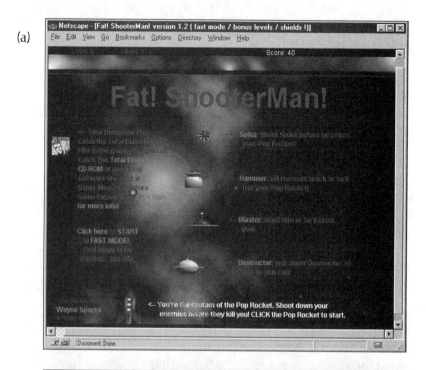

(b)

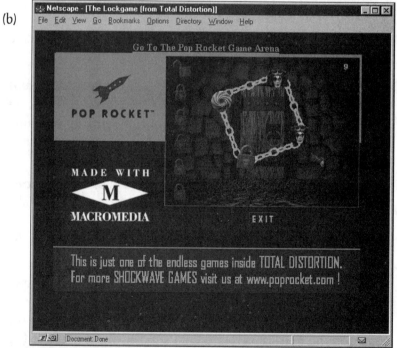

Figure 9.4   These Shockwave movies, Fat! ShooterMan! (a) and Lock (b), play like arcade games. They're fast, loud, colorful, and addictive.

graphic would reduce its file size to about one-quarter of the identical red-and-blue logo saved in 4-bit format.

- "Mix sound effects down to 11 kHz 8-bit mono. Also, cut down on random sounds and have sound loops." By using sound loops strategically, you can provide continuous background music with relatively small file overhead.

- "Every machine runs differently, so you might want different speed modes to adjust [a game's] timing." You could do this by having links on your Web page to identical versions of the game saved in Director at different frames-per-second rates.

- "Use tiles to create a background, with different colors for different levels [of a game]." Tiles in Director work like the tiles you put on a Web page with <BODY BACKGROUND>, except that in Director you can use rectangular tiles in addition to the usual square ones. Tiles are accessed from the Paint|Tiles selection of Director's Paint window.

Web wizard Larry Rosenthal echoes several of these tips, and adds a few more:

- "Segment a large Director movie into small pieces," and then make each piece a separate Shockwave movie.

- "Remember, small is better. Try to make your movie fit in the standard hypercard size of 352 by 240 pixels." The absolute maximum stage size for a Shockwave movie should be 640 by 480 pixels.

- "Quitting a movie becomes an issue [in Shockwave] because the last frame just sits on the screen. Also, the first and last frame of your movie becomes more important for the same reason." This is unlike a Director movie, where the movie ends and the whole window disappears when the user clicks a Quit button that has a small Lingo script attached to it, like this:

```
on mouseUp
  quit
end
```

To let the user stop a Shockwave movie by pressing a Quit button, you'll need a script like this, where "last frame" is a marker for a frame that you want to stay on the screen:

```
on mouseUp
  go to frame "last frame"
end
```

If it's absolutely necessary that the movie not stay on the screen after the user quits, you can send control to a different Web page when the user presses the Quit button with the special *go to NetPage "url"* command:

```
on mouseUp
  go to NetPage "http://www.anywhere.com/newpage.html"
end
```

To attach a script to a cast member, click the Script button in the Cast window, which brings up the Script dialog box with the *on mouseUp* and *end* lines already typed in. Then, just type in the details, close the dialog box, and the script is ready to use.

Your First Shockwave Movie

To add any Shockwave movie to a Web page, follow these three basic steps:

1. Create a Director movie, keeping in mind the Web wizards' tips and the importance of keeping file sizes down.
2. Run AfterBurner on the Director movie to turn it into a Shockwave movie.
3. Use the special <EMBED SRC> HTML tag to put the Shockwave movie on the Web page.

The <EMBED SRC> tag takes WIDTH and HEIGHT attributes that set the size of the movie in pixels, as well as optional ALIGN, PALETTE, and TEXTFOCUS attributes. The WIDTH and HEIGHT attributes are **mandatory** and must match the size of the stage that you set in Director. Otherwise, the movie might crash your browser.

The optional PALETTE attribute can be set to either *PALETTE=foreground* or *PALETTE=background* (the default). If you set it to foreground, the entire page uses the palette from the Director movie, instead of having the movie use the system palette. You might want to do this if you've created a custom palette for the movie, although it might cause a temporary color shift in the browser. The optional TEXTFOCUS attribute can be set to *TEXTFOCUS=never*, *TEXTFOCUS=onStart*, or *TEXTFOCUS=onClick* to indicate when the movie should start responding to input from the user. The ALIGN attribute works like it does for the <IMG SRC> tag.

Some people might already have lots of Director movies lying around, waiting to be shocked, so they can skip the first step. If you aren't one of these people, you'll need to learn how to use Director to make the movies you want to put on your Web pages. While teaching the fine art of creating full-scale Director movies is way beyond the scope of this chapter, I do want to give you a taste of how Director works. A good place to start is with Director's Auto Animate feature, which works kind of like a template: you pick from a limited number of animation options, fill in the details of the particular text or graphic you want to animate, and Director does the rest.

 Director 4.0 for Windows needs to run in 256-color mode. Many of its options, especially in the Paint window, will simply be unavailable if your monitor is set to display thousands or millions of colors. If you have an SVGA monitor, it's probably set to show more than 256 colors, so you'll have to change it before you run Director if you want all of Director's options to be available.

 Here's how you could use Director's Auto Animate feature, together with a sound file, to produce a simple animated Shockwave graph of a company's yearly sales:

1. Select File|Preferences to bring up the Preferences dialog box. Set it up as shown in Figure 9.5 with a custom stage of 352 by 240 pixels, centered on the screen. The *stage* sets the width and height of the finished movie.

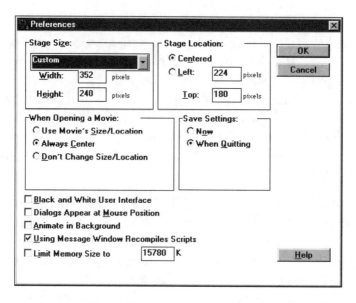

Figure 9.5   These settings will produce an animation 352 pixels wide and 240 pixels square, centered on the screen.

2.   Select Score|Auto Animate. There are lots of easy-to-use choices you could pick from here to do basic animation, but for this example, choose Bar Chart. Fill in the details of the dialog box that appears as shown in Figure 9.6.

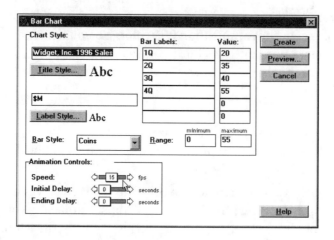

Figure 9.6   The year's sales will be graphed according to the settings in this dialog box, using animations of stacked coins, animated at a rate of 15 frames per second.

3. Click Create to complete the animation and close the dialog box. The stage is still empty, but that's just because you haven't played the animation yet. You'll see lots of new entries in the Score and Cast windows. You might want to move those windows for the next step so they aren't covering the stage, as shown in Figure 9.7.

4. Play the animation you've just created by clicking the Control Panel's Play button, as shown in Figure 9.8.

5. The Auto Animate feature has added several cast members to the score for you, but you're going to add one more yourself, to play a sound file as the animation builds. Choose File|Import, select applaud.wav (an 11 kHz, 8-bit mono sound effect) from the appropriate directory, and click OK. Scroll through the Cast window to find applaud.wav; it should be cast member 10.

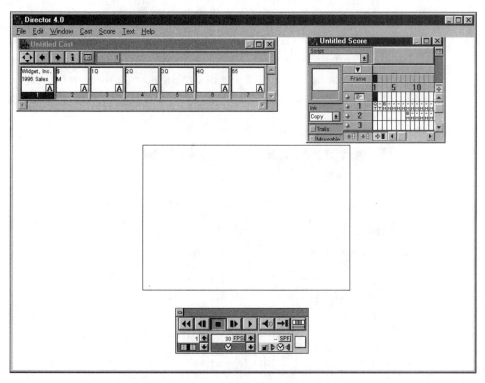

Figure 9.7 Before playing an animation, move the Score and Cast windows out of the way.

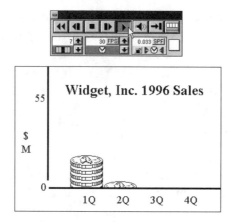

Figure 9.8 When you press the Play button, the animation runs from beginning to end.

6. Put the Score window back onscreen with Window|Score and scroll up through it until you see two "speaker" symbols—that's where sound effects go.

7. Drag applaud.wav from its place in the Cast window to the first little block next to either one of the speakers, and drop it there, as shown in Figure 9.9. This puts the sound effect in the first frame of the animation.

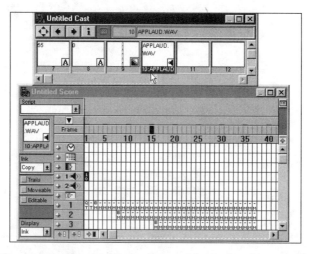

Figure 9.9 The sound effect has been dragged from the Cast window to the first frame of the first sound in the Score window.

8. Now you need to get the sound to play throughout all the frames of animation. In the row of the Score window where you dropped the sound, Shift-click on the frame (cell) in the last column that has anything in it, which should be about frame 70. Since you Shift-clicked, all of the frames in between should be selected; if not, go back and Shift-click the first frame in the sound row.

9. Select Score|In Between Linear to have the sound play from the first frame you selected to the last. If your speakers are turned on and Edit|Disable Sounds is turned off in Director, you should hear the sound of clapping.

10. From the Control Panel, click the Rewind button, then click the Play button to see and hear the mini-animation. You might want to make some changes here, such as copying the last column of sounds and images to another 15 or 20 frames so the clapping seems to continue after the charting is done.

11. When you're ready, choose File|Save As, name the file (I used *widgsale*), and click OK.

12. Close Director and start up AfterBurner. You should see what looks like a normal Open dialog box, as shown in Figure 9.10.

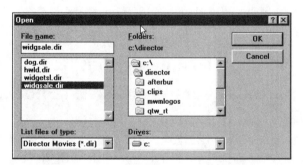

Figure 9.10   Select the Director file that you want "shocked" in AfterBurner's Open dialog box.

13. Select the file you want to turn into a Shockwave movie and click OK.

14. A Save As dialog box appears. Just click OK here and, after a few seconds, AfterBurner will end and your movie will be finished.

It's usually easiest to keep the same name for both the Shockwave and Director versions of a movie. The Director version will have a .DIR extension and the Shockwave version will have a .DCR extension.

15. Start up your favorite HTML editor and create a small file to test out your movie, like this:

```
<HTML>
<HEAD><TITLE>How Shocking Can I Get?</TITLE></HEAD>
<BODY BGCOLOR="white">
<CENTER>
<H1>My First Try at Shockwave</H1>
An animated bar chart with appropriate sound effects should play
here:
<BR><BR>
<EMBED SRC="widgsale.dcr" WIDTH=352 HEIGHT=240>
<NOEMBED>Sorry, you need the Shockwave plug-in to see this chart.
</NOEMBED>
</CENTER>
</BODY>
</HTML>
```

When you test the Web page out in Netscape, you should see something like Figure 9.11. This is a very simple example, but it should give you some idea of how easy and powerful Shockwave is. Note that the finished Shockwave file is only 24 KB, about the same size as a typical static GIF of similar width and height.

"Why Didn't I Think of That?": Supporting Users Who Aren't Shocked

To add support for visitors to your site who don't have the Shockwave plug-in, you can add the <NOEMBED>..</NOEMBED> tag pair. Anything within these two tags will be ignored by browsers that can handle a Shockwave movie, so any messages and/or graphics you put here will only be seen by non-Shockwave-enabled browsers.

Although the <NOEMBED>..</NOEMBED> tag pair lets you add information for visitors who don't have Shockwave, they'll still see a broken link where the Shockwave movie should be. To prevent this,

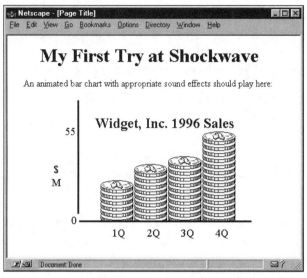

Figure 9.11   An animated bar chart like this makes a nifty little attention-getter with a minimum of effort.

Macromedia has come up with a clever little trick that involves JavaScript (see Chapter 10). Since the same browsers that support JavaScript also support the Shockwave plug-in, you can hide a call to a Shockwave movie in a line of JavaScript code, like this:

```
<SCRIPT>
    <!— Hide from non-JavaScript and non-Shockwave browsers.
      document.write('<EMBED SRC="widgsale.dcr" WIDTH=352
HEIGHT=240'>
    // Done hiding -->
</SCRIPT>
<NOEMBED><IMG SRC="altimage.gif" WIDTH=250 HEIGHT=190></NOEMBED>
```

Browsers that can't handle JavaScript will just ignore what they see as a comment and go on to the stuff after <NOEMBED>, while browsers that can handle JavaScript and Shockwave will ignore the stuff in <NOEMBED>..</NOEMBED> and write the Shockwave movie to the screen. The assumption here is that browsers that can handle JavaScript also have the Shockwave plug-in installed, so they'll load the movie. This is not necessarily the case; it's quite possible to have a JavaScript-enabled browser that doesn't have Shockwave, in which case a visitor would still see a broken link. This trick does solve the problem for most of your visitors, though.

An Interactive Shockwave Game

For a more fully-developed Director movie to shock than the simple animated chart in the previous section, try the interactive Miaws game from Web wizard David Yang of QuantumWave Interactive (http://www.magic.ca/~qwi/). It is on the CD-ROM in .DIR and .EXE form, together with readme files in .TXT and .DOC formats, as miaws.zip (or miaws.sit for Mac users). The opening screen from the game is shown in Figure 9.12.

Yang has included detailed information on how he created the game and the associated Lingo scripts in the readme files. One particularly interesting thing to note is that the entire game takes only 33 cast members (including sounds and Lingo scripts) and 13 frames.

Figure 9.12 This interactive Shockwave game is a good example of how relatively simple Shockwave movies can add value to a site.

If you plan to create interactive Shockwave movies, Miaws.dir is a good file to study, especially its Lingo scripts. Just unzip it and open it in Director. If you want to see how it plays, you can run the stand-alone .EXE file or compile the .DIR yourself into a Shockwave file, even if you don't have Director. First, make sure you have AfterBurner installed (if not, download it from http://www.macromedia.com/Tools/Shockwave/Director/aftrbrnr.html). Then, follow these steps:

1. If you have Director, open the movie and select File|Preferences so you can find out the width and height of the movie's stage size. You'll need these numbers later in the <EMBED SRC> tag. Close Director without saving any changes to the file. (If you don't have Director, the width is 512 and the height is 342.)

2. Run AfterBurner. In the Open dialog box, select the file and click OK.

3. In the Save As dialog box, select the name and location for the Shockwave version of the movie. Click OK to "burn" the movie.

4. Make up a quick test page of HTML, like this:

```
<HTML>
<HEAD><TITLE>A Shockwave Animation from QuantumWave</TITLE></HEAD>
<BODY BGCOLOR="white">
<CENTER>
<H1>Send the cute little miaws back home!</H1>
<BR><BR>
<EMBED SRC="miaws.dcr" WIDTH=512 HEIGHT=342>
</CENTER>
</BODY>
</HTML>
```

Unlike other elements of a Web page, a Shockwave movie is not automatically repositioned when the browser window is resized. If you resize your window several times—say, to test the page at different screen widths—the movie will seem to creep sideways off the screen. To solve this problem, just click the Reload button and the Shockwave movie will be repositioned correctly for the new window size.

Some New Toys to Play With

If you've got some time to goof around on the Web because, say, you're surfing from work, there are all kinds of fun Shockwave games and toys you can play with online. Some of them can also be downloaded to play offline. And really, it's not playing, it's...um, *research*. Yeah, research. You need inspiration for your own Shockwave Web wizardry, right?

Here are a few sources of inspiration to check out, in addition to the QuantumWave and Pop Rockets sites—just be sure to turn down the speakers on your computer first, or you might have to explain to your boss why the sounds of exploding bombs, zooming rockets, heavy-metal music, and screams are coming from your office:

  The movies at M-Squared Productions (http://www.m-squared.com), such as Stranded, shown in Figure 9.13.

Figure 9.13 In this Shockwave movie, the sea creatures move in time to an island-music soundtrack. The movie was designed by Mark Donnelly and programmed by Mark Chipman. Donnelly estimates it took about 50 hours to complete.

- Gary Rosenzweig's Shockwave Arcade at http://www2.csn.net/~rosenz/ shock.html for an assortment of games, toys, and educational movies.

- AfterShock's Arcade Alley at http://www.ashock.com/html/ arcadealley.html for nostalgia-inducing Shockwave versions of arcade games from the early 1980s.

- Headbone Interactive's Velma Apparelizer at http://www.headbone. com/ text/dressvelshock.html—ColorForms with an attitude, as you can see in Figure 9.14.

Figure 9.14   You can dress Velma from the many wardrobe items that show up in her closet. This would be one of the easier types of Shockwave games to implement, since the user is basically just dragging items back and forth across the screen.

Web Wizard's Touchstones for Shockwave

Do   make sure the first and last frames of a Shockwave movie look presentable, since they'll stay onscreen when the movie isn't playing.

Don't   use Lingo's quit command to try to shut down a movie. The *quit* command is disabled by Shockwave, as are the *open* and *saveMovie* commands, along with a few others others. For the complete list of changes to Lingo for Shockwave, see http://www.macromedia.com/Tools/Shockwave/Director/create.html.

Do   set your monitor to display just 256 colors before you run Director 4.0.

Don't   forget to change the display back from 256 colors when you're finished with Director. Otherwise, other things on your screen, including Web pages, might look odd.

Do   keep the file size of the Shockwave movie down as much as possible, by using tricks like sound loops, reduced bit depths for graphics, and the In Between command.

Don't   omit or use incorrect WIDTH and HEIGHT attributes for the <EMBED SRC> tag. These attributes must match the size of the stage you used to create the movie.

Do   use the <NOEMBED>..</NOEMBED> tags to add text or graphics for the benefit of users who don't have the Shockwave plug-in.

JAVA: HOT, FRESH, AND STRONG

Java has all the ingredients of a major Web success. Everything that anyone needs to be able to use it is free and readily available, it's got the backing of most of the major Web players, it can be used to varying extents by anyone from HTML novices to professional programmers, and (perhaps most important) it's got a catchy name that lends itself to clever headlines. Its only real drawback is the one shared by almost every other high-end Web technology: it is not supported by all computer platforms or all Web browsers. In Java's case, its inability to run under Windows 3.x can be a fairly serious shortcoming depending on your hardware requirements, although a port to a Windows 3.x version is supposed to be in the works and might even be available by the time you read this.

Despite its lack of support for Windows 3.x—or, more correctly, Windows 3.x's lack of support for *it*, since 3.x is missing true multitasking and multithreading—Java promises great things for Web wizards. Even if you don't have any programming experience, you can use elements of Java to add animation and interactivity to your Web pages, as you'll see in this chapter.

First, a few general definitions:

- *Java* is a full-fledged programming language, created by James Gosling at Sun Microsystems and first released to the Web-surfing public in January 1995. It is closely related to the C++ language. More loosely, the term *Java* is sometimes used to refer to any use of Java-related tags on a Web page, whether it's a single line of JavaScript, the parameters that run a Java applet, or a call to a full-fledged Java application.

- A *class* is a Java program that's been compiled and is ready to use. It is a file that has the .CLASS extension.

- The *JDK* is the *Java Developer's Kit*, a collection of utilities and classes for creating, debugging, compiling, and testing Java programs. If you plan on writing your own Java programs, you'll definitely need this. You can download it from http://java.sun.com/JDK-1.0/index.html. (Be patient, it's a pretty big download—over 4 MB.)

- *Compiling* means turning lines of Java code into a class that can, more or less, stand on its own. If you try to look at a compiled Java file in a text editor, you'll just see lines of gibberish. I say that compiled Java code can "more or less" stand on its own because you'll need either a Java-enabled Web browser (such as Netscape) or a special program such as the JDK's AppletViewer to run (*interpret*) the compiled code.

- A *script* or *source* refers to Java code that hasn't been compiled into a class.

If you delve into Java or JavaScript programming, you'll see lots of other special terms, especially *object, method,* and (in JavaScript) *property.* There are long, technical definitions of exactly what these things are, but here's how I think of them: An *object* is a Web element, such as the page in the browser or a separate window that can pop up. A *property* is a particular piece of information that a computer can store, such as today's date. A *method* is something you can do with or to an object, such as rounding a number or writing something on the page in the browser. The syntax is:

```
object.property
object.method(Depending on the method, these parentheses might be empty or
have stuff in them, such as a string to write)
```

Consider this line of JavaScript:

```
document.write("Last modified: ", document.lastModified);
```

It uses the *document* object twice, first with the *write* method and then with the *lastModified* property. If you put this line between the <SCRIPT>..</SCRIPT> tags, a JavaScript-enabled browser would write a message like this on the current Web page (which in JavaScript is referred to as the document):

```
Last modified: Mon May 13 13:46:54 1996
```

Methods and properties are case-sensitive, so be extra-careful how you type them. For example, document.lastmodified wouldn't do anything at all—not even produce an error message—while document.lastModified would give the last time the Web page was changed.

The Three Flavors of Java

In order to be able to understand and (more importantly) swipe from Java-related material on the Web, it's important to know how to use the three main varieties of Java, which I've already alluded to: Java applets, JavaScript, and Java itself. If they were really types of coffee, they'd be something like flavored instant coffee, regular drip, and espresso, respectively.

If you're a new or occasional coffee drinker, you probably prefer sweet, flavored coffee because it's not that different from cocoa, milkshakes, and other drinks that you're already used to. Similarly, Java applets are added to a Web page using HTML much like you're already used to. A Java applet is a program that has already been written by a Java expert for some fairly specific purpose, such as animating lines of text. Usually, freeware and shareware Java applets have already been compiled, too, making them ready to use right away (and hiding the source code from inquisitive eyes).

Java applets are lots of fun and easy to use. They provide a great way to add "extras"—things like sounds, animations, clocks, graphs, and simple calculators—to your Web pages. The trade-off for a particular Java applet's ease of use is that it's fairly limited. For example, you might not be able to find one that provides options to animate a billboard in exactly the way you want it animated. In such a case, your choices are either to change your expectations or move on to one of the more robust varieties of Java.

You can tell when any Java script is compiled because it ends with the .CLASS extension. If it isn't compiled, it ends in .JAVA instead. You can't use an applet on your Web pages until it's been compiled. You can compile it yourself using the javac program included in the JDK, by typing a line like this:

javac EverythingButTheKitchenSinkProgram.java

Assuming that there are no errors in the code, you should get the file EverythingButTheKitchenSinkProgram.class, ready to use at your site.

JavaScript is a step up from "canned" Java applets in both flexibility and difficulty. JavaScript is kind of like a macro language that's been incorporated into Netscape starting with version 2.0. Unlike a Java applet or a true Java script, the lines of a JavaScript program are actually included right in the HTML file itself instead of being kept in a separate file that's called from the HTML. Also, unlike Java itself, JavaScript is programmable in Windows 3.x. (I know it's confusing that a JavaScript script isn't the same as a Java script. A little later in this chapter, when you've seen them both in action, it should be clearer; just bear with me for now.)

It's certainly possible to use JavaScript to write applications, but JavaScript is more often used for simpler things like the famous (or infamous) scrolling text in the status bar. Since JavaScript is embedded in a Web page's HTML, anyone who visits the page can see the JavaScript code by choosing to view the source. If you don't want to make your code available to the whole Web-surfing world, therefore, you have to move up to Java itself (at least as of this writing).

Java is a full-fledged, object-oriented language based on C++ . If you already have some knowledge of C or C++, you probably won't have any problem picking up Java syntax. For example, Web wizard Morgen Sagen is a C++ programmer who started experimenting with Java one Friday and had written several clever applets by Monday, including those shown in Figure 10.1. You can see them in action at http://www.aimnet.com/~morgen/. On the other hand, if you

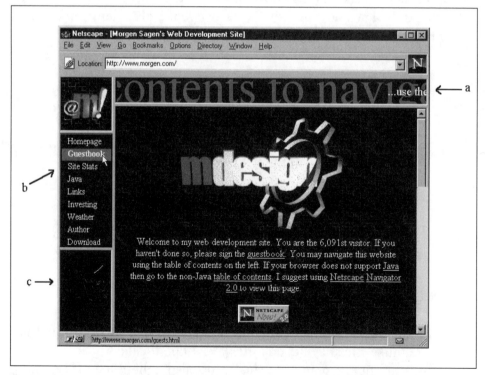

Figure 10.1 This page has three custom Java applets, each in its own frame: an animated "billboard" (a), a table of contents whose entries change color as the mouse passes over them (b), and a group of tiny, animated sprites (c). The Webmaster for this site wrote these applets from scratch in Java, but you can accomplish similar results using public-domain and shareware applets.

don't have much experience with a high-level computer language, writing Java will be a challenge, to put it rather mildly.

Although you'll get a taste of Java code here, actually teaching Java programming is way beyond the scope of this chapter. Instead, most of this chapter is devoted to Java applets and JavaScript. For most aspiring Web wizards, Java applets and small JavaScript routines give a better return on the investment of your time than full-blown Java programming.

If, after experimenting with Java applets and JavaScript, you decide that you want to take the plunge into Java programming itself, a good book to look for is *Java Programming Explorer* by Neil Bartlett, Alex Leslie, and Steve Simkin (Coriolis Group, 1996). It's down-to-earth, easy to read, and only as technical as absolutely necessary (and I'm not just saying that because it's published by the same company as this book). It's also very *big*, weighing in at over 800 pages.

The Wizards Speak: Java's Overflowing Options

Who better to talk about Java than members of the New Media Marketing lab, part of Sun Microsystems, the company where Java was "born"? These three Web wizards:

- Eric Harshbarger, Web specialist and Java programmer
- Mark Holt, the product development manager for New Media Marketing
- Mark Sacoolas, a member of New Media Marketing's technical staff

have developed some of the coolest freeware applets around for spicing up your Web pages, and made them available at the Café del Sol (http://www.xm.com/cafe/).

Harshbarger, in particular, has written several of the applets discussed in detail later in this chapter. His own favorite applet at the moment is Comix2.class (shown in Figure 10.2 and included on the CD-ROM) because, he says, "It's not too terribly difficult to use, but it's cute and flashy; I tried to make it as versatile and open-ended as possible. It lets people put images on a page and pass dialog to the images, which it draws as little cartoon bubbles. The bubbles can appear and disappear, so you can have a dynamic comic strip on a Web page."

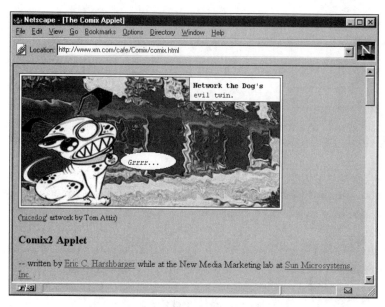

Figure 10.2 You could use this little Java applet purely for amusement or as an alternative to static text and graphics for conveying information.

Sacoolas's current favorite is a scrolling image map shown in Figure 10.3 (made up of ScrollMap.class, MyImage.class, and ImageLoader.class on the CD-ROM) where each part of the scrolling image can have a different target. This provides, he says, "a nonintrusive way to supply lots of URLs." Holt, on the other hand, tends to favor the game applets, such as a crossword-puzzle applet that members of New Media Marketing are currently working on. The applet works, he explains, by being "fed a solved file through the server. It runs through the Web page, so there's no need for the user to download anything."

Although Java applets can be lots of fun for Web developers, Harshbarger cautions, "a huge program with a big sound file takes too long to download when most people are still on 14.4 and 28.8 modems. Keep it small and simple; don't try to push the limit." Holt agrees, "Don't do it just for the sake of the technology. Only use [Java applets] when needed." A good rule of thumb is to try to keep the whole page, including any applets and their supporting files, down to 100 KB.

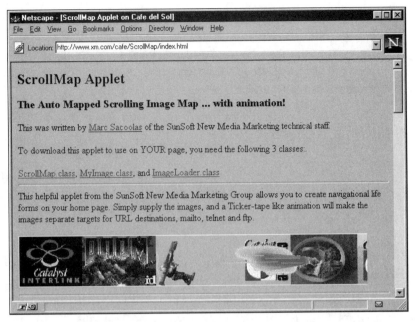

Figure 10.3 As the images scroll by, the user sees animation and hears sounds, such as the "Doom guy" shooting a bazooka (at least, I think that's what that big gun is). Messages in the status bar tell the user what a click at a particular place on the image would do.

As for the future of Java, Holt sees libraries of very generic Java applets being made available, either commercially or as freeware, as opposed to the specific, relatively small applets that are currently being written. "People don't want to write their own applets" for every specific situation, he says. "They want [Java libraries] to download and use at their Web pages much like CGI and Perl libraries."

Generally, though, all three of these Web wizards have moved beyond focusing on fairly simple Java applets to writing full-fledged Java applications. That, they claim, is the real power of Java. As Sacoolas explains, "It's not just an animation tool. You can make it do whatever your imagination can do. Java could be used to write Web browsers, paint programs—you could even write Shockwave in Java."

But why would you want to program in Java instead of an older language like C? According to Holt, "Portability is Java's trump card. With Java on the horizon, developers won't have to worry about recompiling for each platform, and users won't have to worry about making sure they download, say, the PC version of a program, not the Mac or Unix version. You only have to write an application once and release it through the Web, which will cut down on development costs dramatically at software companies."

For example, a Java-based streaming audio server was recently debuted at a trade show (for more on streaming audio, see Chapter 8). The user selects from a jukebox-like interface on a Web page and begins hearing his or her selection immediately, without any buffering (wait time) and without having to download, install, and configure a separate audio-player add-in to the Web browser.

There seems to be a minor bug in Netscape regarding the alignment of Java applets, according to Harshbarger. "The documentation says you can use any of the ALIGN attributes with an applet just like you can with an image," he says, "but in my experience, only TOP, CENTER, and BOTTOM work." Not a tremendously big deal, but a good thing to keep in mind as you're constructing your Web pages.

Java Applets So Good, Nobody Will Know They're Instant

One of the deep, dark secrets of Web wizards is that many of them don't write their own Java programs from scratch. Instead, they depend on the customizable freeware and shareware applets found at Web sites like these:

 The Café del Sol at http://www.xm.com/cafe/, a product of Sun Microsystem's New Media Marketing lab

 Gamelan at http://www.gamelan.com/

 The Java Boutique at http://weber.u.washington.edu/~jgurney/java/

 Sun Microsystem's "Cool Applets We've Written" at http://java.sun.com/applets/applets.html

 The Java Applet Rating Service (JARS) at http://www.jars/

These sites include Java applets for games, various kinds of animation, and utilities like specialized clocks, graphs, and calculators. Several of the best applets from these sources are included on the CD-ROM. To call one of them in an HTML file, the only new tags you need to add are the <APPLET>..</APPLET> pair and <PARAM>. Lines of <PARAM> statements are placed between <APPLET> and </APPLET> to supply the variables that make the applet do what you want it to. The most common attributes for <APPLET> and <PARAM> are given in Table 10.1.

The complexity of the <PARAM> lines is dictated by the type of Java applet and by the person who wrote it. Applets that provide lots of opportunities for customization typically also require lots of <PARAM> lines. Java applets usually come pre-compiled, so there are only two ways to know exactly how the <PARAM> lines for a particular applet should look: rely on the programmer's (hopefully detailed) instructions, or make educated guesses based on viewing the source of pages that use the applet.

THE INCREDIBLE TALKING BUTTON

Consider the button on the Web page in Figure 10.4. It was made with a nifty little Java applet for animating buttons called ButtonPLUS2.class (included on the CD-ROM), created by Web wizard Eric Harshbarger at Café del Sol. This highly adaptable Java applet can take up to 11 <PARAM> lines, depending on how many options you want to customize:

- <PARAM NAME=URL VALUE=*URL without http://*> to tell the browser where to go when the button is clicked
- <PARAM NAME=HIGHLIGHT VALUE=*number*> for the amount of beveling on the button
- <PARAM NAME=BGCOLOR VALUE=*RGB color value such as 0,0,0*> to specify the color of the button
- <PARAM NAME=TEXTCOLOR VALUE=*RGB color value such as 0,0,0*> to specify the color of the button's text
- <PARAM NAME=FONT VALUE=*font name*> for any special font to be used for the button's text

For This Tag:	This Attribute:	Does This:	Optional or Required?
\<APPLET\>	CODEBASE=	Provides the URL for the applet, if it's different from the HTML file	Optional
\<APPLET\>	CODE=	Holds the name of the applet itself	Required
\<APPLET\>	WIDTH=	Sizes a graphic applet in pixels	Required
\<APPLET\>	HEIGHT=	Sizes a graphic applet in pixels	Required
\<APPLET\>	ALIGN=	Aligns an applet using the TOP, CENTER, and BOTTOM values	Optional
\<APPLET\>	VSPACE=	Adds space above and below the applet, in pixels	Optional
\<APPLET\>	HSPACE=	Adds space before and after the applet, in pixels	Optional
\<PARAM\>	NAME=	Provides the name of the particular variable, as specified by the applet's author; sometimes case-sensitive	Required
\<PARAM\>	VALUE=	Gives the value for the variable in \<PARAM\>, such as text, a color, or a file	Depends on the variable

Table 10.1 There are two tags involved in putting a Java applet on your page, \<APPLET\> and \<PARAM\>. Each one can have several attributes.

- \<PARAM NAME=FONTSIZE VALUE=*number*\> for the font size of the button's text

- \<PARAM NAME=TEXT VALUE="*first message\second message\third message*"\> to hold the text displayed on the button when nothing's happening, when the mouse rolls over the button, and when the button is clicked

- \<PARAM NAME=SOUND VALUE="*first sound file\second sound file*"\> to hold the sound files (AU format, 8 kHz, m-law mono only) to be played when the mouse rolls over the button and when the button is clicked

@ <PARAM NAME=IMAGE VALUE="*first graphic file\second graphic file\third graphic file*"> to hold graphic (GIF or JPEG) files to use as a button when nothing's happening, when the mouse rolls over the button, and when the button is clicked

@ <PARAM NAME=TEXTALIGN VALUE=*left, center, or right*> to align the text horizontally on the button

@ <PARAM NAME=VTEXTALIGN VALUE=*top, middle, or bottom*> to align the text vertically on the button

Fortunately, Harshbarger includes detailed instructions for exactly how to use each parameter on the same Web page as the applet (http://www.xm.com/cafe/ButtonPLUS/button.html). It's relatively easy, therefore, to create a Web page like the one shown in Figure 10.4 with just a few steps:

1. Record or acquire the sounds that play when the button is rolled over or clicked with the mouse, using your favorite sound editor. Make sure whatever sounds you use are short (less than five seconds) and sampled at 8 kHz. For this example, I used GoldWave (included on the CD-ROM and discussed in detail in Chapter 8) to record the sounds.

2. Edit the sounds as necessary. For a "cartoon" effect, I applied GoldWave's Smurf effect to the sound of my voice by selecting Effects|Doppler|Shapes|Smurf.

3. Save the sound files as AU 8 kHz, m-law mono. This is important; it's the only sound format supported by the applet.

4. Write the HTML for the applet, using the information supplied by the applet programmer to code the <PARAM> statements:

```
<APPLET CODE=ButtonPLUS2.class WIDTH=200 HEIGHT=30>
<PARAM NAME=URL VALUE=www.anyisp.net/~user/funland.htm>
<PARAM NAME=HIGHLIGHT VALUE=4>
<PARAM NAME=FONTSIZE VALUE=14>
<PARAM NAME=TEXT VALUE="Roll your mouse here|Now click|Pretty cool,
huh?">
<PARAM NAME=TEXTCOLOR VALUE=0,0,0>
<PARAM NAME=SOUND VALUE="clickme.au|herego.au">
</APPLET>
```

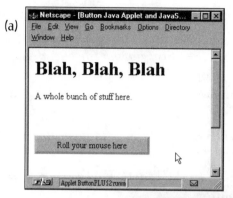

Figure 10.4a, 10.4b, 10.4c The deceptively plain-looking beveled button (a) changes its message (b) and plays a sound file that says "Click me!" when the mouse moves over it. When the user clicks, the message on the button changes again (c) as it plays a sound file announcing "Here we go!"

5. Add the other HTML for the page, including some text and/or graphics to be displayed instead of the Java applet for users without Java-enabled browsers:

```
<HTML>
<HEAD><TITLE>Button Java Applet and JavaScript command</TITLE></
HEAD>
<BODY BGCOLOR=white>
<H1>Blah, Blah, Blah</H1>
A whole bunch of stuff here.
<BR><BR><BR>
<APPLET CODE=ButtonPLUS2.class WIDTH=200 HEIGHT=30>
<P>If you had a Java-enabled browser, you'd get a talking _
   button here.
```

```
<PARAM NAME=URL VALUE=www.anyisp.net/~user/funland.htm>
<PARAM NAME=HIGHLIGHT VALUE=4>
<PARAM NAME=FONTSIZE VALUE=14>
<PARAM NAME=TEXT VALUE="Roll your mouse here|Now click|Pretty _
  cool, huh?">
<PARAM NAME=TEXTCOLOR VALUE=0,0,0>
<PARAM NAME=SOUND VALUE"clickme.au|herego.au">
</APPLET>
</BODY>
</HTML>
```

Note that parameter variables that aren't specified with <PARAM> lines are set to whatever default the programmer picked. In this example, the button is standard gray because I didn't include a <PARAM NAME=BGCOLOR VALUE=..> line specifying some other button color. Also, for this particular applet, the NAME variables have to be typed in uppercase, i.e., *BGCOLOR*, not *bgcolor*.

Any regular HTML code that's within the <APPLET>..</APPLET> tag pair will be ignored by Java-enabled browsers, while all the Java-related lines in <APPLET>..</APPLET> will be ignored by other browsers. This provides an easy way to add messages on your Web pages for people who can't see your Java applets. Just add the appropriate lines of HTML between <APPLET> and </APPLET>, like this:

```
<APPLET CODE=AGraphic.class WIDTH=100 HEIGHT=100>
<PARAM NAME=image VALUE=biglogo.gif>
<IMG SRC="nojava.gif" WIDTH=100 HEIGHT=100>
<P>If you had a Java-enabled browser, you'd see an animated version
of this graphic.
</APPLET>
```

A Puzzle to Put on Your Page

Do you remember the little puzzles that you used to get as party favors when you were a kid, where you had to slide the tiles around to reassemble a picture? Well, they're back, and they're on the Web. In fact, you might have seen them already, perhaps at a big, corporate Web site like the Buena Vista division of Disney, as shown in Figure 10.5.

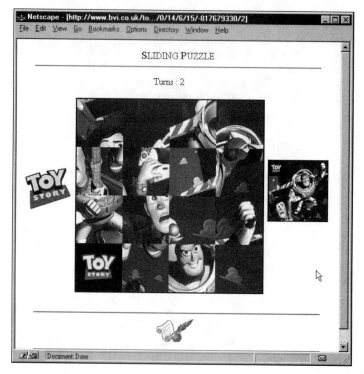

Figure 10.5   You can have interactive slider puzzles like this at your Web site, too.

It's amazingly easy to add this bit of interactivity to your Web pages, with the help of another clever Java applet by Eric Harshbarger at Sun Microsystems. This applet, Slider.class, requires two other classes in order to run: BrightFilter.class and DarkFilter.class. All of them are included on the CD-ROM. Once you've got them in the same directory as your HTML files, it's just a matter of finding an appropriate GIF or JPEG and whipping up a few lines of HTML code. There are only three possible parameters for this applet (as with the previous applet, the NAME variables must be all uppercase):

- <PARAM NAME=IMAGE VALUE=*a square GIF or JPEG graphic*>
- <PARAM NAME=GRID VALUE=*a number, probably 3, 4, or 5*>
- <PARAM NAME=SOUND VALUE=*a sound file in AU 8 kHz, m-law mono format to play each time a tile moves*>

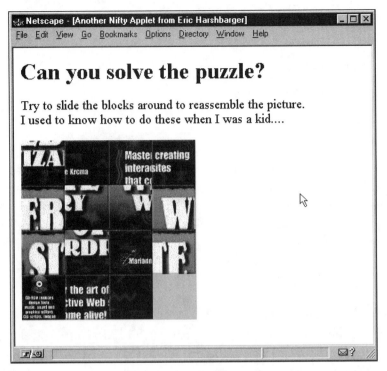

Figure 10.6 Thanks to the Slider.class applet, this puzzle is a lot easier to add to a Web page than it is to solve!

The page in Figure 10.6 took only three quick steps to create:

1. Create or acquire a square GIF or JPEG as the basis of the puzzle. Using Paintshop Pro, I cropped a copy of this book's cover art to make it 249 pixels square.

2. Create or acquire the sound you want to play when the tiles slide, if any. For this example, I just downloaded click.au from Sun Microsystem's FTP site.

3. Write a page of HTML to call the applet:

```
<HTML>
<HEAD>
<TITLE>Another Nifty Applet from Eric Harshbarger</TITLE>
</HEAD>
<BODY bgcolor="white">
<H1>Can you solve the puzzle?</H1>
<FONT SIZE=+1>
<P>Try to slide the blocks around to reassemble the picture.<BR>
I used to know how to do these when I was a kid....</FONT>
```

```
<BR><BR>
<applet code=Slider.class width=249 height=249>
<P>For Java-enabled browsers, an interactive slider puzzle shows up
here.
<param name=IMAGE value=bkcover.jpg>
<param name=GRID value=4>
<param name=SOUND value=click.au>
</applet>
</BODY>
</HTML>
```

Generating the puzzle can be a little processor-intensive, so it's best to pay even more than the usual attention to keeping file sizes small. In this example, the JPEG is only 18 KB and the sound file is 4 KB. For the same reason, don't divide the puzzle up into too small of a grid—Harshbarger advises a grid value of 4 or 5, resulting in a puzzle of either 16 or 25 squares.

A NOT-SO-BASIC BILLBOARD

Suppose you're the unofficial computer guru at the EuroTours travel agency. One day, your boss tells you that the agency has decided to launch a Web site, and—surprise!—you're in charge of it. Your first task is to put up some Web pages advertising the off-season specials. Your boss expects pages with plenty of pizzazz, but without hiring any outside help or buying any expensive Web "toys."

What do you do? Subscribe him or her to the alt.convict.lovers newslist? Start polishing up your résumé? No, you're a great Web wizard; there's no need to panic.

You just surf the Web looking for a likely shareware or freeware Java applet. You find one at the JARS site (http://www.jars.com/). It's called the Dynamic Billboard, written by Robert Temple at Embry-Riddle University (http://www.erau.edu/). The file (dynamic_billboard.zip on the CD-ROM) comes with all of the necessary classes, plus the source code and a detailed, well-documented example. All you have to do is put it on your hard disk, unzip it, and you're ready to go.

As you can see from Figure 10.7, this applet creates a billboard that cycles through several different graphics, with special effects to transition from

Figure 10.7   The sample Web page that comes with the Dynamic Billboard applet illustrates its various effects.

one graphic to another. Each graphic can have a link to a Web page and a message that appears in the status bar when the mouse rolls over the billboard area. The applet comes with six different transitions to choose from, each in a separate CLASS file, including fading, rotating, and a "shutter" effect. It takes five possible parameters, where multiple values are separated by commas without spaces in between:

@ <PARAM NAME="delay" VALUE=*"a number for the delay in milliseconds such as 2000 for two seconds"*>

@ <PARAM NAME="billboards" VALUE=*"the number of panels"*>

@ <PARAM NAME="billx" VALUE=*"a GIF or JPEG, a URL to go to when the panel is clicked, a message to display in the status bar when the mouse*

moves onto the billboard area">—There will be one of these <PARAM> lines for each panel, starting with bill0. Note that the value elements must be separated by commas without spaces.

 <PARAM NAME="transitions" VALUE=*"the number of transitions, the list of transitions separated by commas">*

 <PARAM NAME="bgcolor" VALUE=*"a hexidecimal color value such as #000000">*

With all of the necessary files for the applet installed, you simply follow these steps to create a Web page with an animated billboard:

1. Create the graphics that will be used for each "panel" of the billboard. These graphics can be either GIF or JPEG, but they should all be the same width and height, and have fairly small file sizes—preferably smaller than 20 KB. To illustrate this example, I modified some clip art from Micrografx to produce frtour.jpg, engtour.jpg, iretour.jpg, and switour.jpg, which are shown in Figure 10.8. Each piece of art is 400 pixels wide by 150 pixels high.

2. Decide on the links, messages, and transitions for the panels, as well as the delay time between changing the panels. The number of transitions should match the number of panels; for this example, the ColumnTransition, RotateTransition, Tear-

Figure 10.8 These are the four panels of the dynamic billboard.

Transition, SmashTransition are used. The applet will choose a transition at random, but it won't choose the same transition twice in a row.

3. Start up your favorite HTML editor and create the page. The easiest way to do it is to copy and paste from the index.html file that is included with the applet. Here's the code for the page shown in Figure 10.9:

```
<HTML>
<HEAD><TITLE>EuroTour Travel Agency</TITLE></HEAD>
<BODY BACKGROUND="etlogo1.gif" LINK="#FF0080">
<CENTER>
<H1><FONT COLOR="#8000FF"><FONT SIZE="7">W</FONT>ELCOME TO <FONT
SIZE="7">E</FONT>URO<FONT SIZE="7">T</FONT>OUR!</FONT></H1>
<I>Where the most memorable journeys start with a single click.</I>
<HR>
<P><FONT SIZE="+1">Many of our most popular destinations are on
sale!</FONT><BR><BR>
<APPLET CODE="DynamicBillBoard" WIDTH="400" HEIGHT="150">
  <PARAM NAME="delay" VALUE="1000">
  <PARAM NAME="billboards" VALUE="4">
  <PARAM NAME="bill0" VALUE="engtour.jpg,http://www.eutour.com/
england.htm,Seven days in England starting at $1000">
  <PARAM NAME="bill1" VALUE="iretour.jpg,http://www.eutour.com/
ireland.htm,Read the latest info about our Irish tours">
  <PARAM NAME="bill2" VALUE="switour.jpg,http://www.eutour.com/
switz.htm,New packages to Switzerland just added">
  <PARAM NAME="bill3" VALUE="frtour.jpg,http://www.eutour.com/
france.htm,Tour France for fewer francs">
  <PARAM NAME="transitions"
VALUE="4,ColumnTransition,RotateTransition,TearTransition,SmashTransition">
  <PARAM NAME="bgcolor" VALUE="#FFFFFF">
  Since you are using a browser that is not Java-enabled, check out
our <A HREF="http://www.eutour.com/specials.html">specials page</A>.
</APPLET>
</CENTER>
<HR>
<FONT SIZE="-1">Last Updated: Thursday, April 18, 1996<BR>
Questions? Comments? Contact the <A
HREF="mailto:webmstrs@eutour.com">Webmistress</A></FONT>
</BODY>
</HTML>

<A HREF="mailto:me@myisp.net"
  onMouseOver="window.status='Send e-mail to the Webmaster.
  Cyberspace can be a lonely place!';return true">
  <IMG SRC="pbox2.gif" WIDTH=68 HEIGHT=60 BORDER=0 ALIGN=middle>
</A>
```

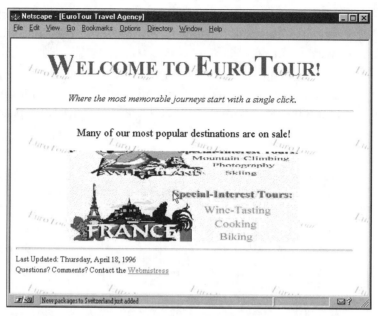

Figure 10.9 Here, the Dynamic Billboard applet is applying a rotate transition from the panel about Switzerland to the one about France. Notice the custom message in the status bar.

What's that! You say you don't want to bother with <PARAM> lines, but you still want Java-based animation on your Web pages? Well, you're in luck. There are a few freeware and shareware programs available that, essentially, fill out the <PARAM> lines of Java applets for you. One program to try is Egor Animator, from the makers of the popular HotDog Pro HTML editor. You can get information and download a demo of the latest version from http://www.sausage.com/.

A Web Site that Does JavaScript Tricks

JavaScript provides what many Web wizards have been wishing for since the Web began: a way to control how information is presented to the user of a Web page without resorting to CGI scripts. You can use JavaScript to add extra little "goodies" to your page, such as customizing the status bar or adding the current date and time to the page. Anyone can do these little tricks with just a few lines of code, as you'll see in the following pages. For more tricks, see Charles Goodin's JavaScript page at http://tanega.com/java/java.htm\.

You can also use JavaScript to write actual programs, complete with variables, functions, conditional statements, etc. If you've ever written a batch file or a Word macro, you can learn to write JavaScript. Two sample JavaScript programs are included in this section.

A MESSAGE IN THE STATUS BAR

You've probably seen Web pages that take control of your status bar to display an advertisement or some other information. All of the Web wizards I spoke to about this practice recommend against it, however. They cite the fact that it's annoying, it acts inconsistently (the scrolling sometimes speeds up when your mouse moves), and it overwrites the valuable information that normally appears on the status bar.

There is a way, though, to add a custom message in the status bar that appears when the mouse is over a particular link or button, as shown in Figure 10.10. When something else needs to be displayed in the status bar, such as information about a file that's downloading, the custom message is automatically "kicked out" of the status bar. Here are the tags that produce the message in Figure 10.10:

```
<A HREF="mailto:me@myisp.net"
  onMouseOver="window.status='Send e-mail to the Webmaster.
  Cyberspace can be a lonely place!';return true">
  <IMG SRC="pbox2.gif" WIDTH=68 HEIGHT=60 BORDER=0 ALIGN=middle>
</A>
```

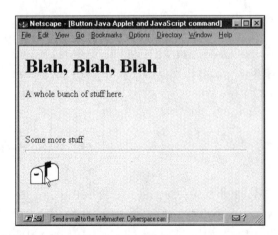

Figure 10.10 With the mouse pointer on the mailbox icon, a message appears in the status bar.

To use this trick on your pages, all you need to do is replace the message in single quotes with your own message. The *onMouseOver* command tells the browser to display the message when the mouse rolls over the item referred to between <A HREF> and </A>. The *window.status* object says to put the message in the status bar of the window, and *return true* just finishes the JavaScript and returns control to the place on the page where it left off.

OTHER WAYS TO GET YOUR MESSAGE ACROSS

JavaScript's *window* object can take several other methods and properties in addition to the *status* property that puts a message in the status bar. Two of these methods, *alert* and *confirm*, provide separate boxes to hold your message, as shown in Figure 10.11.

Figure 10.11 With single lines of code, you can create your own versions of these message boxes.

There are lots of ways you could use these JavaScript elements. For example, you could have a message appear when a user first loads your page, using JavaScript's *onLoad* event (an *event* is, basically, a command saying "when this happens, do this") in the <BODY> tag, like this:

```
<BODY BGCOLOR="white" onLoad="window.alert('Thanks for stopping by! Be sure
to check out the new downloads added last week.');">
```

Similarly, you could use the *confirm* method to bring up a box with the standard OK and Cancel buttons when a user clicks a particular link. If the user clicks OK, the action continues; otherwise, it ends. Here's how such a line might look:

```
This link will take you
<A HREF="elsewhere.htm"
```

```
onClick="if(confirm ('Are you sure you want to go to the top of this
page?')) alert('On you go!');">out of here.
</A>
```

There is an onUnload event that is supposed to do the opposite of onLoad, displaying a message when the user leaves a page. This could be helpful if used sparingly, especially if the user was supposed to do something specific at the page, like fill out a contest entry. Unfortunately, onUnload crashed Netscape every time I tried to use it.

This brings up an important point: JavaScript is not, as of this writing, a finished, stable product. It's changing every day, so be sure to check sites like the JavaScript FAQ at http://www.freqgrafx.com/411/jsfaq.html for the latest developments.

A BETTER BACKGROUND

Picking a background color for your page that all your visitors will like and that will look good regardless of the monitor it's viewed on can be a chore. Why not let the visitors pick the background for you? A few simple lines of JavaScript can produce a page like the one in Figure 10.12. Although you obviously can't see it on this black-and-white book page, clicking a button does, indeed, turn the background the indicated color. (You can test it by opening the jstricks.htm file on the CD-ROM.) Here's the code that produces the page:

```
<HTML>
<HEAD><TITLE>JavaScript commands</TITLE></HEAD>
<BODY bgcolor="white">
<H1>Some simple JavaScript Tricks</H1>
<BR>
Would you like a different background color? Try one of these:
<FORM>
<INPUT TYPE="button" VALUE="Off White"
  onClick="document.bgColor='ivory'">
<INPUT TYPE="button" VALUE="Light Gray"
  onClick="document.bgColor='whitesmoke'">
<INPUT TYPE="button" VALUE="Pale Green"
  onClick="document.bgColor='honeydew'">
<INPUT TYPE="button" VALUE="Pale Pink"
  onClick="document.bgColor='mistyrose'">
```

```
<INPUT TYPE="button" VALUE="Light Blue"
  onClick="document.bgColor='lightblue'">
<INPUT TYPE="button" VALUE="Reset"
  onClick="document.bgColor='white'">
</FORM>
<BR>
<HR>
<A HREF="mailto:me@myisp.net" onMouseOver="window.status='Send e-mail to
the Webmaster. Cyberspace can be a lonely place!';return true">Send feed-
back</A>
</BODY>
</HTML>
```

Note that instead of the normal hexidecimal RGB values in document.bgColor, actual color names are used here. The hexadecimal values would work just as well, but the names tend to be favored by JavaScript wizards.

All of the color names in Table 10.2 can be used instead of the hexadecimal values in document.bgColor. They can also be used in the BGCOLOR, TEXT, LINK, VLINK, and ALINK attributes of the <BODY> tag and in the COLOR attribute of the <FONT> tag. Some of the names don't seem to bear a particularly strong relationship to the colors they're supposed to be describing; for example, lightskyblue is a fairly dark blue on my SVGA monitor. Your best bet, like with the hexadecimal color values, is to experiment until you find some that you like, and make note of them for later use.

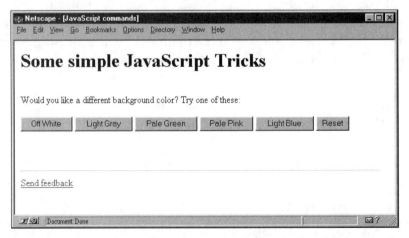

Figure 10.12   Giving the visitor control over the background color is a clever and helpful touch.

azure	aqua	beige	aquamarine	antiquewhite	aliceblue
blueviolet	blue	brown	blueviolet	blanchedalmond	bisqueblack
burlywood	cade	cornflowerblue	coral	chartreuse	cornsilk
darkgoldenrod	darkblue	darkgray	darkcyan	cyan	cadetblue
darkorange	darkmagenta	darkorchid	darkolivegreen	darkkhaki	crimson
darkslategray	darkseagreen	darkturquoise	darkslateblue	darksalmon	darkgreen
dodgerblue	deepskyblue	firebrick	dimgray	deeppink	darkred
ghostwhite	fuchsia	gold	gainsboro	forestgreen	darkviolet
honeydew	green	hotpink	greenyellow	gray	floralwhite
lavender	ivory	lavenderblush	khaki	indigo	goldenrod
lightcoral	lightblue	lightcyan	lightblue	lemonchiffon	indianred
lightseagreen	lightpink	lightskyblue	lightsalmon	lightgray	lawngreen
limegreen	lightyellow	linen	lime	lightsteelblue	lightgreen
mediumvioletred	mediumblue	mediumpurple	mediumorchid	maroon	lightslategray
mediumseagreen	mediumspringgreen	midnightblue	mediumturquoise	mediumslateblue	magenta
orchid	moccasin	oldlace	navajowhite	mistyrose	navy
peachpuff	orange	palegoldenrod	orangered	olivedrab	mintcream
red	palevioletred	peru	papayawhip	paleturquoise	olive
sandybrown	salmon	rosybrown	purple	plum	palegreen
slategray	skyblue	seagreen	salmon	saddlebrown	pink
thistle	tan	snow	slateblue	silver	royalblue
whitesmoke	wheat	tomato	teal	steelblue	sienna
lightgoldenrodyellow	mediumaquamarine	yellow	white	violet	springgreen
				seashell	turquoise

Table 10.2 All of these color names can be used instead of the hexadecimal RGB values.

The only real problem with setting the background color with a JavaScript command is that transparent graphics will show the background color set by the <BODY> tag instead of being transparent. That's why I used a text link in Figure 10.12 instead of the mailbox graphic used in Figure 10.10.

You might be wondering if there is a similarly simple trick to change background tiles. Unfortunately, there isn't—at least, not at this writing. Also, although there are fgColor, linkColor, alinkColor, and vlinkColor properties that work like document.bgColor in JavaScript programs, this trick doesn't work to change them on the fly.

If you use a graphic in a line of JavaScript, make sure to include the HEIGHT and WIDTH attributes in the <IMG SRC> tag. Otherwise, the JavaScript might not work.

Here are a few more JavaScript hints and "gotchas" as of this writing:

- To put a line break in a JavaScript alert box, status box, or similar message area, use the \n escape sequence. I used several of them for the messages in Figure 10.11.

- Any text placed on a Web page with JavaScript will not print out by choosing File|Print, even though it appears onscreen.

- There is no way to call a JavaScript program from the server like you can call a CGI script; you have to embed the JavaScript in a Web page. Eventually, server-side JavaScript should be possible by giving the JavaScript file a .JS extension and calling it as you would a CGI script.

When you put all of the tricks discussed here together, you get a page such as the one in Figure 10.13. Here's the HTML (and JavaScript) that makes it:

```
<HTML>
<HEAD><TITLE>JavaScript Tricks</TITLE></HEAD>
<!-- There are six little JavaScript tricks on this page. -->

<!-- 1. The onLoad JavaScript event brings up an alert box whenever the
page loads. -->
<BODY bgcolor="white" onLoad="window.alert('Thanks for stopping by! If you
like what you see, add a bookmark.');">
<H1>Some simple JavaScript Tricks</H1>
<BR>Would you like a different background color? Try one of these:

<!-- 2. The onClick JavaScript event changes the background color when the
button is clicked. -->
<FORM>
<INPUT TYPE='button" VALUE="Off White" onClick="document.bgColor='ivory'">
<INPUT TYPE="button" VALUE="Light Gray"
onClick="document.bgColor='whitesmoke'">
<INPUT TYPE="button" VALUE="Pale Green"
onClick="document.bgColor='honeydew'">
<INPUT TYPE="button" VALUE="Pale Pink"
onClick="document.bgColor='mistyrose'">
<INPUT TYPE="button" VALUE="Light Blue"
```

```
onClick="document.bgColor='lightblue'">
<INPUT TYPE="button" VALUE="Reset" onClick="document.bgColor='white'">
</FORM>

<!-- 3. This little script, hidden from non-Java browsers, writes the
current Mo/Day/Yr. -->
<SCRIPT>
<!-- Hiding
  today = new Date()
  document.write("Today is: ", today.getMonth()+1,"/",today.getDate(),"/
",today.getYear());
// Done hiding -->
</SCRIPT>
<BR><BR><BR>

<!-- 4. The onClick event brings up a confirm box when the link is clicked.
-->
This link will take you <A HREF="somewhere.htm" onClick="if(confirm('Are
you sure you want to leave?')) alert('On you go!');">out of here.</A>
<BR><BR><BR><HR>

<!-- 5. The onMouseOver event changes the message in the status bar when
the mouse rolls over the link -->
<A HREF='mailto:me@myisp.net' onMouseOver="window.status='Send e-mail to
the Webmaster. Cyberspace can be a lonely place!';return true">Send feed-
back</A>
<BR><BR>

<!-- 6. This little script writes the date and time when the page was last
changed. -->
<SCRIPT>
<!-- Hiding
document.write("Last modified: ', document.lastModified);
// Done hiding -->
</SCRIPT>
</BODY>
</HTML>
```

THE MYSTERIOUS MAGIC 8-BALL

Are you ready for a full-fledged JavaScript program? Unlike the JavaScript tricks you've seen so far, a JavaScript program includes variables and functions to truly interact with the user. You can write a fairly easy JavaScript program to create the famous "fortune cookie" type of Web toy, where the user gets an apparently random message by clicking a button. Figure 10.14 shows such a Web page.

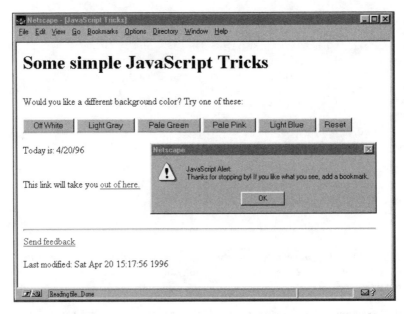

Figure 10.13 There are six separate JavaScript tricks incorporated in this page of HTML, which is only about 35 lines long.

Although this page might not be the most practical bit of JavaScript ever written, it involves basic program elements that are usable under lots of different circumstances, including these:

◎ *JavaScript functions in the <HEAD>..</HEAD> area of the page.* Like other programming languages, a function in JavaScript is designed to accomplish a specific task, such as clearing the screen, whenever it is called. In order to be general-purpose, a function is usually written so that it acts on a variable that gets passed to it from elsewhere on a Web page. Consider a function like this one:

```
function message(name) {
    document.write("Thank you for visiting, ",name);
}
```

All functions must be set up like this, with the curvy brackets as shown. This one would write *Thank you for visiting, Joseph* onscreen (to the document) if it were called with message("Joseph"). Functions are usually placed within the <HEAD> and </HEAD> tags of a Web page so they get loaded into memory before the rest of the page.

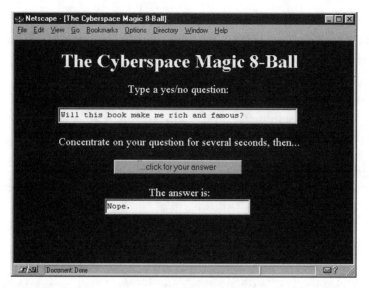

Figure 10.14   There's no truth in these things, is there!

ⓐ *A random or pseudo-random element.* The easiest way to get a random number (at least until the Math.random object is implemented for Windows-based versions of JavaScript) is to start with the time from the computer's internal clock, and then manipulate it in some way. You can, for example, combine the current minute and the current second into one string to get 6,060 possible numbers, like this:

```
today = new Date()
rannum = today.getMinutes() + today.getSeconds()
```

For the magic 8-ball example, you don't need that many different possibilities, so just storing the current second is enough.

ⓐ *Conditional statements.* Conditional, or *branching*, statements are common to all computer languages. JavaScript has the usual ones, including IF..ELSE, FOR loops, and WHILE loops.

ⓐ *Form elements combined with JavaScript.* Forms, discussed in Chapter 7, provide the perfect way to get information from the user, which JavaScript can then process. If you read the previous sections in this chapter on JavaScript, you've already seen a little about how this works. Basically, you add another attribute to the particular form tag that sends information to the JavaScript function, like this:

```
<INPUT TYPE=text NAME="fname" SIZE="20" onFocus="clear(this.form)">
```

When the user clicks in the text box (called *focusing* in JavaScript), the clear() function is called, with instructions to act on the contents of this form.

◎ *JavaScript comments.* JavaScript comments start with two slashes, //. Remember to use them instead of HTML's style of commenting (*<!-- this is a comment -->*) whenever you want to add explanations within the <SCRIPT>..</SCRIPT> tag pair.

Here, then, is the commented code to make the 8-ball page do its magic. To read the code, start with the <BODY> tag and follow the onFocus and onClick events back to the appropriate JavaScript functions:

```
<HTML>
<HEAD><TITLE>The Cyberspace Magic 8-Ball</TITLE>

<!-- Put the JavaScript in the Head area, hidden from non-Java browsers
     by putting it all in HTML comments -->

<SCRIPT>
<!-- Hide JavaScript from browsers that are not Java-enabled

// Two functions make up this little program.
// The first one, answer(form), gets the current second from the computer's
clock
// using the built-in new Date() command. It then puts one of ten _
   different fortunes
// in the form's giveback text box, apparently at random but actually
// depending on the second when the user submitted the question.

    depending on the function answer(form) {
     time = new Date()
     second = time.getSeconds()
     if (second <= 6)
       fortune=("Definitely!")
     else if (second <= 12)
       fortune=("I don't think so.")
     else if (second <= 18)
       fortune=("Maybe.")
     else if (second <= 24)
       fortune=("Nope.")
     else if (second <= 30)
       fortune=("It seems likely.")
     else if (second <= 36)
       fortune=("Try again later.")
     else if (second <= 42)
       fortune=("Not today.")
     else if (second <= 48)
       fortune=("The signs say yes.")
```

```
      else if (second <= 54)
        fortune=("Impossible.")
      else
        fortune=("Yes, indeed.");

// This is how to pass a value back from a JavaScript routine to a form:
// use the syntax "form.form-element-name.value=(message)," followed
  // by a semicolon.
        form.giveback.value=(fortune);
  }

// The clear(form) function replaces values in the question and giveback
// text boxes with nothing. It is called when a user clicks in a text box.
  function clear(form) {
    form.question.value = "";
    form.giveback.value = "";
  }
// Done hiding-->
</SCRIPT>
</HEAD>

<!-- Start of the actual Web page -->
<BODY BGCOLOR="black" TEXT="white">
<CENTER>
<H1>The Cyberspace Magic 8-Ball</H1>
<FONT SIZE="+1">Type a yes/no question:

<!-- The onFocus event sends for the clear function when the user clicks
     (focuses) in the text box. The clear function erases anything in the
     text boxes automatically for the user. -->

<FORM METHOD=POST>
<INPUT TYPE=text NAME="question" SIZE="50" onFocus=clear(this.form)>
<P>Concentrate on your question for several seconds, then...<BR><BR>

<!-- The onClick event sends the value in this form to the answer function.
     The value in this.form is really just a dummy value.
     It's not used for anything other than a way to start up the function.
-->

<INPUT TYPE="button" VALUE="...click for your answer"
onClick=answer(this.form)>
<P>The answer is:<BR>
<INPUT TYPE=text NAME="giveback" SIZE="30" onFocus=clear(this.form)>
</FORM>
</FONT>
</CENTER>
</BODY>
</HTML>
```

A Custom Calculator

Suppose you are responsible for the Human Resources functions of an internal Web site (also called an *intranet*, discussed in Chapter 12). You'd like to have pages at the site where people could figure out some of the details of their benefits packages themselves, instead of calling or memoing your staff. For example, the profit-sharing plan at your company has different levels of vesting depending on the employee's length of service. An employee who has worked for the company for fewer than two years is only entitled to the amount he or she contributed. At two years, an employee is 20% vested in the matching funds that the company has contributed. He or she is 50% vested at three years, 70% vested at four years, and fully vested at five years.

You decide to create a JavaScript "calculator" that figures out the amount of money in an employee's profit-sharing account, based on the number of years worked and the amount he or she has contributed, as shown in Figure 10.15. Notice that the form elements are in a table so the page looks kind of like a real calculator. Here's the code that makes this page, commented so you can follow what's going on:

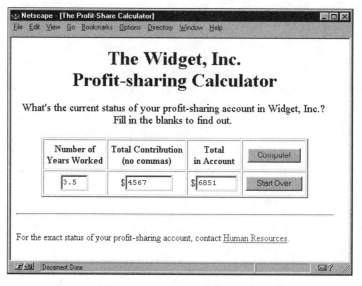

Figure 10.15 There are all kinds of possible variations on this basic JavaScript calculator, depending on the purpose of your Web site.

```
<HTML>
<HEAD><TITLE>The Profit-Share Calculator</TITLE>
<SCRIPT>
<!-- Hide JavaScript

// The chknum function is a pretty standard bit of JavaScript
// for making sure the user enters a valid number in each text box.
// It gets passed two pieces of information, the value in the text box
// and either the word Years or the word Contribution.

function chknum(input, msg) {
   msg = msg + " box does not contain a valid number.";
   for (i = 0; i < input.value.length; i++) {
       ch = input.value.substring(i, i + 1)

// Check the value from the text box character by character,
// making sure each one is either a number between 0 and 9 or a period.
// If any other character is found, give a customized message in an
// alert box to tell the user exactly what is wrong.
// The || means OR, the && means AND, and the != means not equal.

       if ((ch < "0" || "9" < ch) && ch != '.') {
           alert(msg);
       }
     }
}


// The answer function starts by having two variables declared.
// The coshare variable will hold the company contribution and
// the totshare variable will hold the total amount in the
// profit-sharing account. You do not have to declare variables
// in JavaScript, but I did it here so you could see how it works.

function answer(form) {
    var coshare = 0;
    var totshare = 0;

// Check to make sure there is something in the years and contrib _
  text boxes.
// The == is JavaScript syntax for a regular equal sign in a comparison.

       if ((form.years.value == null) ||(form.contrib.value == null)) {
          return;
       }

// Figure out how much the company contributes, multiplying the employee
// contribution by a constant depending on the entry from the years box.

       if (form.years.value >= 5)
          coshare = eval(form.contrib.value)
```

```
        else if (form.years.value >= 4)
            coshare = form.contrib.value * 0.7
        else if (form.years.value >=3)
            coshare = form.contrib.value * 0.5
        else if (form.years.value >=2)
            coshare = form.contrib.value * 0.2
        else
            coshare = 0;

// Get the total amount and use the built-in Math.round object to round it.

        totshare = Math.round(coshare + eval(form.contrib.value));

// Pass the totshare value back to the form in the total textbox.

        form.total.value = totshare;
}

// The clear function clears the form when a user clicks Start button.
// It is essentially the same as the one from the 8-ball JavaScript.

function clear(form) {
    form.years.value = "";
    form.contrib.value = "";
    form.total.value = "";
}


// Done hiding-->
</SCRIPT>
</HEAD>
<!-- Start of the actual Web page -->
<BODY bgcolor="white">
<CENTER><H1>The Widget, Inc.<BR>Profit-Sharing Calculator</H1>
<FONT SIZE="+1">What's the current status of your profit-sharing account in
Widget, Inc.?
<BR>Fill in the blanks to find out.</FONT>

<FORM METHOD=POST>
<TABLE BORDER=2 CELLPADDING=5>
<TR>
<TH>Number of<BR>Years Worked</TH>
<TH>Your Contribution<BR>(no commas)</TH>
<TH>Total<BR>in Account</TH>
<TH><INPUT TYPE="button" VALUE="Compute!" onClick=answer(this.form)></TH>
</TR>
<TR ALIGN=center>
<TD><INPUT TYPE=text NAME="years" SIZE="5" onChange=chknum(this,'Years')></
TD>
<TD>$<INPUT TYPE="text" NAME="contrib" SIZE="9"
onChange=chknum(this,'Contribution')></TD>
```

```
<TD>$<INPUT TYPE="text" NAME="total" SIZE="8"></TD>
<TD><INPUT TYPE="button" VALUE="Start Over" onClick=clear(this.form)></TD>
</TR>
</TABLE>
</FORM>
</CENTER>
<HR>
<P>For the exact status of your profit-sharing account, contact
<A HREF=mailto:msmith@hr.widget.com>Human Resources</A>.
</BODY>
</HTML>
```

Are you wondering how you would know where to begin programming such a calculator? As with most other bits of Web wizardry, the best way to begin is to study what other Web wizards have done at their sites. For example, to develop this calculator, you'd search for similar ones on the Web, such as UC Berkeley's grade-point average calculator (http://www.aad.berkeley.edu/gpacalc.html), the metric-to-English measurement calculator at http://cyberstation.net/~jweesner/conv.html, and Netscape's own example at its JavaScript site (http://proto.netscape.com/comprod/products/navigator/version_2.0/script/). You're probably at least a little familiar with JavaScript's syntax by now, so it's not too hard to see how you could adapt calculator-related JavaScript from other sites into your own calculator. Once you've got the basic idea down, you can use it for all kinds of things, such as interest-payment calculators, currency converters, calorie-counters, and tax calculators, to name just a few.

As you've probably guessed, you'll need to keep some JavaScript documentation handy that gives the syntax of all the available objects, properties, events, etc. as you write and debug your JavaScript code. Netscape has produced just such documentation in the form of a collection of HTML files. You can view pieces of it or download the whole thing as a ZIP file from http://home.netscape.com/eng/mozilla/2.0/handbook/javascript/index.html.

The Wizards Speak: The Real Thing

As I mentioned earlier in this chapter, JavaScript is not Java. With JavaScript, you have a relatively limited number of possibilities. There are only a certain number of JavaScript objects, properties, methods, and events, and these things can only act the way they've been created to act. For example, a JavaScript alert box must look a particular way; you can't make it as big as you want, or any color that you want.

In Java itself, *you* create the objects and methods, so you can program a window object called "alert" that looks however you tell it to look and displays a message in the way you decide. This makes Java far more powerful than JavaScript, but also far more complicated to write.

At this stage in Java's short life, therefore, full-fledged Java applications on the Web are relatively rare. One of the best ones currently available is the WallStreet Web at http://www.bulletproof.com/ WallStreetWeb/, whose home page is shown in Figure 10.16. Scott

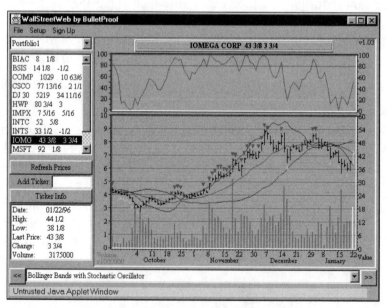

Figure 10.16 The WallStreet Web is a full-fledged Java application.

Milener, the director of marketing at BulletProof.com, reports that it took several programmers over six months to create the WallStreet Web, which debuted in early January 1996. The entire application is called from the Web by the line

```
<applet code = chartwiz.class width=10 height=10>.
```

The WallStreet Web is a good indication of the power of Java programming. A visitor to the site starts out in a free area that provides, among other things, a live stock ticker. There is also a subscription-based area where the user can save such personal preferences as a ticker list of preferred stocks and customized chart set-ups. A user can have a search like "Out of all North American companies, show the ones that went up in volume 30%" performed almost instantly, or have the application send a message when a particular stock reaches a certain price. And, unlike HTML, changes pop up automatically, without the user having to click a submit button.

Finding a way to quickly access all of this data from a Web page was difficult, Milener says. "We needed something to handle database connectivity," he explains, "but having [database] sessions stay open is extremely consuming on the server." BulletProof.com's solution was to develop a proprietary program, called JAGG, that it now licenses to other companies. Milener says that JAGG is "a combination of a Java class and a server engine." The server engine is an .EXE file compiled in C that gets placed on the server in the cgi-bin directory. The class handles the passing of SQL queries to and responses from the server engine.

For other people interested in writing large-scale Java applications, Milener advises, "Test [your application] on each platform." While Java itself might be platform-independent, "even Netscape from Sun to Windows doesn't treat the code the same."

Because BulletProof.com was one of the very earliest adopters of Java, it had to write almost everything at the WallStreet Web from scratch. This experience, Milener says, taught the company that Java "is a difficult language to build an interface in. It's very tedious to lay out." Still, he believes "Java is the way people are going," at least for the foreseeable future.

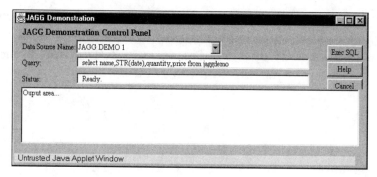

Figure 10.17   This window is created by the Java code in JaggDemo.java.

Just so you can get a feel for what Java code looks like, here is an excerpt from BulletProof.com's JAGG application. It produces the window in Figure 10.17:

```
./*
 * Taken from the BulletProof.com JAGG demo.
 */

import java.applet.*;
import java.awt.*;
import java.io.IOException;
import java.net.MalformedURLException;
import java.util.StringTokenizer;
import java.util.Vector;
import java.util.Enumeration;

public class JaggDemo extends Applet {
  Frame f;

  public void init() {
    setBackground(Color.lightGray);
    setFont(new Font("TimesRoman", Font.PLAIN, 12));
    //setLayout(null);
    f = new JaggConsoleLO();
    f.pack();
    f.reshape(10, 0, 610, 260);
    f.show();
  }

  public boolean handleEvent(Event e) {
    switch (e.id) {
    case Event.WINDOW_DESTROY:
      System.exit(0);
      return true;
    default:
      return false;
```

```
        }
    }

}

/*
 * Screen console layout.
 */

class JaggConsoleLO extends Frame {
    String    SQL = new String("select name,STR(date),quantity,price
from jaggdemo");
    Choice    jDSN;
    TextField jSQL;
    List      jOUTPUT; // Main output area.
    TextField jSTATUS; // Status output area.

    //
    // Constructor.
    //

    JaggConsoleLO() {
        super("JAGG Demonstration");
        setFont(new Font("TimesRoman", Font.PLAIN, 12));
        Panel mainPanel = new Panel();
        Panel centerPanel  = new Panel();
        Panel rightmainPanel = new Panel();
        Panel rightPanel   = new Panel();
        Panel leftPanel = new Panel();
        Panel botPanel      = new Panel();
        Panel outPanel      = new Panel();

        // Set all the main panel layouts.
        setLayout(new BorderLayout());
        mainPanel.setLayout(new BorderLayout());
        centerPanel.setLayout(new GridLayout(3,1,4,4));
        leftPanel.setLayout(new GridLayout(3,1,4,4));
        rightPanel.setLayout(new GridLayout(3,1,4,4));
        outPanel.setLayout(new GridLayout(1,1,4,4));
        botPanel.setLayout(new BorderLayout());

        // TITLE
        Label titlelabel = new Label("JAGG Demonstration Control
Panel", Label.LEFT);
        titlelabel.setFont(new Font("TimesRoman",Font.BOLD,14));

        // RIGHT PANEL, buttons and spacing below
        Button butt1 = new Button("Exec SQL");
        Button butt2 = new Button("Help");
        Button butt3 = new Button("Cancel");
        rightPanel.add(butt1);
        rightPanel.add(butt2);
        rightPanel.add(butt3);
```

```
buttl.setFont(new Font("TimesRoman",Font.PLAIN,12));
butt2.setFont(new Font("TimesRoman",Font.PLAIN,12));
butt3.setFont(new Font("TimesRoman",Font.PLAIN,12));

// Row1
leftPanel.add(new Label("Data Source Name:", Label.LEFT));
Panel row1Panel = new Panel();
row1Panel.setLayout(null);
jDSN = new Choice();
jDSN.addItem("JAGG DEMO 1");
jDSN.addItem("JAGG DEMO 2");
row1Panel.add(jDSN);
jDSN.reshape(0,5,200,30);
centerPanel.add(row1Panel);

// Row2
leftPanel.add(new Label("Query:", Label.LEFT));
Panel row2Panel = new Panel();
row2Panel.setLayout(null);
jSQL = new TextField(SQL);
jSQL.setEditable(false);
jSQL.setBackground(Color.white);
row2Panel.add(jSQL);
jSQL.reshape(0,0,400,20);
centerPanel.add(row2Panel);

// Row3
leftPanel.add(new Label("Status:", Label.LEFT));
Panel row3Panel = new Panel();
row3Panel.setLayout(null);
jSTATUS = new TextField("Ready.");
jSTATUS.setEditable(false);
jSTATUS.setBackground(Color.white);
row3Panel.add(jSTATUS);
jSTATUS.reshape(0,0,400,20);
centerPanel.add(row3Panel);

// Bottom panel
jOUTPUT = new List(6,false);
jOUTPUT.setBackground(Color.white);
jOUTPUT.addItem("Ouput area...");
outPanel.add(jOUTPUT);

// Setup the panel heirarchy.
rightmainPanel.add("Center", rightPanel);
mainPanel.add("North", titlelabel);
mainPanel.add("Center", centerPanel);
mainPanel.add("West", leftPanel);
mainPanel.add("East", rightmainPanel);
botPanel.add("East", new Panel());
botPanel.add("West", new Panel());
botPanel.add("Center", outPanel);
mainPanel.add("South", botPanel);
```

These same steps should work to compile and run most Java files, so don't hesitate to test out some source code that you've found on the Web—or maybe written yourself!

For a look at an another full-fledged Java application, point your browser to The Great Reality Caper at http://vwv.is.co.za/reality/. It's a traditional graphic adventure game, with objects to collect and puzzles to solve, written in Java and playable in realtime on the Web. (A screen shot from it shown in Figure 10.18.)

One of the great things about a Web-based game is that it never needs to end; updates and extensions can be continually added. As one of The Great Reality Caper's creators, Graham Leggett, says, "So far we have approximately 2.5 MB of data that make up the game, with about 180 separate usable objects in 60 locations. And we're still busy at it.."

Figure 10.18   The Great Reality Caper uses Java and frames to produce a real, Web-based, graphic adventure.

Web Wizard's Touchstones for Java

Do   download and install the Java Developer's Kit. It's essential for compiling any uncompiled Java applets that you come across, or for writing your own Java code. Best of all, it's free!

Don't   rely on Java to convey critical information at your site unless you're sure most visitors have Java-enabled browsers.

Do   provide some alternative to a Java applet for visitors who won't be able to use it, by embedding the appropriate HTML tags for the alternative text and graphics between <APPLET> and </APPLET>.

Don't   put a Java or JavaScript applet on your Web pages without thoroughly testing it on different versions of Netscape to make sure it won't crash.

Do   take advantage of the free, easy-to-use Java applets available at sites like Gamelan (http://www.gamelan.com/) and Café del Sol (http://www.xm.com/cafe/).

Don't   expect the user to be able to print out anything you've put on a Web page with JavaScript. Currently, it doesn't work.

Do   carefully read and follow the instructions from the programmer who wrote the Java applet you're using. Pay special attention to case-sensitivity, quotation marks, and the required use of any special characters such as the pipe symbol (|).

Don't   omit the WIDTH and HEIGHT attributes of any <IMG SRC> tags you use in your JavaScript code.

Do   download and study the available source files for Java programs (the ones with .JAVA extensions) if you're interested in writing Java code yourself.

Don't   give up if your first efforts at writing JavaScript or Java result in cryptic error messages! Debugging is a art of programming.

Do   check for these common mistakes if you get error messages from JavaScript or Java: incorrect use of uppercase or lowercase letters, typos in reserved words, incorrect use of single or double quotes, and missing semicolons, parentheses, or curvy brackets.

XI

VRML PUTS PLACES IN CYBERSPACE

"**W**elcome," says Web wizard Larry Rosenthal at his VRML home page, "to the wonderfully underfinished world of VRML." That pretty accurately sums up the current state of the *Virtual Reality Modeling Language*, or *VRML*.

If you're the kind of person who really wants to be on the cutting edge, you might feel like you've already missed getting in on the ground floor of other Web technologies like frames or Shockwave—after all, they're beginning to stabilize at this point, and people have pretty much figured out some logical uses for them. VRML, on the other hand, is still largely unexplored territory. If you hurry, you can stake your claim as one of its pioneers.

VRML is the stuff that science fiction stories are made of. Or, more accurately, science fiction is the stuff that VRML is made of. Science fiction novels like *Nueromancer* by William Gibson and *Snow Crash* by Neal Stephenson have predicted and influenced the virtual worlds that VRML will make possible—worlds filled with computer-generated representations of people and things that have many of the properties of real people and things, plus attributes that would be impossible for their real-world counterparts. While VRML is a long way from the dreams and nightmares of science fiction novelists, it's still a pretty amazing thing to explore.

But what is it, exactly? VRML is a computer language that was first proposed in the Spring of 1994. There is currently a formal VRML 1.0 standard (also called a *spec*, short for specification), which specifies exactly what elements are allowed in the language and what their syntax should be. You can get a copy of the VRML 1.0 spec at http://www.virtpark.com/theme/, among other places. There is also a proposed VRML 2.0 spec. However, companies that don't want to wait for it to be formally accepted have gone ahead on their own with various extensions to do things like add animation to their VRML *worlds* (the equivalent of Web sites). Sounds a lot like the evolution of HTML so far, doesn't it?

Also like HTML, VRML is designed to be interpreted by some kind of browser software. Netscape, for example, has added the ability to handle VRML to Navigator starting with version 2.0. Its VRML add-in is called Live3D. There are lots of specialized VRML browsers from other companies that you can use as add-ins or stand-alone VRML browsers, too. Check a Web directory like Yahoo for the most recent list (http://www.yahoo.com/Computers_and_Internet/Internet/World_Wide_Web/Virtual_Reality_Modeling_Language__VRML_/Browsers/). VRML might be following a similar evolutionary path to HTML, but it doesn't look much like HTML. Consider this short VRML file (on the CD-ROM as simple.wrl), adapted from an example in the VRML 1.0 spec:

```
#VRML V1.0 ascii
Separator {
    DirectionalLight {
        direction 0 0 -1  #Light shining from viewer into scene
    }
    PerspectiveCamera {
        position    -8.6 2.1 5.6
        orientation -0.1352 -0.9831 -0.1233  1.1417
        focalDistance        10.84
    }
  WWWAnchor { #The hypertext link
  name "http://www.spheroid.com/spheres.wrl"
  description "Jump to a made-up VRML world"
      Separator {   #The green ball
          Material {
              diffuseColor 0 1 0   #The color green
          }
          Translation { translation 3 0 1 }
          Sphere { radius 3 }
      }
    }
}
```

Figure 11.1 shows how this little world would look to a user with a VRML-enabled browser. The VRML file, which is just straight ASCII text with a .WRL extension, produces three items (*objects*): a light source, a *camera* that basically indicates which direction you're coming from, and the green ball. Anchored to the green ball is a link to another URL. This link could be to a page of HTML, a CGI, or anything else you could put on the Web, but in this particular example it links to another VRML world. It works just like an <A HREF> tag in HTML: when the user clicks the ball, he or she will go to the new location.

Because this example is so very simple, the code is quite short. Most VRML files, however, are much longer, usually running to several thousand lines of code. If you take a look at the code for a world such as the one in Figure 11.2 with View|Document Source (in Netscape), you'll see line after line of mostly unintelligible mathematical matrices, like this made-up fragment:

```
TransformSeparator {
  MatrixTransform {
     matrix
```

```
                0.000 1.000 -0.000 0
               -0.707 0.000 0.707 0
                0.707 0.000 0.707 0
                0.000 0.000 0.000 1
        }
    DEF InfLight_3 DirectionalLight {
        color 0.698 0.698 0.698
        intensity 1.000
        on TRUE
        direction 0.000 0.000 1.000
    }
}
WWWAnchor {
    name "http://www.myisp.com/something.html"
    description "Some Web page"
    Separator {
        MaterialBinding {
            value OVERALL
        }
        Material {
            ambientColor [
                0.100 0.100 0.100,
            ]
            diffuseColor [
                0.082 0.824 0.047,
            ]
            specularColor [
                0.100 0.100 0.100,
            ]
            emissiveColor [
                0.000 0.000 0.000,
            ]
            shininess [
                0.000,
            ]
            transparency [
                0.000,
            ]
        }
        MatrixTransform {
            matrix
                1.000 0.000 0.000 0
                0.000 -0.000 -1.000 0
                0.000 1.000 -0.000 0
                0.000 1.000 -0.000 1
        }
        Coordinate3 {
            point             [
                0.000 0.000 1.000,
                0.000 0.000 -1.000,
                0.195 0.000 0.981,
```

```
        0.180  0.075  0.981,
        0.138  0.138  0.981,
        0.075  0.180  0.981,
       -0.000  0.195  0.981,
        0.075 -0.180 -0.981,
        0.138 -0.138 -0.981,
        0.180 -0.075 -0.981,
    ]
  }
```

Some people, presumably, understand this stuff. Fortunately, *you* don't have to. There are freeware, shareware, and commercial programs currently available to help you generate VRML worlds, with several more on the horizon. At this point, these "world-building" packages are considerably more complicated to use than, say, your average HTML editor, but they're still a huge step up from defining all those rows of numbers yourself.

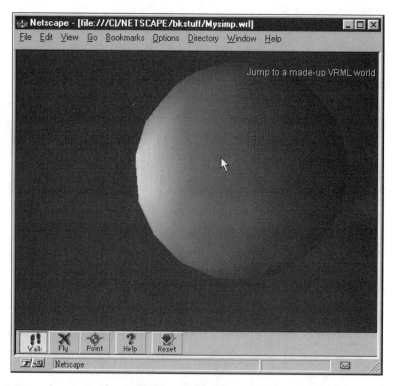

Figure 11.1 A user with a VRML-enabled browser would be able to move all around, over, under—or even through—this ball. A click on the ball itself would take the user to a different site, as indicated by the onscreen message.

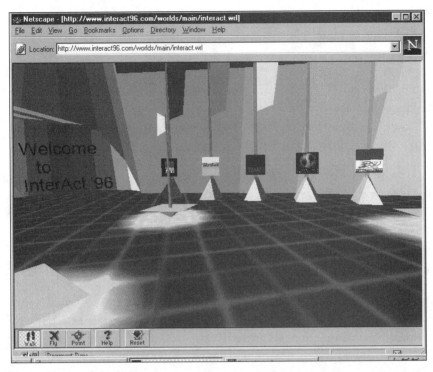

Figure 11.2 The VRML code for this world would take up several chapters' worth of space in this book. It shows a view of the VRML counterpart to a real-world conference on virtual reality. You can walk up to the "stands," click one, and be transported to that company's virtual world.

The matrices of numbers that you'll see when you view VRML code are there to geometrically describe that particular world. Everything in the world is described with these rows of numbers, plus a set of reserved words (called nodes). An object, for example, is described by rows of numbers that give the vertices (corners) of all of its faces (like the facets on a jewel).

Tools for Virtual Worlds

To create a virtual world on the Web, you need the following specialized software:

- A modeling program to create the 3D objects.
- Libraries of objects and textures.

@ A "world-building" program to put the objects together and add any sounds, links, or animation.

@ A converter to turn the virtual world into VRML.

In some cases, all of these items come together in a single package, such as Caligari's trueSpace (http://www.caligari.com/). Other programs, such as the entry-level Virtual HomeSpace Builder (VHSB) from ParaGraph (http://www.paragraph.com/), have most, but not all, of these elements.

VHSB, shown in Figure 11.3, has only very basic modeling functions, but makes up for it with easy-to-use libraries of textures that users can simply drag onto a world, and ready-made "templates" that provide the basic elements of various types of worlds. Its ease of use and low price (about $50 for noncommercial use) make it a popular choice with apprentice VRML wizards—you can try it out from the CD-ROM.

Your library of objects and textures can come from public-domain sources or commercial collections. The best-known and most popular source for public-domain 3D building materials and software is Avalon. It was originally funded and run by the U.S. government, but has been turned over to Viewpoint DataLabs (http://www.viewpoint.com/), which also has commercial collections for sale.

Note, though, that many of the most beautiful and highly detailed objects in both public and commercial collections have very large file sizes, often several hundred kilobytes—and unlike regular graphics, you can't decrease the file size by making the object physically smaller. Therefore, keep a sharp eye on file size when you consider using an object from these kinds of libraries in your own VRML projects.

Textures are bitmaps of things like grass, stone, and bricks that get repeated over and over again to cover objects. Does that sound familiar? It might, since that's the same thing that background tiles do on a Web page. In fact, tiles and textures are the same thing. Any GIF or JPEG you're using for a background is a candidate for a texture, so you might already have the beginnings of a texture library. (You definitely do, since several are included on the CD-ROM.)

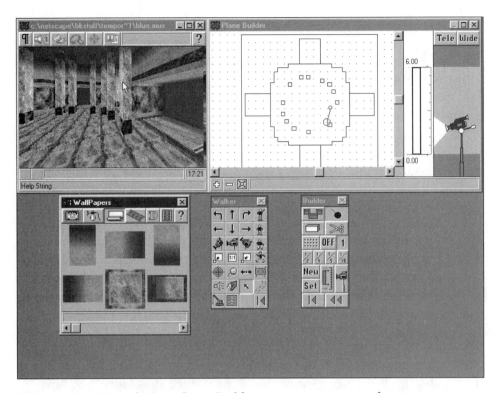

Figure 11.3   Virtual HomeSpace Builder is an inexpensive and easy-to-use way to experiment with VRML. A special version of VHSB is included on the CD-ROM. For full-color screen shots of the kind of worlds you can make with it, see the gallery on the CD-ROM.

To keep the file sizes of your virtual worlds small, limit the textures you use, advises Web wizard Bill Murphy. "They're what make worlds big," he says. "It doesn't really matter how complex your objects are because they're just data. But when you start putting all kinds of textures on them, download times really go up. Try to use solid colors instead."

Some Web wizards also compress their virtual worlds to keep the file sizes small. You can spot a compressed world by the .GZ extension on the end of the file name.

Once you've collected the software for world-building, you'll need a powerful machine to run it. This type of software demands far more from your computer than just about any other type you can think of; so realistically, you'll need a fairly fast Pentium or PowerMac with at least 16 MB of RAM and plenty of hard disk space. Viewing virtual worlds will be less frustrating if you have a good monitor (at least 15 inches and 0.28 dot pitch) capable of displaying true (16-bit) colors and powered by at least 1 MB of VRAM. It also helps if you have a video accelerator board, especially during the *rendering* process (when objects are converted from rows of numbers into 3D graphics). Right now, these boards are fairly unusual, but some Web wizards predict they'll soon be as common as sound cards.

Even with state-of-the-art hardware, you will still probably have a disorienting time lag between doing something and seeing any result onscreen. This is partly a bandwidth issue, but mostly a result of hardware limitations. Despite attempts by world builders to keep their file sizes as small as possible, all the on-the-fly rendering required by the client computer (yours) in VRML can make navigating fairly awkward.

Bandwidth and hardware limitations are nothing new to Web wizards, and as always, they find ingenious ways around them. One possibility is to have the basic elements of a virtual world stored on the client's hard disk, where it can be accessed faster. In such a world, you build your own "rooms" with the same basic building blocks as everyone else in the world uses and store the results on someone else's server using some proprietary VRML-type technology. Eventually, you'll probably have to lease this kind of real estate, but at this stage, it's free from companies like AlphaWorld at http://www.worlds.net/.

As you can see from the screen shot in Figure 11.4, AlphaWorld is actually a completely separate program that you run instead of or in addition to your usual Web browser. If you are a registered user (registration is free at this point), you can do all the things you might typically do in a Web-based chat room, but with visual and auditory elements added.

More important, you can stake your own claim and build your own "homestead" using objects that AlphaWorld supplies, such as walls, arches, trees, and waterfalls. You can link all the typical Web elements to your objects, in addition to adding (limited) sound and animation. A visitor could, for example, hear your choice of music playing in the background while using a 3D mailbox in front of your virtual castle to send email to your usual account. Many companies and institutions, in addition to individuals, are busy staking their claims in cyberspaces like AlphaWorld. Other companies that are doing similar things to AlphaWorld include OnLive (http://www.onlive.com/) and Black Sun Interactive (http://www.blacksun.com/).

Figure 11.4   AlphaWorld is one of a handful of Web-based virtual environments that provide an existing framework for your virtual world. It's not, strictly speaking, VRML, but it's free (at least for now) and the building process is relatively easy, although somewhat tedious.

The Wizards Speak: The Virtual View from Here

Bill Murphy is the founding partner of the Webology Group (http://www.webology.com), a Web consultancy to Fortune 500 and Fortune 100 companies. The Webology Group's VRML work is done with Caligari trueSpace on Unix and Windows NT machines with 64 KB of RAM. The 3D modeling is done with LightWave on Macs. LightWave, like other full-featured 3D modelers, isn't cheap. One 3D modeling program Murphy likes that *is* relatively cheap is Poser, which sells for about $99. It renders human figures on the fly in a variety of poses, which can be very handy for world-building as well as more traditional graphic design.

Murphy sees exciting times ahead with the combination of VRML and Java. "That's what we're excited about; that's where we're heading," he says. "With Java, you can actually have things happen in

VRML. For example, average users could build their own VRML worlds on the Web and, with a Java-based coordinate-tracking system, keep track of where people are in them. You'd know automatically, then, when a friend drops by your site because you'd see that person walking toward you. Java will be the programming engine to make cooler things happen in a VRML world."

Right now, though, he acknowledges, "Moving through [VRML] rooms can be frustrating, especially if you don't have gravity. It's easy to spin out of control or go the wrong direction. You end up pressing the Reset button a lot." He also questions the usefulness of trying to build things like shopping malls with the current state of VRML on the Web. Instead, he looks for the combination of VRML and Java to lead to more interaction between people. Sites like AlphaWorld already have that, to a limited extent, through their use of avatars. Murphy sees more interactive avatars "that won't just float around. You'll be able to make them do animated things like walk up and shake someone's hand or give someone an object."

"Imagine," he continues, "that you're a customer-support person for a computer manufacturer. You'll be sitting at home, but working, logged into a virtual world as an avatar. People with a problem come into the world, and you'll be there to help them. If they have a problem with, say, a CD-ROM drive, you can give them a virtual CD-ROM drive and have them show you what's wrong. Your full-time job will be to interact with people in a virtual environment.

"Or suppose you like to garden. You could have VRML objects that were seeds. You virtually plant the seeds, then [using Java] see how they'll look in five months. You could also wander through other people's gardens at various times of the year. There are also all sorts of applications or interactive games or just about anything else you'd want to do."

Murphy predicts that applications like these will be "really huge in a few years, but there's lots more hard-core programming to do" before they become a reality. Interestingly, bandwidth would not be much of an issue in turning these kinds of scenarios into a reality. The initial download would probably be fairly large, on the order of several megabytes, but after that, using the world would mostly involve updating the objects. And since these objects are really just rows and rows of numbers, they wouldn't take too much bandwidth. Again, this is already proving to be the case, on a limited scale, at sites like AlphaWorld.

For the short term, Murphy, like the other Web wizards interviewed for this book, advises against using any Web technology—in this case, VRML—just because it's there. He urges, "Simplify. If you're going to build VRML rooms or worlds, keep them simple. Have them link to 2D pages when that's more appropriate, like to present lists of things, then come back to VRML when you want to, say, let users spin and examine an object. When you combine 2D and 3D, HTML and VRML, your site becomes more functional. Don't get locked into trying to use one technology for everything."

 Trying to move around in a 3D world can be disorienting, especially since many of them don't have the physical properties you're used to in the real world, such as gravity and mass. Here are a few tips that apply to most VRML browsers and add-ins to make navigation easier:

- Click and drag the left mouse button to move left and right or in and out of a scene.

- Click and drag the right mouse button to rotate you up, down, and around the scene.

- Click and hold the left mouse button to keep moving at a steady pace in whatever direction you're currently heading.

- In some browsers, you can double-click the left mouse button on a "hot" object to zoom to it. Be careful, though: if the object has a link attached, you might end up jumping to another page or world instead.

- If you move the mouse and nothing happens, wait a moment for the rendering to catch up with you. If you jiggle your mouse back and forth trying to get the view to move instead, you'll probably see a nauseating effect onscreen when the computer catches up and rapidly replays your mouse movements.

- Most browsers have a Reset button that will take you back to where you started if you get lost.

A World to Call Your Own

With the help of a program like Caligari Pioneer, shown in Figure 11.5 and available from http://www.caligari.com/, creating a simple Web world in VRML is not that much more complicated than creating a Web page with HTML. (Pioneer is a "light" version, free for noncommercial use, of Caligari's commercial trueSpace program.) The interface, however, takes some getting used to.

Here are the steps to create a little world that will give you some practice with world-building software and VRML. Before you start, you should have Caligari Pioneer installed and running.

1. Select File|Scene|New to start a new file and switch to world-building mode.

2. Start your new world by selecting the texture for the ground. To select a texture, click the Material Library button to bring up its dialog box, and select the brick texture from the box, as shown in Figure 11.6.

URL: http://www.virtpark.com/theme/home.wrl

Figure 11.5 The interface of Caligari Pioneer is different from the typical Windows interface, as you can see. Most of the buttons have several different tools attached to them. Some tools come up when you right-click, others when you click and hold the left mouse button.

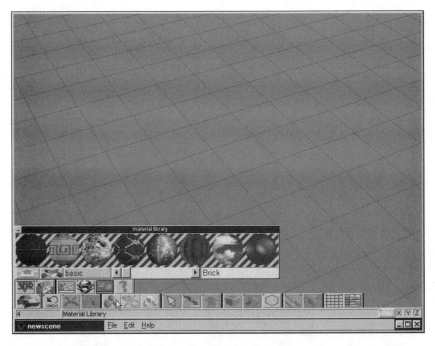

Figure 11.6   The materials library has the brick texture selected, so whatever object you create next will automatically be "wallpapered" in brick.

3. Now, create the "ground." Click and hold the polygon tool to bring up the Polygon mode box. Click and drag the double-sided arrow on the box until the number of polygons is 4. Starting in the middle of the world grid, click and drag to create the four-sided polygon. Make it about six squares across. When you let go, you should have something like Figure 11.7.

4. Now you're ready to put some 3D objects in your world. First, select the texture for a cylinder as in step 2. Since it's going to be the trunk of a tree, wood is a good texture. Then, click the Primitives Panel button to bring up the Primitives toolbox and select the cylinder. A wooden cylinder will appear in your world.

5. You'll probably need to move and resize (rescale) the cylinder. To move or resize an object, it must be currently selected. If it is, a big arrow will be pointing at it, as shown in Figure 11.8. To select an object, click the arrow button in the middle of the lower toolbox, then click the object. (If you've just been walking or flying through

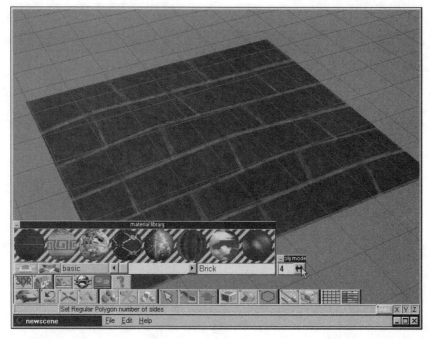

Figure 11.7 Clicking and dragging will create a flat rectangle if you choose the Polygon tool and specify 4 in its box.

the world, you'll see a pair of feet or an airplane instead of an arrow. When that happens, click and hold the button to bring up its pop-up menu and select the arrow.)

6. The Move and Rescale tools are on the same button, to the right of the arrow button. Again, you change from one to the other by clicking and holding the button to bring up its pop-up box. The Move tool (a double-sided arrow) should be currently selected. To move or rescale an object horizontally, click and drag the left mouse button. To move or rescale vertically, click and drag the right mouse button. To move or rescale in both dimensions at once, click and hold both mouse buttons while dragging. After you've moved the cylinder where you want it, switch from the Move tool to the Rescale tool (remember, they're on the same button on the toolbar) and rescale it to look more like a tree trunk.

7. Select a new texture for the rest of the tree. You could use the China texture for a surreal look, or choose one of the plastic textures, click the Paint Face tool, and change its color to green.

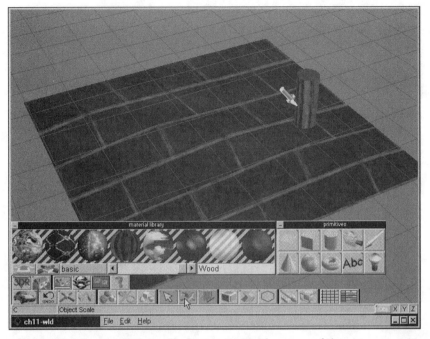

Figure 11.8   You can tell the cylinder is selected because of the arrow pointing to it. The cylinder has been moved and resized to look more like a tree trunk. Note also that the Object Scale tool is currently selected.

After choosing your texture, click the Cone primitive. Move and rescale it to put it on top of the trunk.

8. Add a few more objects to the scene. I chose a box with the fabric texture and a floating sphere with the bullion texture, as shown in Figure 11.9. (The reason I'm using so many textures is that my version of Netscape's VRML add-in renders them better than plain colors created by Pioneer.)

9. You can link any Web file to a VRML object. Just select the object, click the Attach a Hyperlink button, and fill in the dialog box that comes up, as shown in Figure 11.10.

10. With all your links in place, choose File|Scene|Save As and name it in the dialog box, making sure to indicate that it's a .WRL file. This file is named ch11-w2.wrl.

11. When you click OK, you'll get the dialog box in Figure 11.11. For details about what all these options mean, check out the Help file that comes with Pioneer. For now, just click OK again.

Figure 11.9   All of the objects are in place. Now it's time to add a few links.

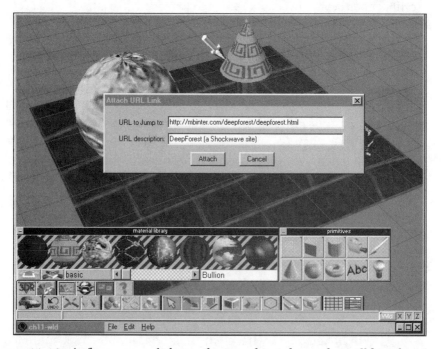

Figure 11.10   When a user clicks on the tree object, he or she will be taken to DeepForest's HTML home page.

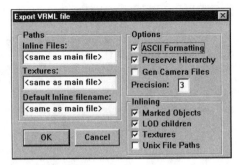

Figure 11.11   This dialog box gives you control over exactly how your world should be exported to .WRL format.

12. At this point, your world would be ready to go, but with a plain gray background. To add a background image, open the file in any text editor and manually add the lines that are shaded in the following code fragment:

```
#VRML V1.0 ascii
#Fountain (tm) was used to create this VRML file.
Separator {
   CALIGARISceneInfo {
      fields [ SFVec3f background, SFVec3f environ,
      SFVec3f fogColor, SFBool fog, SFLong fogNear,
      SFLong fogFar, SFString envName, SFString backgroundName ]
      background 0.502 0.502 0.502
      environ 0.000 0.000 0.000
      fogColor 0.502 0.502 0.502
      fogNear 1
      fogFar 500
      fog FALSE
   }
   DEF BackgroundImage Info {
      string "bg-blue.jpg" # Any GIF, JPEG, or BMP could go here
   }
   Switch {
      whichChild 0
```

Test the new world you've created by opening it in Netscape or another VRML-enabled browser. You might find that objects that looked okay in Pioneer are positioned incorrectly or have strange-looking textures. If so, go back to Pioneer, load the file, make changes, and test it again. Eventually, you should get something like Figure 11.12.

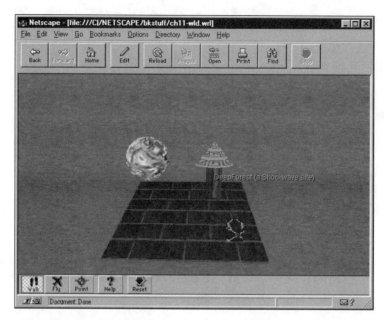

Figure 11.12 This world, including all the textures, takes about 65 KB of disk space. Note the message that the user receives when the mouse passes over the tree.

Supporting non-VRML Browsers

The VRML language itself doesn't provide any backward compatibility. Therefore, if you link directly with a VRML world using a line of HTML like

```
<A HREF="mywrld.wrl">Enter the castle</A>
```

users who don't have VRML-enabled browsers will just get an error message about an unsupported file type. As long as you make it clear on the referring page of HTML that a VRML browser is required to view the link, this shouldn't be too much of a problem.

Another alternative, according to Leonid Kitainik, Vice-President and General Manager of ParaGraph's consumer division (the makers of Virtual HomeSpace Builder), is to use the <EMBED> tag to add the world right into a page of HTML. An example of this from ParaGraph's site is shown in Figure 11.13. Here's the relevant HTML from this Web page:

```
<html>
<head>
<title>ParaGraph International VRML Web Site</title>
```

```
</head>
<body bgcolor="#ffffff" text="#000000" link="#0000f0"
vlink="#0000f0" alink="#f00000">
<center>
<embed SRC="http://vrml.paragraph.com/3dhome/main/mainhall.wrl"
 align=center width=425 height=263 alt="3D Home Page">
<br>
If you are not using Netscape Navigator 2.0, or if you prefer to
watch full-window 3D,<br>
please click
<a href="http://vrml.paragraph.com/3dhome/main/mainhall.wrl">here</
a> (VRML browser required!)
</center>
</body>
</html>
```

When you use <EMBED> with a VRML file, you can set the height and width to any values that make sense to you. Since the VRML world is created mathematically, it will be scaled properly for the size you set. Note the use of the ALT attribute in the <EMBED> tag. By including ALT, users with browsers that support <EMBED> but not VRML will see a message instead of a broken link.

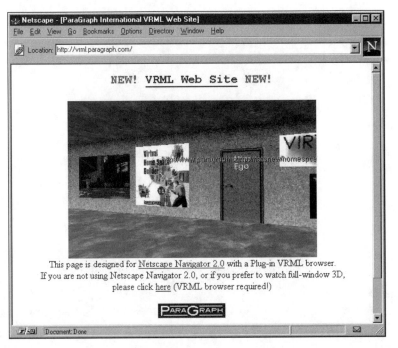

Figure 11.13   Using the <EMBED> tag, you can add a virtual world right on a page of HTML, instead of making it a separate link.

You could extend support for non-VRML browsers even further by putting some alternative to the VRML file, such as a screen shot, in a <NOEMBED>..</NOEMBED> tag pair:

```
<NOEMBED>
  <IMG SRC="mywrld.jpg" WIDTH=400 HEIGHT=250 ALIGN=center>
</NOEMBED>
```

Netscape, which is the most popular VRML-enabled browser, will ignore everything in <NOEMBED>..</NOEMBED>. Only non-Netscape browsers (and therefore, we're assuming, non-VRML-enabled browsers) will show the screen shot.

Web Wizard's Touchstones for VRML

Do   look through your collection of GIF and JPEG background tiles for files that would make good VRML textures, but keep an eye on file sizes.

Don't   use VRML for things that are better implemented in HTML, like reports and articles.

Do   thoroughly test any worlds you make, especially since problems with VRML tend to crash Netscape.

Don't   link directly to a VRML world without letting people know they'll need a VRML browser. There's no way to add backward compatibility in a .WRL file, so users whose browsers can't handle VRML will just get an error message.

Do   consider the <EMBED> tag as a way to put a VRML world on a page of HTML. That way, you can use the ALT attribute and the <NOEMBED>..</NOEMBED> tag pair to support users who don't have VRML-enabled browsers.

Don't   get too frustrated if you have a hard time moving through 3D worlds at first. Spend some time getting used to the different ways your mouse works in 3D, read the help that comes with your particular 3D browser, and remember the Reset button!

Do   check out the VRML 1.0 and 2.0 specifications, and the various extensions from different companies and organizations. You can find them at sites like the VRML Repository, http://www.sdsc.edu/vrml. You don't necessarily have to read the specs line-by-line, but looking through them will give you a feel for how VRML works.

XII

THE INSIDE WORD ON INTRANETS

Intranets are hot. Technologically savvy executives at many organizations have been quick to see how an intranet can speed and centralize the flow of internal information. Intranets can also be very economical, since they're built on the backbone of existing communications technologies and can reduce the costs normally associated with distributing information. But what are they, exactly, and how are they being used in the real world?

Typical Tasks for an Intranet

Unglamorous as it might seem, one of the first things to go on an intranet is usually the company directory/phonebook. It's very easy to turn into HTML, it's essential information that's used by everyone in the organization, and it needs fairly frequent updating—the essential elements of a good intranet publication.

One of the first departments to come online on an intranet is often Human Resources. Many everyday HR functions are related to collecting and routing information such as company procedures, job postings (Figure 12.1), and benefits policies to large numbers of employees. These are perfect candidates for automating via an intranet.

Consider, for example, the typical procedure for announcing job openings without an intranet:

- A manager calls or writes HR about the opening.
- Someone from HR looks up the job requirements in the paper-based or computerized files.
- Someone from HR types up and photocopies the details of this particular opening.
- Someone from HR disseminates copies of the opening to the appropriate people in the various departments.
- Next, any number of things might happen. The announcement might sit in an IN box until it's no longer relevant, or get tacked to a bulletin board, or be read in a meeting, or be photocopied and redistributed.

How much time and effort is spent repeating this procedure over and over in a mid-sized or large company? If an employee wants to apply for the job, the process is just as tedious and resource-consuming.

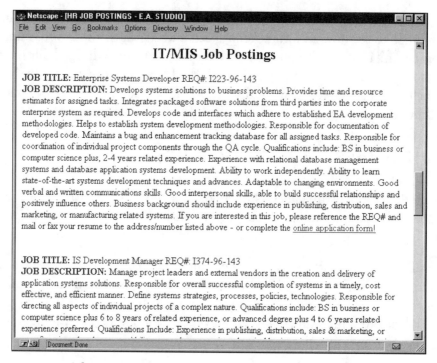

Figure 12.1   Job openings are perfectly suited for posting on an intranet. This is partly because they're time-sensitive and follow a fairly standard format, but also because the information they contain is intrinsically valuable to many members of an organization, so they give people an incentive for using the intranet.

Now, consider how this process might work in an organization that has put this function on an intranet:

- A manager with an opening to fill logs onto the Human Resources internal Web page and clicks the Submit Job Opening link, which displays a form.

- The manager fills out the form with the pertinent information about the opening.

- A CGI script takes the information from the form, combines it with information from a database of job functions, and automatically creates or appends to an HTML file of job listings.

- Someone from HR reviews and approves the new job listings, if necessary.

The job opening is immediately made known to everybody who has access to the intranet, whether they're two doors down from Human Resources or in another country. To respond, an employee just clicks a link and fills out another form, the results of which are immediately relayed back to HR. The technology to implement such a system is not particularly difficult to master using the information in the previous chapters of this book: some text-based pages of HTML (Chapter 3), a few forms (Chapter 7), and a CGI script (also Chapter 7). The hardest part would be writing the CGI script, which could be outsourced, if necessary.

Other popular "test sites" for intranets are the marketing department and the communications department. In a large manufacturing company, for example, the savings in publishing thousands of pages' worth of technical documentation on an intranet instead of on paper can itself pay for the intranet. And posting company news and press releases on an intranet as well as an external Web site (Figure 12.2) helps to ensure that employees are informed and up-to-date. With an intranet, you should never have the problem of employees finding out about corporate news by reading it in the newspaper.

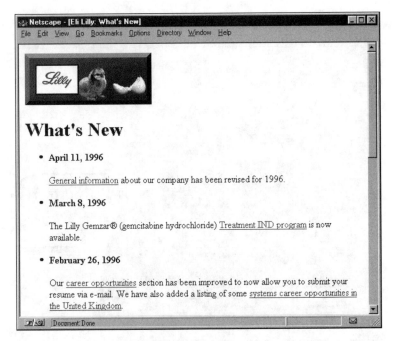

Figure 12.2 Here's how a simple "corporate news" page might look. This one is from a public-access Web site, but it could just as easily be on an intranet.

The Wizards Speak: An Intranet for a Medium-Sized Organization

John Luoma and David Yunck are the MIS manager and marketing specialist, respectively, of Frontier Technologies Corporation (http://www.frontiertech.com/), whose home page is shown in Figure 12.3. Frontier is one of the companies specializing in providing Intranet software. The company intranet, which Luoma manages, is used by its approximately 150 employees in several states around the country.

"An intranet," says Luoma, "is really the same concept as the Internet, but running on a closed network—a LAN or WAN. A company's intranet is usually a separate, stand-alone entity from the Internet, although they can be connected under certain circumstances. You can do everything on an intranet as on the Internet." In fact, many of the coolest new technologies that are difficult to run on the Web because of bandwidth issues are actually easier and more effective on an intranet.

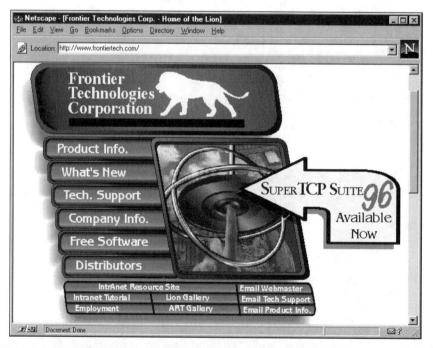

Figure 12.3 Frontier Technologies is one of the companies offering turnkey intranet products.

The big question for many people about intranets is how they fit together with the LAN, email system, and groupware that an organization might already have. According to Luoma, "You still need a LAN as a data repository, to store things like databases. If you want to get to a piece of information on a LAN, though, you have to know specifically where it is—what directory it's under and how to get there. An intranet, on the other hand, gives common accessibility. A user doesn't have to know where something is in the directory structure.

"An intranet is a publishing tool for information that you want to make widely available within the organization. You wouldn't use it for a file that's only going to a few people—email would be more efficient for that. But for things like telephone lists, marketing documents, pricing information, and company news, it's ideal."

The hardware and software costs of an intranet are minimal for an organization that already has a LAN. For a medium-sized company, Yunck estimates $3,000 to $5,000 for the intranet server, and from $99 to several thousand dollars for the server software. Yunck suggests an NT-based server for a small or mid-sized organization, and a Unix-based one for large organization. Choices for intranet-specific server software include Frontier's own products, Microsoft's IIS, and Netscape's Commerce Server and Communications Server. Most intranet server installs are fairly straightforward for network-administration people, he says. In fact, you don't need intranet-specific software at all, but it does make issues of organization and—especially—security easier. At the client level, you can use any browser you'd use for the Web itself.

Many companies that sell intranet software tools have free demos and beta versions at their Web sites. The Useful Intranet Links site (http://www.infoweb.com.au/intralnk.htm) is a good place to start looking for them. Download, install, and experiment with some of them, risk-free, as you plan your intranet.

After installation, the personnel costs vary widely from one organization to another, depending on how big a role the intranet plays in the information flow and how it's managed. Some companies use a very distributed model, where each department is basically responsible for its own space, and they can publish just about anything they want, however they want it, in that space. Other companies use a very centralized model, where everything that is to be published on the server goes through a single source. At Frontier, they started off with a centralized approach, with basically one person responsible for the entire intranet. "As people at the departmental level get more educated about and comfortable with the intranet," says Luoma, "there is more management at that level. Then, the central Webmaster moves to planning organizational things and keeping the information fresh."

Luoma stresses that keeping information fresh on an intranet is crucial to its success: "If people know they can always find new information, they're much more interested in using it. You need to make the server exciting to use, basically do some internal marketing. Try to have a little 'hook' to make people look at it every day, until it becomes a habit." When Frontier's intranet first came online, Luoma put different graphics up each day, including the popular "magic eye" stereograms. Frontier has also occasionally put information on their intranet that isn't directly related to the company, but is helpful for employees. At tax time, for example, they made all the federal tax forms available by linking right to the IRS's Web site.

Security is the other big issue for intranets. At Frontier, Luoma says, "Security is handled very much like Novell's password scheme of inherited rights. Each member of a group can have access to certain documents based on membership in that group. When planning an intranet, it's very important to think about security. For example, if a certain group has access to a particular folder, you can't then have a subfolder containing something they don't have access to."

When an intranet first comes online, it will take some effort to get people used to using it. This is partly a matter of formal training, partly internal marketing, and partly persistence. When someone calls or stops by for information that's available on the server, the first question should be "Did you check the intranet?" As Web wizard John Luoma puts it, "It takes a while before people figure out how much easier it is to look on the server than to wander around the building."

The Wizards Speak: Intranets for Large Organizations

Bill Murphy is a Web consultant whose company, The Webology Group (http://www.webology.com), designs intranets for organizations such as a large computer manufacturer and an international financial institution with over 2,000 employees all over the world. For such large companies, the efficient flow of internal communications is a major goal, and intranets are widely seen as a big step in that direction.

The sheer volume of information produced by a large company can make managing its intranet a daunting task. For example, Murphy cites a situation where a company's new-product announcements were done in five different formats from different departments. One suggestion for putting these documents on the intranet involved bringing them all into Word, and then using a combination of Word style sheets and its built-in Internet Assistant to convert them to HTML. Murphy saw this process as flawed, however, because "it's too easy for people to make mistakes in Word." Tables, for example, could get misaligned or cut off, and the wrong styles could get applied to text.

Instead, he implemented a forms-driven system, written in Visual Basic, with field validation done on the fly. The results are sent to a Microsoft Access database, from which they can be output in any format necessary—including dynamically created HTML. Creating pages dynamically is very important for large intranets; manually coding the HTML would take far too much resources. Murphy calls sites created this way "smart sites." While he tends to use Visual Basic as the engine to drive these smart sites, he acknowledges that languages such as Java and Perl could also be used.

A big consideration when planning an intranet in a large company is deciding who owns it. In other words, which people in which departments decide what goes on the intranet, where it goes, and how it looks? In one company that Murphy consulted for, he says the intranet "started with programmers building it on their own time, however they wanted it. Then, when the big Web wave hit the media, they got to show off what they'd done. At that point, management quickly jumped to take over the project—even though they didn't know anything about the Web." Now, things have stabilized into a Web "swat team" consisting of systems administrators, programmers, and key departmental managers who set the standards for the internal Web sites.

Security is an issue with all intranets. It's even more important in large companies that deal with vast amounts of sensitive information. As long as the intranet stands alone, it can be made relatively secure with standard password-protection schemes. If it interacts with the Web like the one in Figure 12.4, though, access control is handled mainly through *firewalls*.

"Firewalls," Murphy explains, "are like bouncers in a bar or ticket-takers at Disney World. They control who gets to go where by reading *packets* of data that indicate where it comes from, what it contains, and what should be done with it." Most of the time, *packet-filtering* is done to restrict access to or from certain sites according to their *IP address* (a long string of numbers, separated by periods, that uniquely identifies an Internet server). Some companies, however, go so far with packet-filtering as to stop any messages containing particular words from entering or leaving the intranet.

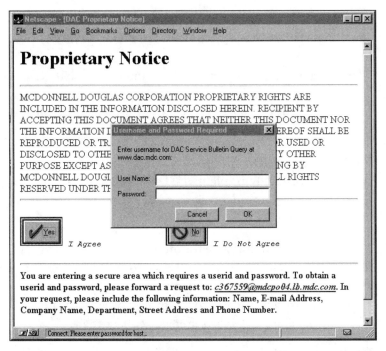

Figure 12.4 If you want to access information from McDonnell Douglas' intranet via the Web, you need to have a user ID and password with the proper rights. Firewalls provide additional behind-the-scenes security.

One of the keys to a successful large intranet, according to Web wizard Bill Murphy, is to make it global. "Give everyone the capability to have their own page. Have the pages generated dynamically from a forms interface, so even people who don't know anything about HTML can make them." These personal pages can contain information about where employees went to school, where they worked previously, what their hobbies are, and so on. Such seemingly mundane information can actually be very important in large organizations where people don't always get a chance to meet their counterparts face-to-face.

Web Wizard's Touchstones for Intranets

Do automate the production of an intranet's Web pages as much as possible, using such tools as CGI scripts, Java scripts, and commercial software, so that it will be easy for people in the organization to create and maintain their own pages.

Don't put sensitive information on the intranet until you have thoroughly implemented security systems. Many commercial intranet server products can provide fairly rigorous security.

Do provide training on the intranet and "hooks" to get people interested in it. Some ways to build interest are with contests, attractive graphics, and information that's intrinsically valuable to lots of employees, such as the schedule at a local sports arena or concert hall.

Don't try to bring all parts of a large organization online on the intranet at once. It's usually better to start with a few localized, departmental test cases.

Do provide clear and easy-to-use guidelines for publishing on the intranet, but...

Don't make the publishing process too restrictive. The most successful intranets tend to give employees a considerable amount of freedom to experiment with their personal pages.

Do consider an intranet if your organization has one or more of these elements:

- Over 100 employees
- Geographically disbursed workforce
- Reliance on outside vendors and contractors
- Large volumes of printed materials that need frequent updating

APPENDIX

Web Site Bibliography

The following is an annotated list of the Web sites I referred to in writing this book, grouped by topic. A hypertext version of this list is available on the CD-ROM as bookmks.htm.

General Reference

The Coriolis Group - Visual Interactive Zine
http://www.coriolis.com/

You didn't think I'd leave out my publisher's Web site, did you?

iWORLD Developer's Forum
http://netday.iworld.com/devforum/

An excellent resource for info and news, broken down by departments: VRML, Shockwave, multimedia, Java, etc. and updated weekly.

Off the Net
http://home.netscape.com/assist/net_sites/off_the_net.html

Straight-up source for what's hip and what's just over-hyped in Web wizardry.

The Ultimate Collection of Winsock Software
http://ftp.ameritel.net/mirrors/tucows/

The well-known "Tucows" site; rates the software it includes on a basis of one to five cows.

Welcome to Feed
http://www.feedmag.com/

One of the better zines for Web developers.

Welcome to Pepsi World
http://www.pepsi.com/

Wanna see how the big boys play with "soft marketing" on the Web? This is the place.

Sites of Web Wizards Quoted or Referred to in the Book

AlphaWorld
http://www.worlds.net/alphaworld/docs.html

Find out about this 3D super-chat-world, download the proprietary browser software, and read the "immigration procedures."

alt.coffee... coffee, computers, comfy chairs
http://www.altdotcoffee.com/

There's lots going on at this cybercafe, including frames, Shockwave, and VRML.

BETHESDA - Ars Est Celare Artem
http://www.bethsoft.com/

Light on content when I visited, but some great graphics and image maps.

Bonnie Carasso—Multimedia Design Samples
http://www.carasso.com/design/northsamples.html

A Web-based graphic artist; note the use of thumbnails at her site.

Caligari Home World
http://www.caligari.com/

The makers of popular VRML world-building software, including the professional-level trueSpace and the entry-level Pioneer.

The Color Table Of Way Grooviness
http://nwlink.com/~catanza/colors.html

My current fave for hexadecimal color codes online.

Discovery Channel Online
http://www.discovery.com/

Inventive use of tables and image maps.

Excel 5.0 to HTML Table Converter
http://www710.gsfc.nasa.gov/704/dgd/xl2html.html

Frontier Technologies Corp.
http://www.frontiertech.com/

A vendor of turnkey intranet products.

The Great Reality Caper
http://vwv.is.co.za/reality/welcome

An absolutely amazing use of frames and Java to create a real, online, graphic adventure game. From South Africa Airlines, but the marketing is extremely subtle and unobtrusive.

Headbone—Shockwave Velma
http://www.headbone.com/text/dressvelshock.html

The Web-based version of ColorForms, and a source of inspiration for that first venture into interactive Shockwave.

Impact Online
http://www.impactonline.org/

An extremely well-designed site. Note the elegant use of text and image maps. And it's a good cause, to boot!

An Interactive History of the Wienermobile
http://www.oscar-mayer.com/wienermobile/history.html

Uses streaming RealAudio synchronized to graphics to create a filmstrip effect.

Javascript
http://tanega.com/java/java.html

Charles Goodin's collection of quick and easy JavaScript tricks.

Morgen Sagen's Web Development Site
http://www.morgen.com/main.shtml

Notable for some clever little Java applets.

New Media Marketing's CAFE DEL SOL
http://www.xm.com/cafe/

An indispensible source of freeware Java applets for adding sound and animation to your home page. The applets are well-documented, too.

Pop Rocket's Game Arena
http://www.poprocket.com/shockwave/arena.html

There are some very cool, addictive Shockwave games at this site, with more being added all the time.

QBullets
http://www.matterform.com/mf/qbullets/aboutqbullets.html

There's a nice collection of tiny buttons (the qbullets) here, but I particularly liked the clean design based on image maps.

Relocation Salary Calculator
http://www.homefair.com/homefair/cmr/salcalc.html

A good use of frames combined with nifty and useful information—find out how far your salary would (or wouldn't) stretch in another state.

Sound Wire's Home Page
http://www.soundwire.com/

A music store featuring online ordering and music clips in several different formats.

Stranded! Shockwave Movie
http://www.m-squared.com/shock1.htm

A cute little Shockwave animation.

THUNKWORLD
http://www.thunk.com/

One of the sites of Web designer Larry Rosenthal, featuring Shockwave and VRML.

Up All Night: Index
http://www.allnight.com/

Web-based graphic artists. Their home page features a cheery, geometric look.

Virtual Home Space Builder
http://www.paragraph.com/vhsb/

VHSB is a very popular and reasonably priced entry-level VRML program. Get information, download demos, and preview libraries of templates and objects from here.

WallStreetWeb by BulletProof.com
http://www.bulletproof.com/WallStreetWeb/

The first full-blown online Java application. Note that it can take several minutes to load, though.

The Webology Group
http://www.webology.com

Web wizard Bill Murphy's consultancy.

Welcome to Haywood & Sullivan
http://www.hsdesign.com/

Web site designers and scanner experts.

Windows95.com 32-bit Shareware
http://www.windows95.com/apps/

Well-organized, frequently updated source of Win95 shareware, featuring a very clean, intuitive image-map interface.

X Files Terminal Now Accessed
http://www.neosoft.com/sbanks/xfiles/xfiles.html

Great site for fans of the TV show. Its home page has the distinction of being the only Web page I've seen with a justifiable use of the BLINK attribute.

Graphics and GIF Animation

Animated Pages! The MicroMovie MiniMultiplex
http://www.teleport.com/~cooler/MMMM/MMMM.html

Lots of inspiration here if you're interested in any kind of Web-based animation.

Ask the Graphics Oracle Page
http://www.mccannas.com/sketch/oracle.htm

Questions and answers on graphics-related topics, especially regarding Photoshop.

CSC Image Index Page
http://www.widomaker.com/~spalmer/

GIF Animation on the WWW
http://member.aol.com/royalef/gifanim.htm

Many clever examples of GIF animation.

Kai's Power Tips and Tricks for Photoshop
http://the-tech.mit.edu/KPT/

OZONE
http://www.winternet.com/~drozone/home-index.html

Doc Ozone's personal site. It's a bit frames-heavy for my taste, but the good Doc gives away nice images and backgrounds.

Resources for Icons, Images, and Graphics
http://osiris.colorado.edu/~brumbaug/graphics.html

Some Building Blocks and Icons
http://www.nas.nasa.gov/NAS/WebWeavers/icons.html

Texture Land
http://www.meat.com/textures/

An excellent source of free files to use as HTML backgrounds and VRML textures.

WebGround - Free background textures
http://www.ip.pt/webground/

Image Maps

Emergent Media | Blue Book
http://www.emergentmedia.com/

I love the metaphor—turning the famous "blue books" used for college exams into image maps.

HTML Support - Client Side Images
http://www.microsoft.com/windows/ie/imagemap.htm

Information and links on creating client-side image maps.

Imagemap Authoring Guide and Tutorial Sites
http://www.cris.com/~automata/tutorial.shtml

Information on server-side image maps.

Frames

Frame-o-rama
http://www.ECNet.Net/users/gallery/webwork/frames/frame1/frame1.html

F U R L intro
http://www.dscnet.com/furl/

Wish I'd thought of this clever combination of frames and Java.

Forms, CGIs, SSIs, and Counters

CGI Applications
http://www.comvista.com/net/www/cgi.html

The CGI Collection
http://www.wolfenet.com/~rniles/cgi.html

CGI Form Handling in Perl
http://www.bio.cam.ac.uk/web/form.html

A CGI Programmer's Reference
http://www.best.com/~hedlund/cgi-faq/

CGI Programs on the Web
http://www.cyserv.com/pttong/cgiprog.html

Counter Definition Page
http://www.microserve.net/~john/counter-def.html

A way to put an access counter on your page.

Dave's List of CGIs
http://www.cyserv.com/pttong/cgi.html

Form/CGI Creator
http://the-inter.net/www/future21/formpro.html

A form with CGI script that creates forms with CGI scripts. How Escher-esque!

HTML Access Counter 4.0
http://www.webtools.org/counter/

Surf here for a very easy-to-use access counter, form-driven, with lots of customizable options. Just hope it can continue to handle all the traffic it gets!

Matt Kruse's Perl Scripts
http://cs.sau.edu/~mkruse/www/scripts/

Matt's Script Archive
http://www.worldwidemart.com/scripts/

Selena Sol's Public Domain CGI Script Archive and Resource Library
http://www2.eff.org/~erict/Scripts/

The premier source for generally well-documented, public-domain CGI scripts.

Shakespearean Insult
http://www.nova.edu/Inter-Links/cgi-bin/bard.pl

A funny and clever variation on the "fortune" CGI script that generates random insults Elizabethan-style.

Writing CGI scripts
http://www.cs.ucl.ac.uk/staff/jon/book/node86.html

Yahoo's page of CGI-related links
http://www.yahoo.com/Computers_and_Internet/Internet/World_Wide_Web/ CGI___Common_Gateway_Interface/

A good place to start your script search.

Sounds and Music

The Capitol Steps
http://pfm.het.brown.edu/people/mende/steps/index.html

Political satire from a locally famous (in the D.C. area) improv group made up of former lobbyists, Congressional aides, and similar types. More important for the purposes of this book, it's a place to test your audio plug-ins.

Directory of /pub/4th_Eye
http://ftp.southern.com/pub/4th_Eye/

One of the rare sources for copyright-free sound clips.

Harmony Central: Map of Harmony Central
http://harmony-central.mit.edu/map.html

Index of free sound effects from Sun microsystems
http://sunsite.unc.edu/pub/multimedia/sun-sounds/sound_effects/

MACOS Web Site
http://www.io.org/~macos/

An organization pushing for more sharing of audio and music files, without lots of usage restrictions. Check here for audio clips that are specifically legal for use on Web sites.

MULTIMEDIA MUSIC
http://www.wavenet.com/~axgrindr/quimby.html

Good, royalty-free music loops in AIFF format. Several are included on the CD-ROM.

Premier Radio Networks: Main Entrance
http://www.premrad.com/

As its home page says, "laughs, movie reviews,...and other nonproductive time killers."

Shareware Music Machine
http://www.gil.com.au/~mcontact/smm/

You'll find music shareware to download here.

Syntrillium
http://www.netzone.com/syntrillium/

Site of the CoolEdit sound editor.

Virtual Noise
http://www.virtualnoise.com/

A site devoted to indie music. Lots of audio clips in various formats. Even if you're not into the music, it's a good way to test whether your various audio plug-ins are working.

Welcome to Real Audio!
http://www.realaudio.com/

Find out what it is, where to get it, and how to do it.

The World Wide Web Virtual Library: Audio
http://www.comlab.ox.ac.uk/archive/audio.html

Yahoo's page of MPEG-related links
http://www.yahoo.com/Computers_and_Internet/Multimedia/Video/MPEG/
Technical_Information/

Shockwave Stuff

DC Comics - Sovereign 7 Kit
http://www.macromedia.com/Tools/Shockwave/Gallery/Shocked.sites/
Dc.comics/index.html

One of the first large-scale uses of Shockwave, and a good one, at that.

Macromedia: Interactive Gallery
http://www.macromedia.com/Gallery/index.html

M/B Interactive presents Deep Forest
http://mbinter.com/deepforest/deepforest.html

Ambient, new-age music with funky animations, all done in Shockwave.

The ShockeR List says Woah! Cool Site
http://www.shocker.com/shocker/cool.html

Shockwave Web Sites
http://www.teleport.com/~arcana/shockwave/

Java and JavaScript

Caffeine Connection
http://www.online-magazine.com/cafeconn.htm

An online Java zine with a good search engine for Java applets. Note, though, that you have to fill out an application form to get to this page.

Cool Applets We've Written
http://java.sun.com/applets/applets.html

Find out what they're up to at Sun Microsystems, where Java was "born."

Gamelan
http://www.gamelan.com/

Probably the best-known source of Java and JavaScript news, applets, links, and reference material.

JARS
http://www.jars.com/

The Java Applet Rating Service, which has one of the largest, best-organized collections of Java-related material around.

The Java(tm) Boutique
http://weber.u.washington.edu/~jgurney/java/

Another source of Java applets, including some commercial ones. Also employment opportunities for Java programmers.

The Java(tm) Developers Kit
http://www.javasoft.com/java.sun.com/JDK-1.0/index.html

A must-have if you're interested in Java programming. It includes a compiler and debugger, plus reference material and samples.

JavaScript 1040EZ at Home Pages, Inc.
http://www.homepages.com/fun/1040EZ.html

Study the source here to help you figure out how a real-world JavaScript application works.

JavaScript 411 Home Page
http://www.freqgrafx.com/411/

Good, step-by-step JavaScript tutorials. There's also a "snippet library" of JavaScript functions and programs ready to cut and paste onto your own pages.

JavaScript FAQ
http://www.freqgrafx.com/411/jsfaq.html

JavaScript Index
http://www.c2.org/~andreww/javascript/

The Unofficial JavaScript Resource Center
http://www.intercom.net/user/mecha/java/index.html

VRML

Aereal Inc.
http://www.aereal.com/
A vendor of popular VRML products.

Dimension X, Inc.
http://www.dimensionx.com/

The home page of the makers of Free Tea and Liquid Reality, two VRML programs.

Interact96
http://www.interact96.com/worlds/main/interact.wrl

A virtual VRML conference. Walk through the exhibit hall, clicking on the "booths" to go to the exhibitors' 3D spaces.

SteelStudio —Virtual Reality
http://www.marketcentral.com/vrml/vrml.html

A Web consultancy with a nice collection of VRML worlds on display.

3d graphics for the Worldwide Web
http://WWW.Stars.com/Graphics/3d-demo.html

Viewpoint DataLabs
http://www.viewpoint.com/

A vendor of 3D objects and the maintainer of the important Avalon repository of public-domain 3D objects and related software.

Virtual Reality Center
http://www.newtype.com/NewType/vr/index.htm

News, how-tos, games.

Virtual Reality on the Net
http://wchat.on.ca:80/public/vr/

Source for news and software related to VRML.

Virtus Corporation: Home Page
http://www.virtus.com/

Another vendor of popular VRML products.

VRML Repository
http://www.sdsc.edu/vrml/

A very famous site in the VRML world. It's even spawned a spoof, "The VRML Suppository."

VRML Review
http://www.imaginative.com/VResources/vrml/

A monthly VRML zine.

VRML 2.0
http://www.hyperstand.com/SITE/Awesome/05vrml/VRML_2.0_Takes_Flight.html

The latest news on the VRML 2.0 spec.

Yahoo's page of VRML-related links
http://www.yahoo.com/Computers_and_Internet/Internet/World_Wide_Web/Virtual_Reality_Modeling_Language__VRML/

Intranets

The Intranet Exchange(sm)
http://www.brill.com/intranet/ijx/index.html

Web-based, moderated Intranet bulletin board with a very active and helpful group of participants.

iWORLD's Business.Net
http://netday.iworld.com/business/

Check out the "Inside Intranets" column here, updated each Thursday, and find back issues.

Netscape Customer Profiles
http://home.netscape.com/comprod/at_work/customer_profiles/index.html

Case studies of companies that have implemented intranets using, of course, Netscape's products. Advertorial, but lots of good detailed info, too.

Useful Intranet Links
http://www.infoweb.com.au/intralnk.htm

WebMaster's Notebook
http://www.cio.com/WebMaster/wm_irc.html

Home of the "Intranet Resource Center," with links, news, articles, and—best of all—case studies.

INDEX

Coriolis Group World Wide Web Home page

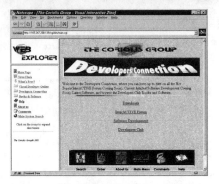

Delphi EXplorer—An incredible resource for Delphi programmers. Includes: commercial demos, dozens of shareware controls, sample code, articles, and two complete chapters from *Delphi Programming Explorer* by Jeff Duntemann, et al.

Explore the Grand Canyon—Take a Web wide view of this incredible new multimedia package produced by the Coriolis Group. Read the press releases, learn about amazing new NetSeeker technology, and view a few of the thousands of images from the software!

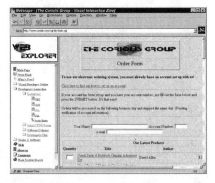

Online Ordering—Set up an account with the Coriolis Group and you can order all of your programming books over the Web. And not just Coriolis Group Books, you can order any of the books from our Developer's Club catalog!

Come visit us at:
http://www.coriolis.com